BUILDING CONTENT TYPE SOLUTIONS IN SHAREPOINT® 2007

DAVID GERHARDT AND KEVIN MARTIN

Charles River Media

A part of Course Technology, Cengage Learning

COURSE TECHNOLOGY
CENGAGE Learning

Australia, Brazil, Japan, Korea, Mexico, Singapore, Spain, United Kingdom, United States

COURSE TECHNOLOGY
CENGAGE Learning™

**Building Content Type Solutions
in SharePoint® 2007
David Gerhardt and Kevin Martin**

**Publisher and General Manager,
Course Technology PTR:** Stacy L. Hiquet

Associate Director of Marketing: Sarah Panella

Content Project Manager: Jessica McNavich

Marketing Manager: Mark Hughes

Acquisitions Editor: Mitzi Koontz

Project and Copy Editor: Marta Justak

Technical Reviewer: Stacia Misner

PTR Editorial Services Coordinator: Jen Blaney

Interior Layout: Shawn Morningstar

Cover Designer: Mike Tanamachi

Indexer: Valerie Haynes Perry

Proofreader: Sue Boshers

For product information and technology assistance, contact us at

**Cengage Learning Customer and Sales Support,
1-800-354-9706**

For permission to use material from this text or product, submit all requests online at
cengage.com/permissions

Further permissions questions can be emailed to
permissionrequest@cengage.com

Microsoft® Office SharePoint® 2007 and Microsoft® SQL Server® are registered trademarks of Microsoft Corporation in the United States and other countries. All other trademarks are the property of their respective owners.

Library of Congress Control Number: 2008940613

ISBN-13: 978-1-58450-669-0

ISBN-10: 1-58450-669-5

Course Technology
25 Thomson Place
Boston, MA 02210
USA

Cengage Learning is a leading provider of customized learning solutions with office locations around the globe, including Singapore, the United Kingdom, Australia, Mexico, Brazil, and Japan. Locate your local office at:
international.cengage.com/region

Cengage Learning products are represented in Canada by Nelson Education, Ltd.
For your lifelong learning solutions, visit **courseptr.com**
Visit our corporate website at **cengage.com**

Printed in Canada
1 2 3 4 5 6 7 11 10 09

Acknowledgments

I would like to thank everyone who helped or offered to help us with this book. Unfortunately, the list of contributors is too long for print. That is probably a good thing, because I would not want to slight anyone, including those who were simply there for moral support. However, there are three groups that I would like to explicitly call out:

- The staff of Charles River Media did a great job of managing this project. The entire production team was very professional and drove us to meet all of our deadlines in a timely manner. I was especially impressed with Stacia Misner, whom our publisher employed as a technical editor. Stacia demonstrated great patience in validating and revalidating our solution.

- Our primary employer, 3Sharp, provides us with many opportunities to develop our professional resumes. Kevin and I have both been there for more than five years, and our technical skill sets have grown exponentially through many projects with them. The 3Sharp partners run a great organization full of many talented people, and having a great day-to-day work experience makes a writing project like this one that much easier.

- Of course, the most patient people of all during this whole process were the members of my immediate family. My wife, Tracey, watched me sacrifice many a weekend and joked that I would never have a sane thought again as I repeatedly burned the midnight oil. My daughters, Anna and Rachel, wondered if I would ever take them back to their favorite park. Despite my "absence" during this effort, Tracey and the girls were my greatest inspiration. Now that the project is over, I look forward to catching up on the quality time that I missed with them.

David Gerhardt

First, I'd like to thank my co-author, David Gerhardt, who was the primary author of this book. Without him asking me to help with this book, I wouldn't have had the opportunity. We've worked together for over five years, and our paths have crossed on more than a few projects, but this was the biggest.

I can't say enough about the Charles River Media staff. Jen Blaney not only gave us the opportunity to write this book, but she also assembled its incredible staff. Stacia Misner provided an immense amount of invaluable feedback as the technical editor while traveling the four corners of the earth (all while writing her own book). Marta Justak kept her wits and sense of humor about her through to the end and helped this first-time author actually finish.

The partners and employees of 3Sharp provided us with the means and opportunity to write the book. I've worked with the people at 3Sharp for the past five years and have enjoyed every single day.

Finally, my family deserves a lot of credit for the book actually getting finished. Like most people, we lead fairly busy lives and probably didn't have the bandwidth to add a project of this size. I spent a lot of late nights creating and reviewing. My wife, Kari, added even more responsibilities around the house to pick up my slack and still continued to succeed at her own full-time career. She gave up a lot of weekends to catch up. I still owe her a Facebook application. My son, Kiel, put on hold all of the projects we were working on together before all of this started. We can get back to discussing those projects over games of pool again.

Kevin Martin

About the Authors

David Gerhardt manages a team at 3Sharp that develops out-of-the-box and custom solutions using Microsoft SharePoint offerings and Office System client applications. He has been consulting with clients since the mid-90s and especially enjoys XML-related technologies. Since 2003, he has done a lot of work with InfoPath and is the author of the Developing InfoPath 2007 Managed-Code Solutions white paper (http://www.microsoft.com/downloads/details.aspx?FamilyID=DB1D99D9-0A31-45DE-8EFB-16C75E194DC3&displaylang=en). He has written several other articles for the MSDN Library and *Windows IT Pro* magazine and has a blog site at http://blogs.3sharp.com/davidg. In his "spare" time, he likes to go on easy-to-moderate hikes with his family in the greater Seattle area and is an avid fan of the National Football League.

Kevin Martin is the owner of Martin Software Solutions, a consulting firm located in Kirkland, Washington. Kevin worked in both product support and development at Microsoft for 11 years and has been a consultant for the last 7 years, working closely with Dave at 3Sharp for the past 5 years. He specializes in .Net and Microsoft Office solution development for small businesses, as well as enterprise level customers.

Contents

Introduction

SharePoint power users, administrators, and developers often need to reference a particular type of content throughout a site collection. With Microsoft Office SharePoint Server 2007, content types were introduced as a means to manage content and ease reuse within sites. This book examines the power of SharePoint content types and walks through the process of creating one in a sample scenario.

WHAT YOU'LL FIND IN THIS BOOK

Within many organizations, different groups employ slightly different versions of the same solution in a SharePoint site collection. Content types offer normalization and management for these solutions and allow for greater reuse throughout the site collection. This book is the only one available that exclusively examines SharePoint content types. Within this book, you will find the following information:

■ A detailed description of Microsoft Office SharePoint Server 2007 content types, with an emphasis on document content types.

■ A step-by-step process to implement a sample performance appraisal solution with a document content type.

■ Examples of how to programmatically manipulate a content type.

WHO THIS BOOK IS FOR

If you have ever created or thought about creating document-centric SharePoint solutions, then this book is for you. The book is intended for IT professionals and is targeted at SharePoint power users, administrators, and (to a lesser extent) developers.

How This Book Is Organized

The authors wanted to appeal to as large an audience as possible, so they chose a simple sequence for this book. The first two chapters provide an overview of content types and can be read by anyone who has had experience with SharePoint. Chapters 3 through 8 are targeted at SharePoint power users and administrators, offer details about the components of document content types, and walk the reader through the process of creating a sample performance appraisal solution. The last two chapters are geared toward developers and describe how to programmatically manipulate the sample performance appraisal solution with Microsoft Visual Studio 2008. The specific content of each chapter is as follows:

Chapter 1, "What Is a Content Type?," provides an overview of document content types and a description of the performance appraisal solution architecture, with some setup steps.

Chapter 2, "Included Content Types," provides an overview of other SharePoint content types.

Chapter 3, "Site Columns," provides details about site columns and describes the step-by-step process for creating the performance appraisal solution site columns.

Chapter 4, "Document Template," provides details about document templates and describes the step-by-step process for creating the performance appraisal solution template, a Microsoft Office Word 2007 document.

Chapter 5, "Document Information Panel," provides details about the Document Information Panel and describes the step-by-step process for creating one for the performance appraisal solution.

Chapter 6, "Workflows," provides details about SharePoint workflows and describes the step-by-step process for creating the workflows for the performance appraisal solution.

Chapter 7, "Information Management Policies and Document Conversions," provides details about information management policies and document conversions and shows examples of both.

Chapter 8, "Out-of-the-Box Solution Walkthrough," offers an end-to-end walkthrough of the sample performance appraisal solution.

Chapter 9, "Automating the Performance Appraisal Solution," introduces a custom workflow activity and the start of a Visual Studio 2008 custom workflow.

Chapter 10, "Completing and Deploying the Appraisal Process," completes the custom workflow from Chapter 9 and introduces Microsoft InfoPath 2007 task form integration into the custom workflows. Deploying the custom workflow is also covered.

MATERIAL FOR DOWNLOAD

In Chapter 4, there is a Microsoft Office Word 2007 document used to build the solution template that is available for download. The authors have also made the source and project files described in Chapters 9 and 10 available for download at www.courseptr.com/downloads.

1 What Is a Content Type?

Whether using Windows SharePoint Services v3.0 or its more robust sister product, Microsoft Office SharePoint Server 2007, you can leverage an abundance of features to build enterprise application solutions. One feature in particular that has stirred us is the content type. This feature allows you to define a collection of metadata and processes for a certain type of content within your organization. For example, a sales proposal would consist of a document, perhaps some attributes that identify the sales representative and customer, and a workflow that routes the document for approval from key stakeholders. Taken together, the sales proposal document, attributes, and workflow process comprise a SharePoint content type.

In addition to having metadata and processes, a content type can be built once and then leveraged throughout your organization. You can create a content type in a site collection, site, or list, and then reuse that site content anywhere within that SharePoint hierarchical level. For example, an expense report content type defined at the site level can be referenced from multiple document libraries within that site. Moreover, when you reference that expense report content type, you can customize it at the document library level without affecting the parent content type on which it was based.

This book is a step-by-step walkthrough for building a performance appraisal content type. This was chosen as an example because we figured that most of you, at some point in your professional lives, have been through an appraisal process— whether formal or informal. The elements described throughout this book therefore should be somewhat familiar. We also elected to build our performance appraisal content type with Office SharePoint Server 2007 Enterprise CAL, which offers similar functionality to Office SharePoint Server 2007 Standard CAL, but with a slightly different user experience. Windows SharePoint Services v3.0 allows you to create content types, but it lacks some powerful features, such as built-in workflow templates and information management policies. In this chapter, we will review the main components of a content type and identify the prerequisites for getting started with the performance appraisal solution.

SharePoint Products Comparison

For more information about the differences between Office SharePoint Server 2007 Enterprise CAL, Office SharePoint Server 2007 Standard CAL, and Windows SharePoint Services v3.0, go to http://office.microsoft.com/en-us/sharepointserver/ HA101978031033.aspx.

CONTENT TYPE COMPONENTS

In our experience, document content types are the most prevalent of the content types used in SharePoint solutions, but they are not the only types available. In Chapter 2, "Included Content Types," we will go into detail about the list of other content types, which includes but is not limited to business intelligence, list, and page layout content types. For the performance appraisal solution, however, the focus is the document content type, and the components for such are as follows:

- Site columns
- Document template
- Document Information Panel
- Workflows
- Information management policies
- Document conversions

SITE COLUMNS

Site columns represent the data layer of a content type. They comprise the metadata that gives your document content type structure. In Chapter 3, "Site Columns," which provides the steps for creating the performance appraisal solution site columns, we use the analogy of an XML schema to illustrate how site columns construe a data model. Each site column has a data type that specifies the type of data a user can associate with that column. Site columns can also be reused across content types within the SharePoint site hierarchy from which they are defined. Figure 1.1 shows some of the site columns and corresponding data types that you will create in Chapter 3.

AppraisalDate	Date and Time
AppraisalPeriodEnd	Date and Time
AppraisalPeriodStart	Date and Time
AppraisalStatus	Choice
AppraiserName	Person or Group
AppraiserOverallComments	Multiple lines of text
EmployeeName	Person or Group
EmployeeOverallComments	Multiple lines of text

FIGURE 1.1 Reviewing some of the performance appraisal solution site columns.

DOCUMENT TEMPLATE

If site columns constitute the data layer of a content type, then the document template represents the presentation layer. For document content types, the template typically is either a Microsoft Office Word 2007, Microsoft Office Excel 2007, or Microsoft Office PowerPoint 2007 document. In all these cases, the template is a client application that uses the data model described by the site columns.

In this book we use an Office Word 2007 document as our template. Technically, any of the aforementioned clients could have worked for the performance appraisal solution. However, Office Word 2007 has three capabilities that collectively give it an edge over the other applications:

■ Content controls that are bound to site columns can be surfaced in the document.

■ User edits can be tracked with the Track Changes feature.

■ Office Word 2007 documents are easier to print.

In Chapter 4, "Document Template," we will walk through the steps for building the performance appraisal solution document template. Figure 1.2 shows an example of the document template being used.

Performance Appraisal

Employee:	[EmployeeName]	**Period Start:**	8/29/2008
Reviewer:	[AppraiserName]	**Period End:**	8/28/2009
Date of Appraisal:	9/10/2009		

Goals

Description	Metric	Comments	Weight	Score
[GoalDescription1]	[GoalMetric1]	[GoalComments1]	[GoalWeight1]	[GoalScore1]
[GoalDescription2]	[GoalMetric2]	[GoalComments2]	[GoalWeight2]	[GoalScore2]
[GoalDescription3]	[GoalMetric3]	[GoalComments3]	[GoalWeight3]	[GoalScore3]
[GoalDescription4]	[GoalMetric4]	[GoalComments4]	[GoalWeight4]	[GoalScore4]
[GoalDescription5]	[GoalMetric5]	[GoalComments5]	[GoalWeight5]	[GoalScore5]
		Totals:	0	0

Employee Comments:	[EmployeeOverallComments]
Reviewer Comments	[AppraiserOverallComments]

FIGURE 1.2 Seeing the performance appraisal document template in use.

DOCUMENT INFORMATION PANEL

In document content types, the template contains a horizontal region at the top that can expose all the site columns or a subset of them. This region is actually an embedded Office InfoPath 2007 form, with controls that map both to site columns and content controls used in the document template. In the performance appraisal solution, only a handful of site columns will be surfaced in the Document Information Panel. The real value comes from the declarative rules engine of Office InfoPath 2007, which allows you to drive business logic in the document template with functionality such as data validation and conditional formatting. Figure 1.3 shows an example of the Document Information Panel, which we will design in Chapter 5, "Document Information Panel."

Performance Appraisal Properties - Server ▼				
Employee Name:	Appraiser Name:	Appraisal Period Start:	Appraisal Period End:	AppraisalStatus:
David Gerhardt	Kevin Martin	1/1/2008	12/31/2009	2 - Goals Finalized

FIGURE 1.3 Seeing the performance appraisal Document Information Panel in use.

WORKFLOWS

Workflows define the business processes in a document content type. Tasks can be automated and list items can be created or updated with SharePoint workflow capabilities. For example, you can collect feedback from different users about a particular performance appraisal document using one of the out-of-the-box SharePoint workflow templates. If you need conditional logic or require actions that are not supported with any of the out-of-the-box templates, Microsoft Office SharePoint Designer 2007 allows you to define codeless workflows and attach them to specific lists. You can also develop custom workflows with Microsoft Visual Studio 2008 and deploy them as features for use by SharePoint content types. In Chapter 6, "Workflows," we will describe how to create codeless workflows with the out-of-the-box templates and with Office SharePoint Designer 2007. In the last two chapters, we'll describe how to use Visual Studio 2008 for the more complex scenarios. Figure 1.4 shows how conditional logic can be used to send email notifications to users in an Office SharePoint Designer 2007 workflow.

FIGURE 1.4 Reviewing conditional logic in an Office SharePoint Designer 2007 workflow.

INFORMATION MANAGEMENT POLICIES

Information management policies allow you to manage your content types to ensure that documents are in compliance with company policy in areas such as document usage and retention. You can define policies that identify auditing events, schedule content disposition when a document expires, or assign barcodes or labels for documents. Collectively, these policies are a quick and easy means to build a unified infrastructure for managing a particular group of documents. In Chapter 7, "Information Management Policies and Document Conversions," we will show how to define information management policies for a content type. Figure 1.5 shows the events that can be audited by a policy.

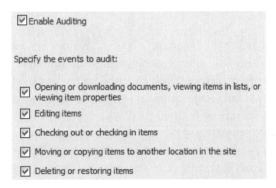

FIGURE 1.5 Reviewing auditing options for an information management policy.

DOCUMENT CONVERSIONS

With content types, you also have the ability to convert documents into Web pages. Converters can be configured for Office Word 2007 documents (with or without macros), Office InfoPath 2007 forms, and XML files. When choosing settings for a converter, you can select a page layout for new Web pages, identify the specific location where Web pages are to be created, and define whether users can continue to work while a conversion is in process. Document conversions will be covered in greater detail in Chapter 7, along with the discussion of information management policies. Figure 1.6 shows an example of how to define a page layout for a converter.

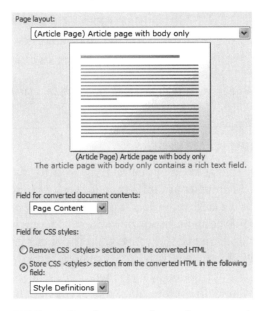

FIGURE 1.6 Creating a page layout for a converter.

SOLUTION REQUIREMENTS

As mentioned in the beginning of this chapter, the performance appraisal solution that we will be building requires Office SharePoint Server 2007 Enterprise CAL. We will assume that most of you have access to a SharePoint server and can implement our solution on an existing Web application that hosts a Shared Service Provider (SSP). For the steps described throughout this book, we will be using the fictional http://moss.litwareinc.com Web application.

SSP Configuration

For more information about creating and configuring SSPs, go to http://technet. microsoft.com/en-us/library/cc303421.aspx.

In addition to Office SharePoint Server 2007, there are four client applications that are needed for the development effort:

- **Office Word 2007**. Needed for the document template.
- **Office InfoPath 2007**. Needed to design the form template for the Document Information Panel.
- **Office SharePoint Designer 2007**. Needed to create codeless workflows that act on a set of conditions.
- **Office Excel 2007**. This application is not required for development, but you will need it to view any auditing reports.

Client Application Installs

These four applications do not need to be installed on the machine that is hosting Office SharePoint Server 2007. They can be run from a client machine that has access to the SharePoint server.

For Chapters 9, "Automating the Performance Appraisal Solution," and 10, "Completing and Deploying the Appraisal Process," we will use Visual Studio 2008 as the tool for developing custom logic. For this solution, Visual Studio 2008 should be installed on the machine that is hosting Office SharePoint Server 2007, mainly to ease the process of deploying custom workflows.

Visual Studio 2008 Configuration

At the time of this writing, having Visual Studio 2008 installed on the same machine with Office SharePoint Server 2007 is supported only in a 32-bit environment.

There are also setup steps for some of the content type components described throughout this book. The following subsections identify the requirements for workflows, information management policies, and document conversions.

WORKFLOW SETUP STEPS

Chapter 6 is devoted to the configuration of workflows, which have actions that notify users about different stages of the performance appraisal solution. Notification comes in the form of email messages, and you must configure outgoing email settings on the SharePoint server in order for messages to be delivered.

To configure outgoing email settings, use the following steps:

1. From the SharePoint server machine, click Start | All Programs | Microsoft Office Server | SharePoint 3.0 Central Administration.
2. On the Central Administration page, click the Operations tab.
3. On the Operations page, in the Topology and Services section, click Outgoing e-mail settings.
4. On the Outgoing E-Mail Settings page, define your mail settings accordingly and then click OK. Figure 1.7 shows an example of outgoing email settings for a SharePoint server.

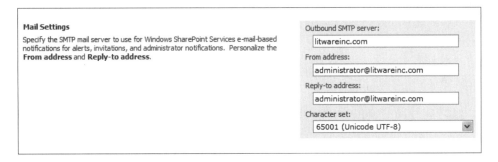

FIGURE 1.7 Defining outgoing mail settings for a SharePoint server.

INFORMATION MANAGEMENT POLICY CONFIGURATION STEPS

In Chapter 7 we will describe how to define information management policies that identify auditing events, schedule content disposition when a document expires, or assign barcodes or labels for documents. In order for these policies to be used within content types, they must be made available on the SharePoint server.

To configure these information management policies for use within content types, follow these steps:

1. In Central Administration, click the Operations tab.

2. In the Security Configuration section, click Information management policy configuration.

3. On the Information Management Policy Configuration page, ensure that all policy features are available, as shown in Figure 1.8

4. If any policy feature is listed as decommissioned, click the corresponding Name link, click Available for use in new site and list policies, and then click Save.

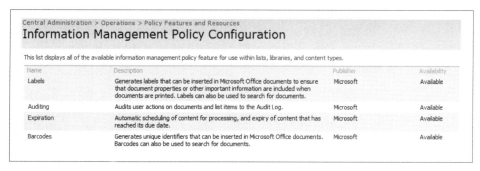

Central Administration > Operations > Policy Features and Resources

Information Management Policy Configuration

This list displays all of the available information management policy feature for use within lists, libraries, and content types.

Name	Description	Publisher	Availability
Labels	Generates labels that can be inserted in Microsoft Office documents to ensure that document properties or other important information are included when documents are printed. Labels can also be used to search for documents.	Microsoft	Available
Auditing	Audits user actions on documents and list items to the Audit Log.	Microsoft	Available
Expiration	Automatic scheduling of content for processing, and expiry of content that has reached its due date.	Microsoft	Available
Barcodes	Generates unique identifiers that can be inserted in Microsoft Office documents. Barcodes can also be used to search for documents.	Microsoft	Available

FIGURE 1.8 Reviewing the availability of policy features.

DOCUMENT CONVERSION SETUP STEPS

In Chapter 7 we will also describe how to configure converters for the performance appraisal solution so that documents can be converted to Web pages. In order for converters to work, you need to start two services on the SharePoint server. To start these services, follow these steps:

1. In Central Administration, click the Operations tab.

2. In the Topology and Services section, click Services on server.

3. On the Services on Server page, review the list of services in the table. If the Document Conversions Load Balancer and Document Conversions Launcher services both show a status of Stopped, as shown in Figure 1.9, then you will need to start both services.

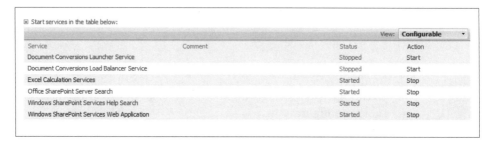

FIGURE 1.9 Reviewing the status of the conversion services.

4. Click the Start action for the Document Conversions Load Balancer service.

5. Click the Start action for the Document Conversions Launcher service.

6. On the Launcher Service Settings page, define settings for the Document Conversions Launcher service accordingly and then click OK. Figure 1.10 shows an example of Document Conversions Launcher service settings.

FIGURE 1.10 Defining settings for the Document Conversion Launcher service.

After these services are started on the SharePoint server, you must then enable document conversions for your solution Web application. To enable document conversions, do the following:

1. In Central Administration, click the Application Management tab.

2. On the Application Management page, in the External Service Connections section, click Document conversions.

3. On the Configure Document Conversions page, click the Web Application list and then click Change Web Application.

4. In the Select Web Application dialog box, click the Web application that you will be using for the performance appraisal solution.

5. On the Configure Document Conversions page, in the Enable Document Conversions section, click Yes to enable document conversions for the selected Web application.

6. Click the Load Balancer server list and then select a load balancer.

7. Specify a conversion schedule and converter settings as needed and then click OK. Figure 1.11 shows an example of how conversions are configured for a particular Web application.

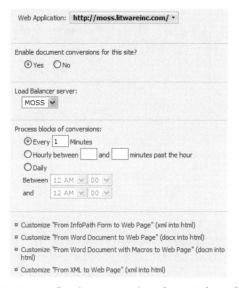

FIGURE 1.11 Configuring conversions for a Web application.

SOLUTION ARCHITECTURE

The architecture for the performance appraisal solution is relatively simple. Within the site collection for the SharePoint Web application, there is a Human Resources site, which contains document libraries for each user that will be managing performance appraisals. Figure 1.12 shows an example of the SharePoint hierarchy for the performance appraisal solution, with the relevant nodes highlighted in gray.

The performance appraisal content type will be defined at the site collection level and then referenced from appraisal document libraries within the Human Resources site. You could also reference the performance appraisal content type from document libraries in other sites, although we will stay within the Human Resources site in this book.

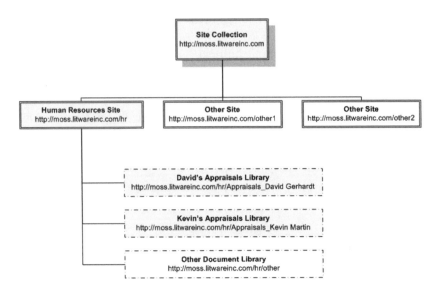

FIGURE 1.12 Reviewing the SharePoint architecture for the performance appraisal solution.

Within the site collection for your SharePoint Web application, you will need to create the Human Resources site and document libraries for each appraiser. The steps to create a document library are described in Chapter 4, where we reference the performance appraisal content type for the first time.

To create a site within your site collection, follow these steps:

1. In the browser, navigate to your site collection home page (for example, http://moss.litwareinc.com).

2. From the Site Actions menu, click Create Site.

3. On the New SharePoint Site page, in the Title box, type **Human Resources** or some other descriptive title for your site.

4. In the Web Site Address section, type **hr** or some other URL that maps to the site.

5. In the Template Selection section, select a site template. Figure 1.13 shows an example of the title, Web site address, and site template being defined.

6. Modify permissions and navigation options, as needed, and then click Create.

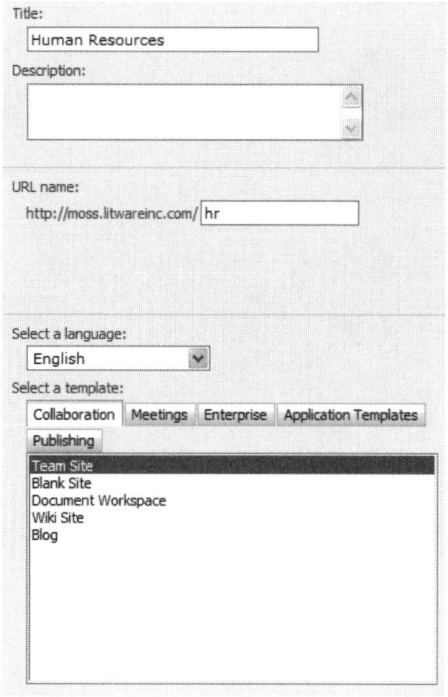

Title:
Human Resources

Description:

URL name:
http://moss.litwareinc.com/ hr

Select a language:
English

Select a template:

Collaboration | Meetings | Enterprise | Application Templates
Publishing

Team Site
Blank Site
Document Workspace
Wiki Site
Blog

FIGURE 1.13 Creating the Human Resources site.

You are now ready to start building the solution. If you are interested in learning more about other content types besides document content types, Chapter 2 provides overview information. Otherwise, if you just want to dive into the development effort for the performance appraisal solution, proceed to Chapter 3.

2 Included Content Types

Chapter 1 introduced the main components of a content type and identified the prerequisites for getting started with the performance appraisal solution. The performance appraisal solution requires a custom document content type. While the rest of the book covers a document content type in depth, we'll introduce and briefly go over other out-of-the-box content types included with SharePoint.

SharePoint organizes content types into a hierarchy. Each content type inherits its attributes from a parent content type. This means that when you create a new content type, you must choose an existing parent content type. The new content type inherits all of the attributes of the parent. When a parent content type is updated, you have the option of updating all of the child content types that derive from the parent. Updating a child content type has no effect on the parent content type.

Windows SharePoint Services 3.0 servers ship with the following parent content types:

- Document content types
- Folder content types
- List content types
- Special content types

Microsoft Office SharePoint Server 2007 offers these additional parent content types:

- Business Intelligence content types
- Page Layout content types
- Publishing content types

After opening the SharePoint site created in Chapter 1, use the following steps to view the list of parent content types in your environment:

1. Click Site Actions, Site Settings, Modify All Site Settings.

2. Under Galleries, click Site content types.

3. Click Create.

4. Expand the Parent Content Type: drop-down.

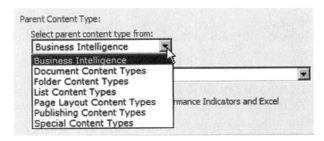

FIGURE 2.1 View the parent content types for a Microsoft Office SharePoint Server.

Content types are stored in groups. When you create a new content type, you can either assign it to an existing group or create a group of your own. Figure 2.2 shows the group selection controls.

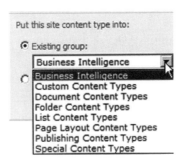

FIGURE 2.2 View the content type groups for a Microsoft Office SharePoint Server.

Click Cancel to return to the site content type gallery.

The rest of the chapter will describe the out-of-the-box content type hierarchy via each parent content type and its associated child content types, and it will demonstrate how to create a custom list content type.

AVAILABLE CONTENT TYPES

The parent content types listed in the previous section are associated with default child content types. We're going to explore the different parent content types and their associated child content types in the next few sections.

Most of the content types are self-explanatory. This makes sense because they are the types that all others are based upon.

DOCUMENT CONTENT TYPES

Document types consist of types that are stored in document libraries. These types are listed below and can be documents, pages, forms, pictures, or links to other documents.

- Basic Page
- Document
- Dublin Core Columns
- Form
- Link to a Document
- Master Page
- Picture
- Web Part Page

This list is pretty self-explanatory with a couple of exceptions:

- **Dublin Core Columns Dublin**. Core Columns are columns from the Dublin Core Metadata set. The Dublin Core metadata element set is a standard for cross-domain information resource descriptions. It provides a simple and standardized set of conventions for describing things online in ways that make them easier to find. Dublin Core is widely used to describe digital materials, such as video, sound, image, text, and composite media, such as Web pages.
- **Link to a Document**. The Link to a Document content type is a predefined type that creates a record in a document library that points to a document in a different document library.

Folder Content Types

Folder content types are listed below.

- Discussion
- Folder

The discussion content type is the basis for discussion boards and folders are just folders. It's pretty straightforward.

List Content Types

The List content types are at the top of the hierarchy. The Item content type is the root of all other content types used by SharePoint. If you review the site content type gallery, you'll see that Item is based upon the System content type and every other type is derived in one way or another from Item. For instance, if you look at the Web Part Page content type, it is based on the Basic Page content type. Basic Page is based on the Document content type, and Document is based on the Item content type.

An example of creating a new Item-based content type is detailed later in the chapter. The List content types are shown below:

- Announcement
- Contact
- Far East Contact
- Issue
- Item
- Link
- Message
- Task

Special Content Types

Special content types contain a single content type, Unknown Document Type. The Unknown Document Type content type is based upon the Document content type mentioned previously. When this type is implemented, users are allowed to upload any document type. Those documents will be treated as their original content type in client applications.

BUSINESS INTELLIGENCE CONTENT TYPES

Business Intelligence, or BI, content types are part of the Microsoft Office Share-Point Server (MOSS) content types. Business Intelligence, as it pertains to Share-Point, is a complex subject worthy of an entire book itself and is out of the scope of this book.

- Dashboard Page
- Indicator using Data in Excel Workbook
- Indicator using Data in SharePoint List
- Indicator used in SQL Server Analysis Services
- Indicator using Manually Entered Information
- Report

PAGE LAYOUT CONTENT TYPES

The page layout content types are installed by the Publishing Resources feature and are available in sites that have the Publishing Resources feature enabled. Each of the child types listed below is associated with templates for a particular kind of page. As with BI, the Publishing Resources feature is available with MOSS and is too broad of a subject to be covered here. There are many resources, both in print and online, that cover the subject matter.

- Article Page
- Redirect Page
- Welcome Page

PUBLISHING CONTENT TYPES

The publishing content types are listed below:

- Page
- Page Layout
- Publishing Master Page

Just like the Page Layout content types, the Publishing content types are installed with the Publishing Resources feature and are only included with MOSS.

CREATING A NEW LIST ITEM CONTENT TYPE

While this book is concerned with creating a document content type for performance appraisals, we're going to look at the List content types. If you peruse the list of List child content types, shown in Figure 2.3, you'll see a few content types that are familiar, such as Announcement, Contact, Issue, and Task.

List Content Types	
Announcement	Item
Contact	Item
Far East Contact	Item
Issue	Item
Item	System
Link	Item
Message	Item
Task	Item

FIGURE 2.3 Child content types of the List content type.

The mechanics of creating a new content type based upon another content type is the same, regardless of the base content type. The difference is the columns you start off with. To keep things simple, we're going to base our new content type on Item. Looking at Figure 2.3, you can see that all of the List content types have a parent type of Item. An Item is a basic content type having only a single column, the Title column, as shown in Figure 2.4.

To get started creating our new content type, we need to have the browser open to the Site Content Gallery page.

1. If not already there, open the browser to the site home page and click Site Actions, Site Settings, Modify All Site Settings.

2. From the Site Settings page, click Site content types under the Galleries heading.

3. On the Site Content Type Gallery page, click Create.

4. Enter the information for the new content type as listed below. See Figure 2.5 for help.
   - **Name.** My Test Content Type
   - **Description.** Test Item content type for book
   - **Select parent content type from.** List Content Types
   - **Parent content type.** Item
   - **New group.** My Test Content Type Group

FIGURE 2.4 Item content type properties.

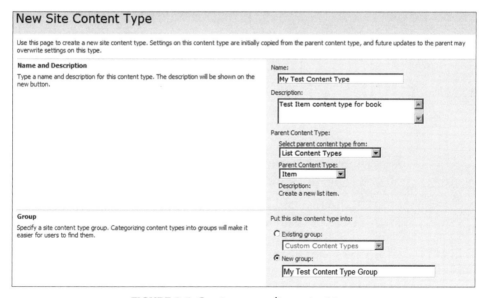

FIGURE 2.5 Create a new site content type.

5. Click OK to create the new content type.

6. Next, you need to add a single field to make the content type different from the Item content type.

7. From the My Test Content Type property page, click Add from new site column, as shown in Figure 2.6.

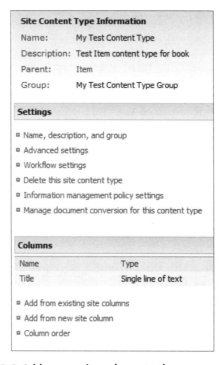

Site Content Type Information

Name:	My Test Content Type
Description:	Test Item content type for book
Parent:	Item
Group:	My Test Content Type Group

Settings

▫ Name, description, and group
▫ Advanced settings
▫ Workflow settings
▫ Delete this site content type
▫ Information management policy settings
▫ Manage document conversion for this content type

Columns

Name	Type
Title	Single line of text

▫ Add from existing site columns
▫ Add from new site column
▫ Column order

FIGURE 2.6 Add a new site column to the new content type.

8. We're going to create a description field for our content type. Enter the information for the new site column as listed below (see Figures 2.7 and 2.8).

   ■ **Column name**. MyItemDescription
   ■ **The type of information in this column is**. Single line of text
   ■ **Put this site column into**. Existing group: Custom Columns
   ■ **Description**. Custom content type description field

9. Keep the rest of the fields as default values and click OK.

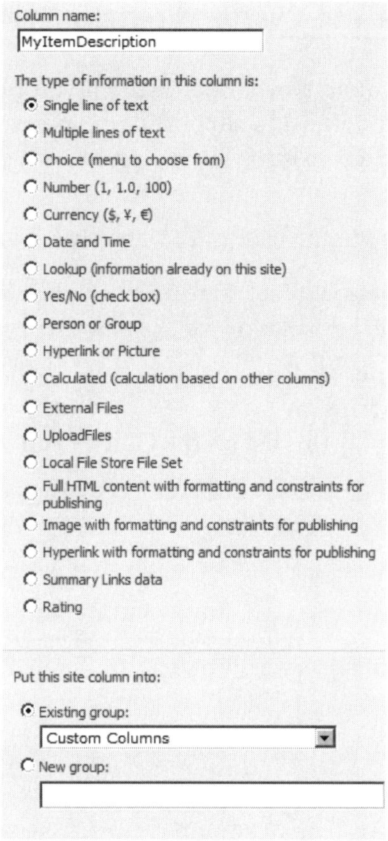

Column name:

MyItemDescription

The type of information in this column is:

- ◉ Single line of text
- ◯ Multiple lines of text
- ◯ Choice (menu to choose from)
- ◯ Number (1, 1.0, 100)
- ◯ Currency ($, ¥, €)
- ◯ Date and Time
- ◯ Lookup (information already on this site)
- ◯ Yes/No (check box)
- ◯ Person or Group
- ◯ Hyperlink or Picture
- ◯ Calculated (calculation based on other columns)
- ◯ External Files
- ◯ UploadFiles
- ◯ Local File Store File Set
- ◯ Full HTML content with formatting and constraints for publishing
- ◯ Image with formatting and constraints for publishing
- ◯ Hyperlink with formatting and constraints for publishing
- ◯ Summary Links data
- ◯ Rating

Put this site column into:

- ◉ Existing group:

  Custom Columns
- ◯ New group:

FIGURE 2.7 Add a description field to the new content type, part 1.

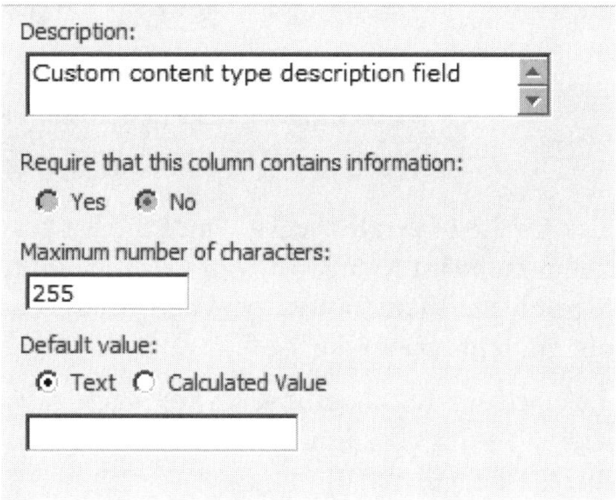

Description:

Custom content type description field

Require that this column contains information:
- ◯ Yes   ◉ No

Maximum number of characters:

255

Default value:
- ◉ Text   ◯ Calculated Value

FIGURE 2.8 Add a description field to the new content type, part 2.

CREATING A LIST FOR THE CUSTOM CONTENT TYPE

A custom list content type is only useful if you can utilize the type in a list. We're going to create a new list to support our content type but the content type can be added to any already existing list. To get started, you need to create your list.

1. From the home page of the site, click Site Actions, View All Site Content.

2. Click Create and then click Custom List under the Custom Lists header.

3. Enter the information for the new list, as shown in Figure 2.9.
   - **Name**. My Test List
   - **Description**. List for test content type
   - **Display this list on the Quick Launch?** No

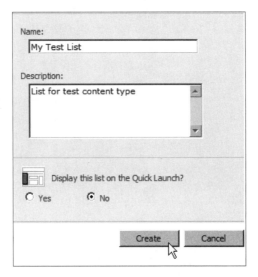

FIGURE 2.9 Create a new custom list.

4. Click Create to create the list. Once the list has been created, you need to configure the list to support your new content type. Newly created lists are based on the Item content type and need to be updated so you can add your content type to the list.

5. Click Settings, List Settings. Next, click Advanced Settings under the General Settings heading. Select Yes under Allow management of content types? (see Figure 2.10).

6. Click OK.

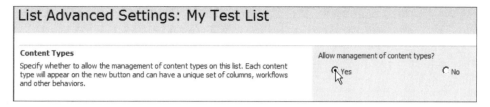

FIGURE 2.10 Add content type management support to the custom list.

7. Now that your list can have multiple content types, you need to add the content type you just created. Click Add from existing site content types, as shown in Figure 2.11.

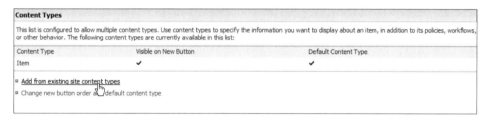

FIGURE 2.11 Add an existing content type to a list.

8. From the Select site content types from: drop-down on the Add Content Types page, select My Test Content Type Group.

9. Then select My Test Content Type from the Available Site Content Types: drop-down and click Add, as shown in Figure 2.12.

10. Click OK to add the new content type to the list.

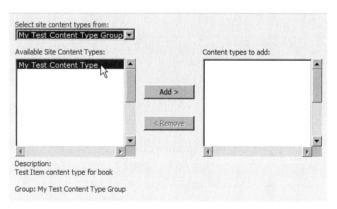

FIGURE 2.12 Select the Content Type for your list.

11. From the list Settings page, click My Test List to get to the list view for the content type list, as shown in Figure 2.13.

FIGURE 2.13 Navigating to the list view.

12. Now when you click the down arrow next to New, you will see two types of items that can be created (as shown in Figure 2.14)—Item and My Test Content Type.

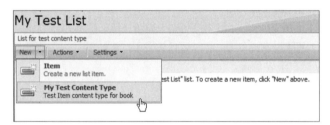

FIGURE 2.14 Creating a custom content type item.

13. Click My Test Content Type, and the new item form shows your content type fields, as shown in Figure 2.15. As this is just a demonstration, click Cancel.

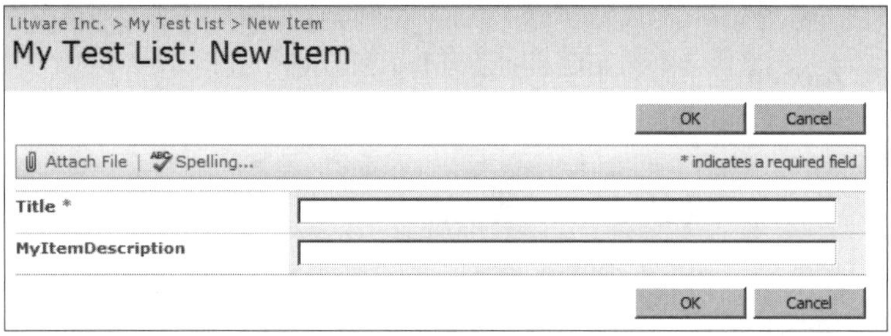

FIGURE 2.15 The new item form for the custom content type list.

Content types are the fundamental data structure utilized by SharePoint. This chapter gave you a flavor for what content types are available and the content type hierarchy, as well as creating a new list content type.

In the rest of the book, you'll create a solution based on a custom content type that you'll develop as you go.

3 Site Columns

Now that you have a high-level understanding of what SharePoint content types offer, let's start building the performance appraisal content type. The first step in the development process is to define the content type metadata. Site columns represent the data model of your solution. They define the content type structure and can map to content controls used in the Office Word 2007 document template. They can also be evaluated or modified by a SharePoint workflow. In this chapter, we will create all the site columns needed for the out-of-the-box performance appraisal solution.

SITE COLUMN COMPONENTS

Before defining the content type structure, it is helpful to understand what comprises a site column. The three components of every site column are as follows:

- Name and Type
- Group
- Additional Column Settings

NAME AND TYPE

Naming a site column is self-explanatory. However, do not underestimate the importance of choosing names wisely. Site columns are used everywhere in a content type. Within SharePoint lists that reference a particular content type, site columns appear as headers in the views. They are also the names of content controls used in Office Word 2007 document templates and the names of data source nodes in the Document Information Panel. When developing SharePoint workflows, you can also use the site column name property to evaluate or modify data. Given this level of prominence within content types, keep your site column names pithy.

In addition to a name, each site column has a distinct data type. Think of a data type much like you would a column in a Microsoft SQL Server table or an element in an XML schema. The data type simply defines what kind of information you can store in the site column. The following list shows the data types that can be associated with a site column:

- Single line of text
- Multiple lines of text
- Choice (menu to choose from)
- Number (1, 1.0, 100)
- Currency ($, ¥)
- Date and Time
- Lookup (information already on the site)
- Yes/No (check box)
- Person or Group
- Hyperlink or Picture
- Calculated (calculation based on other columns)
- What's New Field (this field requires a What's New list in the site)
- Full HTML content with formatting and constraints for publishing
- Image with formatting and constraints for publishing
- Hyperlink with formatting and constraints for publishing
- Summary Links data

The data type you select will help determine the control that is bound to the site column elsewhere in the content type. For example, the Date and Time type is bound to a date picker content control in an Office Word 2007 document template, while a Person or Group type manifests itself as a people picker in the Document Information Panel. We will discuss some of these data types in greater detail later when we create the site columns for the performance appraisal solution.

Group

Grouping is not a requirement for site columns. However, categorizing your columns will make it easier for users to find them when creating content types. Every time you create a site column, you can either place it in an existing group or define a new group. If you define a new group, the new site column will be placed there, and the group name will appear in the Existing group list when you create subsequent site columns.

Site Column Grouping

Grouping does not prevent you from using certain site columns in your content type. You can select site columns from as many groups as you want, or you can have all the site columns come from just one group.

ADDITIONAL COLUMN SETTINGS

Additional settings for your site column will vary depending on the data type you select. For example, the Choice type allows you to identify choices and whether they should be displayed in a drop-down menu, as radio buttons, or as check boxes. Meanwhile, with the Number type, you can specify minimum and maximum allowed values, the number of decimal places, and whether to show the value as a percentage. For most of the data types, you can specify a default value and whether the site column is required to contain data. For all of the data types, you can provide a description for the site column in the Additional Column Settings section.

PERFORMANCE APPRAISAL SITE COLUMNS

Before creating site columns for the performance appraisal solution, you must first consider the structure of the content and answer some basic questions about the data. Are there repeating elements in the data source? Do calculations need to be performed, and, if so, will calculated values be displayed in the document template? Are there any columns that will trigger different stages of a workflow when their values change? The remainder of this chapter shows you how to construct the data model for this solution after you answer some of these questions.

NESTED STRUCTURE

If you were building an XML data model, you would probably start with an XML schema. The schema would define the data type for each element, the sequence and nesting of elements, and other rules for your XML data. With the performance appraisal solution, you could simplify the data model as having two high-level sections:

■ **General Information.** This section would store the name of the employee and appraiser, the appraisal period start and end dates, the appraisal date, the appraisal status, and other general information.

■ **Goal Information.** This section would store repeating goal information. Each goal would include a description, metric, weight, appraiser comments, score, and other goal-specific information. There would also be calculations for each weighted score (weight * score), the weight total (sum of all weights), and overall score (sum of all weighted scores).

An XML representation of the performance appraisal data model with high-level sections for general and goal information is shown below.

```xml
<PerformanceAppraisal>
  <GeneralInfo>
    <Employee>David Gerhardt</Employee>
    <Appraiser>Benjamin Franklin</Appraiser>
    <PeriodStart>2008-01-01</PeriodStart>
    <PeriodEnd>2008-12-31</PeriodEnd>
    <AppraisalDate>2009-01-07</AppraisalDate>
    <EmployeeOverallComments>This seemed pretty fair.</EmployeeOverallComments>
    <AppraiserOverallComments>Nice work overall.</AppraiserOverallComments>
    <Status>4 — Appraisal Draft</Status>
  </GeneralInfo>
  <GoalInfo>
    <Goals>
      <Goal>
        <Description>Project Management</Description>
        <Metric>Manage five projects successfully.</Metric>
        <Weight>.6</Weight>
        <Comments>David managed six projects successfully.</Comments>
        <Score>4.5</Score>
        <WeightedScore>2.7</WeightedScore>
      </Goal>
      <Goal>
        <Description>Personal Profitability</Description>
        <Metric>Achieve a personal profit margin of 25%.</Metric>
        <Weight>.4</Weight>
        <Comments>David had a 22% personal profit margin.</Comments>
        <Score>2.5</Score>
        <WeightedScore>1</WeightedScore>
      </Goal>
      <WeightTotal>1</WeightTotal>
      <ScoreTotal>3.7</ScoreTotal>
    </Goals>
  </GoalInfo>
</PerformanceAppraisal>
```

This data model is pretty straightforward, except for one problem: nesting and repeating structures are not supported in SharePoint content types. In other words, you cannot have a GeneralInfo site column that contains an Appraiser site column (or any other site columns), and you would not be able to define 1:N Goal site columns. This limitation does not mean that the exercise of identifying a nested structure was done in vain. Instead, it is useful in redefining the performance appraisal data model as a flat structure, which is supported in SharePoint content types.

FLAT STRUCTURE

Flattening the data structure shown in the previous section is not complicated. You just need to think of each site column as an individual data-entry point. Since nesting is not supported, you do not need to be concerned with the hierarchical relationships of the data. You just need to define all the column names, their corresponding data types, and any additional settings for the columns. In the subsections that follow, we will build the "General Information" and "Goal Information" site columns for the performance appraisal solution.

General Information Columns

In the XML representation of the performance appraisal data model shown earlier, the GeneralInfo element contained eight nested elements. In the flat structure of a SharePoint content type, those eight elements will be defined as shown in Table 3.1.

TABLE 3.1 General Information Site Columns

Column Name	Data Type
EmployeeName	Person or Group
AppraiserName	Person or Group
AppraisalPeriodStart	Date and Time
AppraisalPeriodEnd	Date and Time
AppraisalDate	Date and Time
EmployeeOverallComments	Multiple lines of text
AppraiserOverallComments	Multiple lines of text
AppraisalStatus	Choice

A couple of things are worth pointing out with these column names. First, there are no spaces in the column names. This is by design for this book, but it is not a requirement for your naming conventions. Space characters are not allowed in XML element names and thus are converted to "_x0020_" strings for the corresponding nodes in the Document Information Panel and elements in the custom XML part of the Office Word 2007 document template. For the development tasks that appear toward the end of this book, working without the "_x0020_" strings is just a little easier. In addition to the usage of space characters (or lack thereof), the names are also more descriptive than the element names shown in the XML representation of the data model. For example, the Status element has been renamed AppraisalStatus for the site column. When naming columns, you should try to avoid overly generic names. A "status" column for a performance appraisal content type will likely store different data than a "status" column for a different content type, such as a status report solution.

Before we start building the data model for the performance appraisal solution, one additional point concerns the level in your SharePoint site structure where the columns are to be created. With SharePoint content types, columns can be created at the site collection, site, or list levels. If you create columns at the site collection level, they can be referenced anywhere within nested sites and lists, thus maximizing their reuse. For the example described in this book, the columns will be created at the site collection level.

EmployeeName

Now we can begin the task of creating the site columns. The first step is to navigate in the browser to the Site Column Gallery page for the site collection:

1. In the browser, navigate to the SharePoint site collection home page.
2. From the Site Actions menu, click Site Settings | Modify All Site Settings.
3. In the Galleries section, click Site columns.

As shown in Table 3-1, the EmployeeName column is defined as a Person or Group data type. This data type is automatically bound to a plain text content control in the Office Word 2007 document template. If users were to use the Office Word 2007 content control to modify the site column data, they could easily make typographical errors. Fortunately, in the Document Information Panel, the Person or Group data type is bound to a people picker control. You can use the address book or "check names" feature of the people picker control to enter valid user data. The user's display name will then be shown in the corresponding Office Word 2007 plain text content control.

For this solution, all site columns will be added to a new Human Resources group. To create the EmployeeName column in this group, use the following steps:

1. On the Site Column Gallery page, click Create.

2. In the Column name box, type **EmployeeName.**

3. Click Person or Group.

4. In the Group section, click New group and then type **Human Resources**.

5. In the Additional Column Settings section, for the Require that this column contains information option, click Yes. Figure 3.1 shows the settings for the EmployeeName column.

6. Click OK.

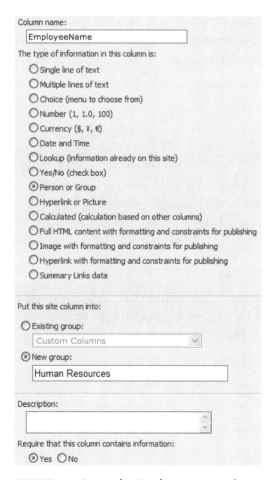

FIGURE 3.1 Create the EmployeeName column.

Although we are not making any additional changes to the EmployeeName column, we should point out some of the options in the Additional Column Settings section for Person or Group columns. You can specify whether to allow multiple selections and whether groups can be selected. By default, only one selection is allowed, and choices are limited to people only. You can also narrow the choice of users to those in a particular group, with the default option being all users. Lastly, you can change the user property that is shown in SharePoint list views. By default, the display name of the user will be shown, although you could choose instead to display the user's email address, for example.

AppraiserName

The AppraiserName column is also defined as a Person or Group data type. As with the EmployeeName column, you will not need to modify any additional column settings. Since you have already created the Human Resources group, you can select from an existing group when creating the column. To create the Appraiser-Name column, do the following:

1. On the Site Column Gallery page, click Create.

2. In the Column name box, type **AppraiserName**.

3. Click Person or Group.

4. In the Group section, from the Existing group list, click Human Resources.

5. In the Additional Column Settings section, for the Require that this column contains information option, click Yes.

6. Click OK.

AppraisalPeriodStart

The AppraisalPeriodStart column is defined as a Date and Time data type and identifies the start of the appraisal period. To create the AppraisalPeriodStart column, use the following steps:

1. On the Site Column Gallery page, click Create.

2. In the Column name box, type **AppraisalPeriodStart**.

3. Click Date and Time.

4. In the Group section, from the Existing group list, click Human Resources.

5. In the Additional Column Settings section, for the Require that this column contains information option, click Yes.

6. Click OK.

We will not be making any additional changes to the AppraisalPeriodStart column, but we will still point out some of the options in the Additional Column Settings section for Date and Time columns. By default, these values are displayed as "date only" in SharePoint list views, but you can change the format to show the date and time. You can also specify a default value, which can be set to today's date, a hard-coded date and time, or a calculated value. The Document Information Panel also offers the ability to set default values and provides the added benefit of allowing conditional logic, so we will save the discussion of default values for a later chapter.

AppraisalPeriodEnd

The AppraisalPeriodEnd column is also defined as a Date and Time data type and identifies the end of the appraisal period. As with the AppraisalPeriodStart column, you will not need to modify any additional column settings. To create the AppraisalPeriodEnd column, do the following:

1. On the Site Column Gallery page, click Create.
2. In the Column name box, type **AppraisalPeriodEnd**.
3. Click Date and Time.
4. In the Group section, from the Existing group list, click Human Resources.
5. In the Additional Column Settings section, for the Require that this column contains information option, click Yes.
6. Click OK.

AppraisalDate

The AppraisalDate column is also defined as a Date and Time data type and identifies the date of the face-to-face meeting between the employee and appraiser. As with the other Date and Time columns, you will not need to modify any additional column settings. To create the AppraisalDate column, do the following:

1. On the Site Column Gallery page, click Create.
2. In the Column name box, type **AppraisalDate**.
3. Click Date and Time.
4. In the Group section, from the Existing group list, click Human Resources.
5. In the Additional Column Settings section, for the Require that this column contains information option, click Yes.
6. Click OK.

EmployeeOverallComments

The choice of whether to define a comments column as either a Single line of text or Multiple lines of text is somewhat nominal in document content types. Both data types are automatically bound to the plain text content control in the Office Word 2007 document template. By default, a plain text content control bound to a Multiple lines of text column is set up to handle multiple paragraphs, but you could modify content control settings to have the same functionality if it were bound to a Single line of text column. However, if you enter multiple paragraphs into a plain text content control using a carriage return between paragraphs and that control is bound to a Single line of text column, then all paragraphs will be consolidated into a single paragraph because the carriage return is ignored by this column type. As a result, we will define each "comments" column with the Multiple lines of text data type. To create the EmployeeOverallComments column, use the following steps:

1. On the Site Column Gallery page, click Create.
2. In the Column name box, type **EmployeeOverallComments**.
3. Click Multiple lines of text.
4. In the Group section, from the Existing group list, click Human Resources.
5. Click OK.

We will not be making any additional changes to the EmployeeOverallComments column, but it is worth noting some of the other options in the Additional Column Settings section for Multiple lines of text columns. By default, the option to allow unlimited length in document libraries is disabled. If you enable this option, a dialog box appears and warns that columns with long text are not supported by most applications for editing documents and could result in a loss of data. You should keep this option disabled unless users will be uploading documents from the SharePoint list and not saving directly from Office Word 2007. Additionally, for Multiple lines of text columns, you can specify the number of lines for editing, whether to allow plain text or rich text (with or without pictures, tables, and hyperlinks), and whether changes should be appended to existing text.

AppraiserOverallComments

The AppraiserOverallComments column is also defined as a Multiple lines of text data type. As with the EmployeeOverallComments column, you will not need to modify any additional column settings.

To create the AppraiserOverallComments column, use the following steps:

1. On the Site Column Gallery page, click Create.
2. In the Column name box, type **AppraiserOverallComments**.
3. Click Multiple lines of text.
4. In the Group section, from the Existing group list, click Human Resources.
5. Click OK.

AppraisalStatus

The AppraisalStatus column is defined as a Choice data type and is the crux for SharePoint workflows in the performance appraisal solution. Each time the appraiser changes this column value, a workflow process is triggered that notifies some user that a task needs to be performed. We will discuss the workflows for the performance appraisal solution in a later chapter. To create the AppraisalStatus column, do the following:

1. On the Site Column Gallery page, click Create.
2. In the Column name box, type **AppraisalStatus**.
3. Click Choice (menu to choose from).
4. In the Group section, from the Existing group list, click Human Resources.
5. In the Additional Column Settings section, for the Require that this column contains information option, click Yes.
6. In the Type each choice on a separate line box, enter the following values on separate lines: 1 - Goals Draft, 2 - Goals Finalized, 3 - Collect Feedback, 4 - Appraisal Draft, and 5 - Appraisal Finalized.
7. Press Tab, which will auto-update the default value. Figure 3.2 shows how the options should appear in the Additional Column Settings section.
8. Click OK.

Choice Default Values

For Choice columns, the default value will initially be set to the first option listed, unless you specify otherwise. You can also choose not to have a default value by clearing this field.

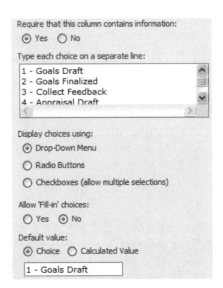

FIGURE 3.2 Create the AppraisalStatus column.

In the Additional Column Settings section, the default option is to display choices using a drop-down menu, which is what we are using here. But you could also have choices displayed as radio buttons or check boxes. Additionally, you could allow users to fill in their own choices, and the default could be a calculated value.

With the AppraisalStatus column created, you should now have eight site columns in your Human Resources group, as shown in Figure 3.3. In the next section, we will add these site columns to a new site content type and then include the goal information site columns.

Human Resources	
AppraisalDate	Date and Time
AppraisalPeriodEnd	Date and Time
AppraisalPeriodStart	Date and Time
AppraisalStatus	Choice
AppraiserName	Person or Group
AppraiserOverallComments	Multiple lines of text
EmployeeName	Person or Group
EmployeeOverallComments	Multiple lines of text

FIGURE 3.3 Review the general information site columns.

Goal Information Columns

We have already mentioned that repeating structures are not supported in Share-Point content types. In the performance appraisal solution, one or more goals are defined for the employee, with each goal having a description, metric, weight, score, weighted score, and appraiser comments. Because a 1:N relationship cannot be created with the out-of-the-box content type, you must instead identify a finite number of goals, and thus a finite number of nested columns. For our solution we will set the goal limit at five, although you could easily add to that at a later time. With the goal limit set, the goal information site columns will be defined as shown in Table 3.2.

TABLE 3.2 Goal Information Site Columns

Column Name	Data Type
GoalDescription1-5	Single line of text
GoalMetric1-5	Single line of text
GoalComments1-5	Multiple lines of text
GoalWeight1-5	Number
GoalScore1-5	Number
GoalWeightedScore1-5	Number
WeightTotal	Number
ScoreTotal	Number

GoalDescription

The GoalDescription column allows users to briefly describe a goal. This column is one of the nested elements and thus will be defined five times using the Single line of text data type. Each unique GoalDescription column will have an enumerator appended to its name. To create the GoalDescription columns, use the following steps:

1. On the Site Column Gallery page, click Create.
2. In the Column name box, type **GoalDescription1**.
3. Click Single line of text.
4. In the Group section, from the Existing group list, click Human Resources.

5. Click OK.

6. Repeat steps 1–5 for the other four GoalDescription columns. Figure 3.4 shows how these columns will appear on the Site Column Gallery page.

GoalDescription1	Single line of text
GoalDescription2	Single line of text
GoalDescription3	Single line of text
GoalDescription4	Single line of text
GoalDescription5	Single line of text

FIGURE 3.4 Create the GoalDescription columns.

In the Additional Column Settings section for Single line of text columns, you can specify the maximum number of characters the user can enter, with the default being 255. You can also specify a default value for the column. Default values can be text or calculated. For the performance appraisal solution, we will not make any changes in the Additional Column Settings section for these columns.

GoalMetric

The GoalMetric column identifies the criteria used by the appraiser to determine a score. This column is also a nested element and will be defined five times using the Single line of text data type. To create the GoalMetric columns, use the following steps:

1. On the Site Column Gallery page, click Create.

2. In the Column name box, type **GoalMetric1**.

3. Click Single line of text.

4. In the Group section, from the Existing group list, click Human Resources.

5. Click OK.

6. Repeat steps 1–5 for the other four GoalMetric columns. Figure 3.5 shows how these columns will appear on the Site Column Gallery page.

GoalMetric1	Single line of text
GoalMetric2	Single line of text
GoalMetric3	Single line of text
GoalMetric4	Single line of text
GoalMetric5	Single line of text

FIGURE 3.5 Create the GoalMetric columns.

GoalComments

The GoalComments column captures feedback from the appraiser about how the employee performed with respect to the specific goal. This column is also a nested element and will be defined five times. Since the appraiser has the option of collecting feedback from other users (for example, project managers or peers), it makes sense to define the column using the Multiple lines of text data type instead of the Single line of text data type. To create the GoalComments columns, do the following:

1. On the Site Column Gallery page, click Create.
2. In the Column name box, type **GoalComments1**.
3. Click Multiple lines of text.
4. In the Group section, from the Existing group list, click Human Resources.
5. Click OK.
6. Repeat steps 1–5 for the other four GoalComments columns. Figure 3.6 shows how these columns will appear on the Site Column Gallery page.

GoalComments1	Multiple lines of text
GoalComments2	Multiple lines of text
GoalComments3	Multiple lines of text
GoalComments4	Multiple lines of text
GoalComments5	Multiple lines of text

FIGURE 3.6 Create the GoalComments columns.

GoalWeight

The GoalWeight column identifies the weight of a particular goal per the overall appraisal. This column is also a nested element and will be defined five times using the Number data type. To create the GoalWeight columns, use the following steps:

1. On the Site Column Gallery page, click Create.
2. In the Column name box, type **GoalWeight1**.
3. Click Number (1, 1.0, 100).
4. In the Group section, from the Existing group list, click Human Resources.
5. In the Additional Column Settings section, in the Min box, type **0**.
6. In the Max box, type **100**.
7. Select the Show as percentage (for example, 50%) check box.
8. Click OK.
9. Repeat steps 1–8 for the other four GoalWeight columns. Figure 3.7 shows how these columns will appear on the Site Column Gallery page.

GoalWeight1	Number
GoalWeight2	Number
GoalWeight3	Number
GoalWeight4	Number
GoalWeight5	Number

FIGURE 3.7 Create the GoalWeight columns.

Percentage values will be displayed as decimals (for example, .65) in the corresponding plain text content controls of the Office Word 2007 document template. In the Additional Column Settings section for Number columns, you can also indicate the number of decimal places and specify a default value (text or calculated).

GoalScore

The GoalScore column identifies the score of a particular goal. This column is also a nested element and will be defined five times using the Number data type. For the performance appraisal solution, the scale used for scoring is 0-5, although you can make adjustments as needed.

To create the GoalScore columns, use the following steps:

1. On the Site Column Gallery page, click Create.
2. In the Column name box, type **GoalScore1**.
3. Click Number (1, 1.0, 100).
4. In the Group section, from the Existing group list, click Human Resources.
5. In the Additional Column Settings section, in the Min box, type **0**.
6. In the Max box, type **5**.
7. Click OK.
8. Repeat steps 1–7 for the other four GoalScore columns. Figure 3.8 shows how these columns will appear on the Site Column Gallery page.

GoalScore1	Number
GoalScore2	Number
GoalScore3	Number
GoalScore4	Number
GoalScore5	Number

FIGURE 3.8 Create the GoalScore columns.

GoalWeightedScore

The GoalWeightedScore column identifies the product of the corresponding Goal-Weight and GoalScore columns. This column is also a nested element and will be defined five times. Because of the calculation, it would seem logical to define each of these columns using the Calculated data type. Unfortunately, Calculated columns do not have bound nodes in the Document Information Panel or bound content controls in the Office Word 2007 document template. Thus, they cannot be displayed in the appraisal accordingly. As a work-around to the display issue, you can define each column using the Number data type and then add declarative logic to the Document Information Panel to perform the calculations.

To create the GoalWeightedScore columns, do the following:

1. On the Site Column Gallery page, click Create.
2. In the Column name box, type **GoalWeightedScore1**.
3. Click Number (1, 1.0, 100).
4. In the Group section, from the Existing group list, click Human Resources.
5. In the Additional Column Settings section, in the Min box, type **0**.
6. In the Max box, type **5**.
7. Click OK.
8. Repeat steps 1–7 for the other four GoalWeightedScore columns. Figure 3.9 shows how these columns will appear on the Site Column Gallery page.

GoalWeightedScore1	Number
GoalWeightedScore2	Number
GoalWeightedScore3	Number
GoalWeightedScore4	Number
GoalWeightedScore5	Number

FIGURE 3.9 Create the GoalWeightedScore columns.

WeightTotal

The WeightTotal column identifies the sum of all the GoalWeight columns. Again, because Calculated columns are not bound to content controls in the Office Word 2007 document template and thus cannot be displayed, you will need to define this column using the Number data type. Declarative logic can then be added to the Document Information Panel that performs the calculation. To create the Weight-Total column, use the following steps:

1. On the Site Column Gallery page, click Create.
2. In the Column name box, type **WeightTotal**.
3. Click Number (1, 1.0, 100).
4. In the Group section, from the Existing group list, click Human Resources.

5. In the Additional Column Settings section, in the Min box, type **0**.

6. In the Max box, type **100**.

7. Select the Show as percentage (for example, 50%) check box.

8. Click OK.

ScoreTotal

The ScoreTotal column identifies the sum of all the GoalWeightedScore columns. Again, because Calculated columns are not bound to content controls in the Office Word 2007 document template and thus cannot be displayed, you will need to define this column using the Number data type. Declarative logic can then be added to the Document Information Panel that performs the calculation. To create the ScoreTotal column, do the following:

1. On the Site Column Gallery page, click Create.

2. In the Column name box, type **ScoreTotal**.

3. Click Number (1, 1.0, 100).

4. In the Group section, from the Existing group list, click Human Resources.

5. In the Additional Column Settings section, in the Min box, type **0**.

6. In the Max box, type **5**.

7. Click OK.

PERFORMANCE APPRAISAL SITE CONTENT TYPE

At this point you should have 40 site columns within the Human Resources group. The next step in the development process is to create a site content type and then add the existing columns. As with columns, content types can be created at the site collection, site, or list levels, and the same referencing rules apply. For the sake of consistency, we will create the content type at the site collection level. We will also create a new Human Resources group, which will make it easier to find the content type when we are ready to reference it from a SharePoint list. Within our site collection, there is a Human Resources site. In subsequent chapters, the content type will be referenced in lists within that site.

To create the Performance Appraisal content type, use the following steps:

1. Navigate to the site collection home page.
2. From the Site Actions menu, click Site Settings | Modify All Site Settings.
3. In the Galleries section, click Site content types.
4. On the Site Content Type Gallery page, click Create.
5. In the Name box, type **Performance Appraisal**.
6. From the Select parent content type from list, click Document Content Types.
7. From the Parent Content Type list, click Document.
8. In the Group section, click New group and type **Human Resources**. Figure 3.10 shows the settings for the Performance Appraisal content type.
9. Click OK.

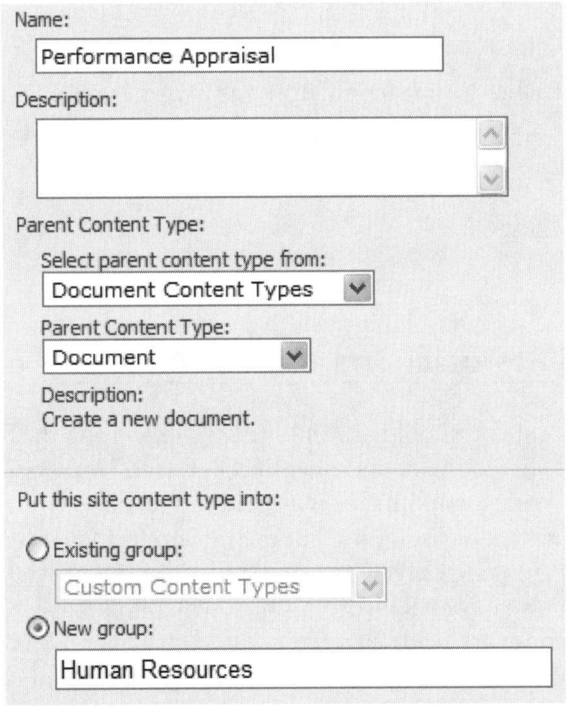

FIGURE 3.10 Create the Performance Appraisal content type.

ADD FROM EXISTING SITE COLUMNS

With the site content type created, you can reference the existing Human Resources site columns from the Site Content Type: Performance Appraisal page. To add these columns to the content type:

1. In the Columns section, click Add from existing site columns.

2. From the Select columns from list, click Human Resources.

3. To select all of the site columns, click AppraisalDate, scroll to the bottom of the Available columns list, press Shift and click WeightTotal.

4. Click Add. Figure 3.11 shows all of the site columns being added for the Performance Appraisal content type.

5. Click OK.

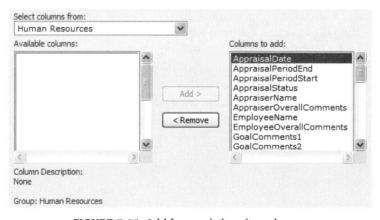

FIGURE 3.11 Add from existing site columns.

When adding existing columns, you can specify whether content types inheriting from the site content type should be updated or not. Notice the statement in the Update List and Site Content Types section: "This operation can take a long time, and any customizations made to these values on the child site and list content types will be lost." However, both performance and inheritance are not an issue at this point, since the Performance Appraisal content type has not yet been referenced. As a result, for the option to Update all content types inheriting from this type, you can leave the default option (Yes) selected.

ADD FROM NEW SITE COLUMNS

In our approach to building the Performance Appraisal content type, the columns were created first and then added to a new content type. That sequence is not a requirement. You could have also created the site content type first and then added new site columns from there. There is also the option of first creating site columns, adding them to a new content type, and then adding new site columns to the content type. In the case of the performance appraisal solution, you may later decide that there should be more than five goals allowed. If you needed to add a GoalDescription6 column, for example, from the Site Content Type: Performance Appraisal page, you would click Add from new site column. The New Site Column page allows you define a site column much like you did earlier in the chapter. The only variation on this page is the option to Update all content types inheriting from this type.

EDIT SITE COLUMNS

Before concluding this chapter, there are some items worth noting when editing existing site columns. Column names can be changed, but the new names will not be reflected in the corresponding nodes in the Document Information Panel. In addition, not all of the data types are available when editing a site column. For example, a Choice column cannot be changed to a Person or Group column, and a Multiple lines of text column cannot be changed to any other data type. In cases like these, it might be best to delete the existing site column and create a new one with the correct data type.

4 Document Template

The Office Word 2007 document template is the presentation layer of the performance appraisal content type. The template provides users with an interface by which they can edit SharePoint metadata and start workflow processes. Within the template, there are content controls that map to the site columns you built in the previous chapter. These content controls are the data-entry points for your users and help transform the template from a word-processing application to a data-collection tool. In this chapter, we will build the document template for the out-of-the-box performance appraisal solution.

DOCUMENT LIBRARY

Before building the document template, we will need a SharePoint document library from which we can reference the performance appraisal content type. This library is required in order for us to add the correct content controls to the template. In this section, we will do the following:

- Create a document library within our site collection
- Set permissions for that library accordingly
- Reference the performance appraisal content type

CREATE A LIBRARY

The document library is where appraisers go to start the document template and commence the performance appraisal solution. It is also the location where performance appraisal documents are subsequently stored. When working with a site content type, you must have at least one document library that references the content type if you want to add content controls to the document template that are bound to the site columns. For the example described in this book, we will create a document library within the Human Resources site of our site collection.

To create the document library, use the following steps:

1. In the browser, navigate to the Human Resources site.

2. From the Site Actions menu, click Create.

3. In the Libraries section, click Document Library.

4. On the New page, in the Name box, type a descriptive name for the document library. Since the document library is a workspace for a particular appraiser, you might want to identify the appraiser in the name of the library, as shown in Figure 4.1.

5. Click Create.

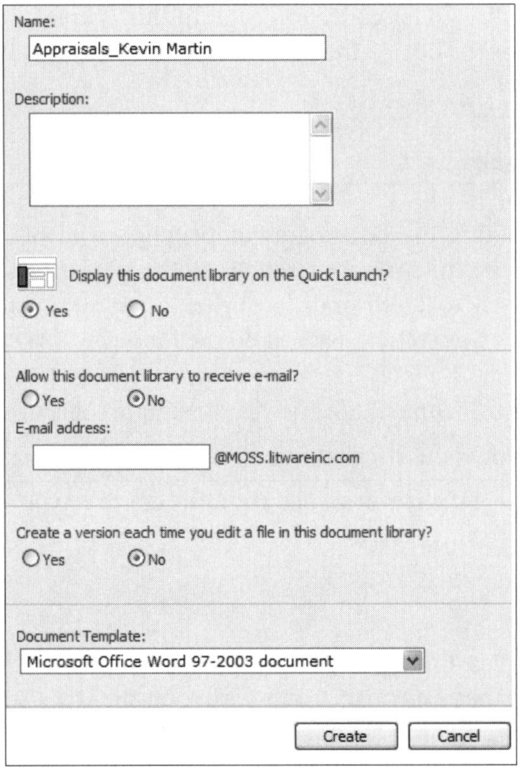

FIGURE 4.1 Create an appraiser document library.

On the New page, we will not be modifying any settings for the document library, although it is worth noting some of the other options. In the Navigation section, you can specify whether a link to the document library should appear in the Quick Launch of your site navigation. Even with the default option (Yes) selected, users who do not have any access to the document library will not see the link displayed in their Quick Launch. You can also specify whether to allow items to be added to the library through email or whether a new version is created each time you edit a file. Versioning can be extremely useful if auditing is required for your appraisal process, but it will significantly increase the size of the SharePoint index. In the Document Template section, you can identify the default application to use for new files created in the document library. The value selected here is immaterial, as we will subsequently suppress the default template when referencing the performance appraisal content type.

SET PERMISSIONS

There are three basic levels of permissions for all pages in your SharePoint site collection. Table 4.1 shows these permission levels and how they pertain to document library content.

TABLE 4.1 Basic SharePoint Permissions

Permission Level	Description
Full Control	Users have full control of the document library, including the ability to set permissions
Contribute	Users can view, add, update, and delete items in the document library
Read	Users can only view items in the document library

All other permission levels are variations of these three. In the performance appraisal solution, we will give the appraiser full control over his document library and remove access for all other users. By default, permissions for a document library are inherited from its parent, in this case the Human Resources site. We will stop inheriting permissions from the site to give the appraiser full control and restrict access for everyone else. The appraiser can then modify permissions for the document library as needed.

To edit permissions for the document library:

1. In the document library you just created, from the Settings menu, click Document Library Settings.

2. In the Permissions and Management section, click Permissions for this document library.

3. On the Permissions page, from the Actions menu, click Edit Permissions.

4. In the Windows Internet Explorer message box, click OK to create unique permissions for the document library.

5. Select the check boxes for all users and groups. An easy way to do this is to select the Select All check box, located to the left of the Users/Groups column header.

6. From the Actions menu, click Remove User Permissions.

7. In the Windows Internet Explorer message box, click OK to confirm the removal of all permissions.

8. From the New menu, click Add Users.

9. On the Add Users page, in the Users/Groups box, type the name of the appropriate appraiser and click the Check Names button control (or press Ctrl+K).

10. In the Give Permission section, select the Full Control - Has full control check box, as shown in Figure 4.2.

11. Click OK.

On the Add Users page, you can also choose whether to send new users a welcome email message. The subject and body of the message can be personalized, with links and information about the site appearing below the personal message. By default, a welcome email message will be sent with a subject that reads Welcome to the SharePoint document library: <<LIBRARY NAME>>.

Welcome Email Message

The ability to send a welcome email message depends on the version of SharePoint you are using. If you recall from Chapter 1, we are using Office SharePoint Server 2007 Enterprise CAL.

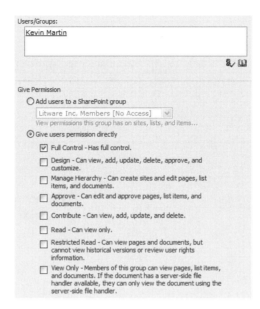

FIGURE 4.2 Give the appraiser full control to the document library.

REFERENCE THE CONTENT TYPE

In the previous chapter you created the Performance Appraisal content type at the site collection level. Here, we will reference that content type from the appraiser document library you just created. A reference allows you to inherit all of the properties of the content type from any list within the site collection. At a later time, users will be able to navigate to the document library and start the document template from the New menu.

By default, the management of content types at the list level is disabled, meaning you cannot reference a content type from the appraiser document library unless you specify otherwise. From the Document Library Advanced Settings page, you will enable this option and then reference the content type:

1. On the Permissions page, in the breadcrumb trail, click Settings.

2. In the General Settings section, click Advanced settings.

3. In the Content Types section, click Yes to allow management of content types.

4. Click OK.

5. In the Content Types section, click Add from existing site content types.

6. On the Add Content Types page, from the Select site content types from list, click Human Resources.

7. With Performance Appraisal selected in the Available Site Content Types box, click Add. Figure 4.3 shows the Performance Appraisal content type being added to the document library.

8. Click OK.

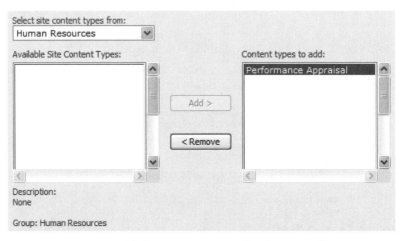

FIGURE 4.3 Add the content type to the document library.

There are now two content types available in the appraiser document library. You just added the Performance Appraisal content type. The default Document content type was included when you created the document library. If you want to change the order in which content types appear on the new menu, change the default content type, or remove a content type, click Change new button order and default content type and make your changes accordingly.

Another point worth mentioning is the fact that content type columns will not be displayed in list views by default. If you want any of the site columns that you created in the previous chapter—along with their corresponding values—to appear in your document library, you must make modifications to the view(s). In our scenario, the appraiser document library has the default All Documents view. In the Views section, click the All Documents link and make your changes accordingly.

OFFICE WORD 2007 DOCUMENT

After you create and configure the appraiser document library, the next step is to add an Office Word 2007 document to the content type. The format and layout of the initial document is a matter of personal preference. We are not UI design specialists, so we traded ornamentation for utility, as can be seen in Figure 4.4. This document layout makes the placement of content controls, which you will do later in this chapter, somewhat obvious.

Document Template Download

To use the same Office Word 2007 document that we used as a starting point, download the file Performance Appraisal.docx from http://www.courseptr.com/ downloads.

Performance Appraisal

Employee: Period Start:
Reviewer: Period End:
Date of Appraisal:

Goals

Description	Metric	Comments	Weight	Score
		Totals:		

Employee Comments:
Reviewer Comments

FIGURE 4.4 Start with a simple Word document.

Regardless of the format and layout you choose, you will need to navigate to the content type settings page to add the initial Office Word 2007 document:

1. In the browser, navigate to the site collection home page.
2. From the Site Actions menu, click Site Settings | Modify All Site Settings.

3. In the Galleries section, click Site content types.

4. In the Human Resources section, click Performance Appraisal.

5. In the Settings section, click Advanced settings.

6. On the Site Content Type Advanced Settings page, in the Document Template section, click Upload a new document template and then click Browse.

7. In the Choose file dialog box, navigate to the location of your initial Office Word 2007 document and double-click it. Figure 4.5 shows how the Document Template section would appear.

8. Click OK.

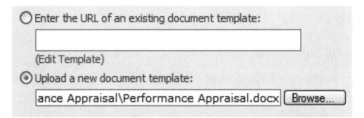

FIGURE 4.5 Add the initial document to the content type.

On the Site Content Type Advanced Settings page, you can set the content type to be read only. By default, the content type is modifiable, which is the setting we will keep for this scenario. In addition, you can specify whether all child site and list content types using this type should be updated with the settings on this page. Since we have already created a document library that inherits from this content type, we will leave the default Yes option selected.

ADD CONTENT CONTROLS

Content controls are mapped to site columns and are the data-entry points for users in the document template. With an initial Office Word 2007 document added to our Performance Appraisal content type, we can now navigate back to the appraiser document library and insert these content controls:

1. In the browser, navigate to the appraiser document library.

2. From the New menu, click Performance Appraisal.

3. If a Windows Internet Explorer message box appears asking for confirmation to open the file, click OK to continue.

When Office Word 2007 starts, you will notice a panel at the top of the document, below the ribbon. This is the Document Information Panel, which is an embedded Office InfoPath 2007 form that can be used to add business logic to the document template. By default, it displays controls for all the site columns of the content type. For now, you can ignore the Document Information Panel, which we will modify in the next chapter. In the next few sections, we will add the content controls in the order that their corresponding headers appear in the initial document.

EmployeeName

The first header seen at the top of the document is Employee, which maps to the EmployeeName site column of our content type. This site column is defined as a Person or Group data type, thus making it bound to a plain text content control in the document. To add the EmployeeName content control, use the following steps:

1. Place the cursor to the right of the Employee header in the document.
2. Click the Insert tab on the ribbon.
3. In the Text group, from the Quick Parts menu, click the Document Property submenu and then click EmployeeName. Figure 4.6 shows the EmployeeName content control added to the document.

FIGURE 4.6 Add a content control to the document.

If the Developer tab is not visible in the ribbon, then you will need to enable it from the Word Options dialog box in order to make modifications to content controls:

1. Click the Office button (File menu) and then click Word Options.
2. In the Word Options dialog box, select the Show Developer tab in the Ribbon check box, as shown in Figure 4.7.
3. Click OK.

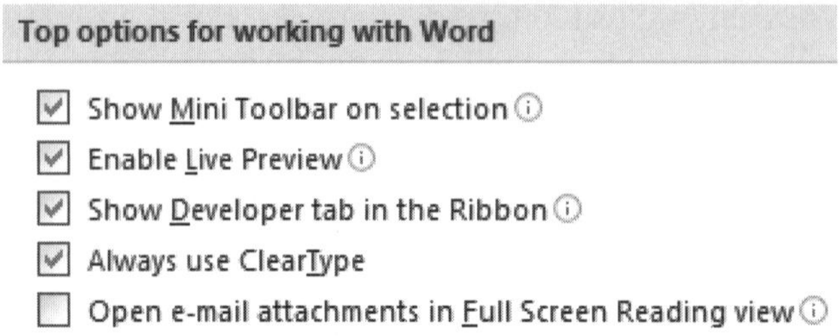

Top options for working with Word

☑ Show <u>M</u>ini Toolbar on selection ⓘ
☑ Enable <u>L</u>ive Preview ⓘ
☑ Show <u>D</u>eveloper tab in the Ribbon ⓘ
☑ Always use Clear<u>T</u>ype
☐ Open e-mail attachments in <u>F</u>ull Screen Reading view ⓘ

FIGURE 4.7 Show the Developer tab in the ribbon.

OFFICE OPEN XML FILE FORMATS

Office Word 2007 provides support for the Office Open XML (OOXML) file formats, which are also supported in Office Excel 2007 and Office PowerPoint 2007. OOXML combines XML and ZIP technologies to offer a standard and extensible file format. In essence, each OOXML document is a ZIP archive that contains numerous XML parts.

One of the XML parts in our performance appraisal document template contains the data source that corresponds to the site columns created in the previous chapter. This part was added automatically when we associated the document template with the Performance Appraisal content type. The content controls that are being added to the document template are actually bound to nodes in the XML part.

For more information about OOXML, go to http://msdn.microsoft.com/en-us/library/aa338205.aspx.

With the Developer tab enabled, you can modify the properties of any content control. You can "lock" a content control so that it cannot be deleted from the document, and you can prevent users from editing its content. We will prevent users from deleting any of the content controls added to the performance appraisal document template. In the case of the EmployeeName content control, we will also prevent users from editing its contents. This choice was made to reduce typos in a plain text content control. To modify the properties of the EmployeeName content control, use the following steps:

1. Click the EmployeeName content control in the document.

2. Click the Developer tab in the ribbon.

3. In the Controls group, click Properties.

4. In the Content Control Properties dialog box, in the Locking section, select the Content control cannot be deleted check box.

5. Ensure that the Contents cannot be edited check box is selected. Figure 4.8 shows how the Content Control Properties dialog box should appear.

6. Click OK.

FIGURE 4.8 Set properties for the EmployeeName content control.

Although we are not making any additional changes to the properties of the EmployeeName content control, we should point out some of the other options in the Content Control Properties dialog box. For plain text content controls, you can specify whether to allow carriage returns (multiple paragraphs). If the Content control cannot be deleted option were not selected, you could choose to remove the content control when contents are edited. For all content controls, you can also use a style to format contents.

AppraiserName

Below the Employee header is the Reviewer header, which maps to the Appraiser-Name site column of our content type. This site column is also defined as a Person or Group data type, thus making it bound to a plain text content control in the document. To add the AppraiserName content control, do the following:

1. Place the cursor to the right of the Reviewer header in the document.

2. Click the Insert tab on the ribbon.

3. In the Text group, from the Quick Parts menu, click the Document Property submenu and then click AppraiserName.

As with the EmployeeName content control, we will modify the AppraiserName content control to prevent users from deleting the content control or editing its contents, relying instead on the people picker control in the Document Information Panel to properly select names. To modify the properties of the Appraiser-Name content control, do the following:

1. Click the AppraiserName content control in the document.
2. Click the Developer tab in the ribbon.
3. In the Controls group, click Properties.
4. In the Content Control Properties dialog box, in the Locking section, select the Content control cannot be deleted check box.
5. Ensure that the Contents cannot be edited check box is selected.
6. Click OK.

AppraisalDate

Below the Reviewer header is the Date of Appraisal header, which maps to the AppraisalDate site column of our content type. This site column is defined as a Date and Time data type, thus making it bound to a date picker content control in the document. To add the AppraisalDate content control, do the following:

1. Place the cursor to the right of the Date of Appraisal header in the document.
2. Click the Insert tab on the ribbon.
3. In the Text group, from the Quick Parts menu, click the Document Property submenu and then click AppraisalDate.

In the case of the AppraisalDate content control, we will allow users to edit contents, since typos are not an issue with the date picker content control. To modify the properties of the AppraisalDate content control, do the following:

1. Click the AppraisalDate content control in the document.
2. Click the Developer tab in the ribbon.
3. In the Controls group, click Properties.
4. In the Content Control Properties dialog box, in the Locking section, select the Content control cannot be deleted check box. Figure 4.9 shows how the Content Control Properties dialog box should appear.
5. Click OK.

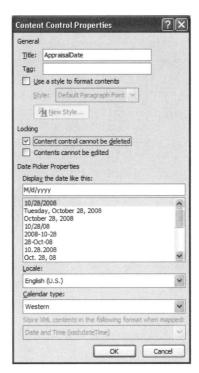

FIGURE 4.9 Set properties for the AppraisalDate content control.

We will not be making any additional changes to the AppraisalDate content control, but we will still point out some of the options in the Content Control Properties dialog box for date picker content controls. By default, the date is displayed in "M/d/yyyy" format, but you can change it to long text, ISO, or some other format. Regardless of which format you select, the date and time will still be stored for the site column. You can also change the locale from the default (English) to Japanese, German, or something else. The calendar type can also be changed from Western to Arabic Hijri or Hebrew Lunar.

The AppraisalDate content control has a red-dashed border around it. This is the result of a date picker content control being mapped to a site column that requires a value. If you were to select a date, using either the date picker content control or the corresponding control in the Document Information Panel, the border would disappear. In the next chapter, we will add declarative logic to the Document Information Panel that adds default values for the AppraisalDate, AppraisalPeriodStart, and AppraisalPeriodEnd content controls.

AppraisalPeriodStart

To the right of the EmployeeName content control is the Period Start header, which maps to the AppraisalPeriodStart site column of our content type. This site column is defined as a Date and Time data type, thus making it bound to a date picker content control in the document. To add the AppraisalPeriodStart content control, do the following:

1. Place the cursor to the right of the Period Start header in the document.
2. Click the Insert tab on the ribbon.
3. In the Text group, from the Quick Parts menu, click the Document Property submenu and then click AppraisalPeriodStart.

Again, note that the AppraisalPeriodStart content control has a red-dashed border around it. As with the AppraisalDate content control, we will prevent users from deleting the AppraisalPeriodStart content control but allow contents to be edited. To modify the properties of the AppraisalPeriodStart content control, do the following:

1. Click the AppraisalPeriodStart content control in the document.
2. Click the Developer tab in the ribbon.
3. In the Controls group, click Properties.
4. In the Content Control Properties dialog box, in the Locking section, select the Content control cannot be deleted check box.
5. Click OK.

AppraisalPeriodEnd

To the right of the AppraiserName content control is the Period End header, which maps to the AppraisalPeriodEnd site column of our content type. This site column is defined as a Date and Time data type, thus making it bound to a date picker content control in the document.

To add the AppraisalPeriodEnd content control, do the following:

1. Place the cursor to the right of the Period End header in the document.
2. Click the Insert tab on the ribbon.
3. In the Text group, from the Quick Parts menu, click the Document Property submenu and then click AppraisalPeriodEnd.

Again, note that the AppraisalPeriodEnd content control has a red-dashed border around it. As with the other date picker content controls, we will prevent users from deleting the AppraisalPeriodEnd content control but allow contents to be edited. To modify the properties of the AppraisalPeriodEnd content control, use the following steps:

1. Click the AppraisalPeriodEnd content control in the document.
2. Click the Developer tab in the ribbon.
3. In the Controls group, click Properties.
4. In the Content Control Properties dialog box, in the Locking section, select the Content control cannot be deleted check box.
5. Click OK.

GoalDescription

In the Goals section of the document template, there are five empty rows, one for each set of "Goal Information" columns that we defined in the previous chapter. Here, we will insert the five content controls that correspond to the Description table header, which map to the GoalDescription site columns of our content type. Each of these site columns is defined as a Single line of text data type, thus making them bound to plain text content controls in the document. To add the GoalDescription content controls, do the following:

1. Place the cursor in the first empty cell below the Description header in the document.
2. Click the Insert tab on the ribbon.
3. In the Text group, from the Quick Parts menu, click the Document Property submenu and then click GoalDescription1.
4. Repeat steps 1–3 for the other four empty cells below the Description header, making sure to add the GoalDescription2, GoalDescription3, GoalDescription4, and GoalDescription5 content controls, respectively. Figure 4.10 shows the GoalDescription content controls added to the Description column.

Goal descriptions are generally pretty concise, so we do not need to allow multiple paragraphs. However, we do need to prevent users from deleting the content controls.

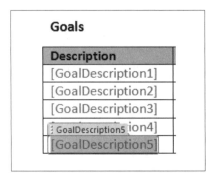

FIGURE 4.10 Add the GoalDescription content controls.

To modify the properties of the GoalDescription content controls, use the following steps:

1. Click the GoalDescription1 content control in the document.
2. Click the Developer tab in the ribbon.
3. In the Controls group, click Properties.
4. In the Content Control Properties dialog box, in the Locking section, select the Content control cannot be deleted check box.
5. Click OK.
6. Repeat steps 1–5 for the GoalDescription2, GoalDescription3, GoalDescription4, and GoalDescription5 content controls.

GoalMetric

We will now insert the five content controls that correspond to the Metric table header, which map to the GoalMetric site columns of our content type. Each of these site columns is defined as a Single line of text data type, thus making them bound to plain text content controls in the document. To add the GoalMetric content controls, do the following:

1. Place the cursor in the first empty cell below the Metric header in the document.
2. Click the Insert tab on the ribbon.
3. In the Text group, from the Quick Parts menu, click the Document Property submenu and then click GoalMetric1.

4. Repeat steps 1–3 for the other four empty cells below the Metric header, making sure to add the GoalMetric2, GoalMetric3, GoalMetric4, and GoalMetric5 content controls, respectively.

Goal metrics, like descriptions, are also pretty concise, so we do not need to allow multiple paragraphs. However, we do need to prevent users from deleting the content controls. To modify the properties of the GoalMetric content controls, use the following steps:

1. Click the GoalMetric1 content control in the document.
2. Click the Developer tab in the ribbon.
3. In the Controls group, click Properties.
4. In the Content Control Properties dialog box, in the Locking section, select the Content control cannot be deleted check box.
5. Click OK.
6. Repeat steps 1–5 for the GoalMetric2, GoalMetric3, GoalMetric4, and GoalMetric5 content controls.

GoalComments

Next, we will insert the five content controls that correspond to the Comments table header, which map to the GoalComments site columns of our content type. Each of these site columns is defined as a Multiple lines of text data type, thus making them bound to plain text content controls in the document. To add the Goal-Comments content controls, use these steps:

1. Place the cursor in the first empty cell below the Comments header in the document.
2. Click the Insert tab on the ribbon.
3. In the Text group, from the Quick Parts menu, click the Document Property submenu and then click GoalComments1.
4. Repeat steps 1–3 for the other four empty cells below the Comments header, making sure to add the GoalComments2, GoalComments3, GoalComments4, and GoalComments5 content controls, respectively.

Goal comments tend to be much more verbose than descriptions or metrics, so multiple paragraphs are allowed, which is the default setting for plain text content controls that are mapped to Multiple lines of text data types. We just need to prevent users from deleting these content controls. To modify the properties of the GoalComments content controls, do the following:

1. Click the GoalComments1 content control in the document.
2. Click the Developer tab in the ribbon.
3. In the Controls group, click Properties.
4. In the Content Control Properties dialog box, in the Locking section, select the Content control cannot be deleted check box.
5. Click OK.
6. Repeat steps 1–5 for the GoalComments2, GoalComments3, GoalComments4, and GoalComments5 content controls.

GoalWeight

Next, we will insert the five content controls that correspond to the Weight table header, which map to the GoalWeight site columns of our content type. Each of these site columns is defined as a Number data type, thus making them bound to plain text content controls in the document. To add the GoalWeight content controls, do the following:

1. Place the cursor in the first empty cell below the Weight header in the document.
2. Click the Insert tab on the ribbon.
3. In the Text group, from the Quick Parts menu, click the Document Property submenu and then click GoalWeight1.
4. Repeat steps 1–3 for the other four empty cells below the Weight header, making sure to add the GoalWeight2, GoalWeight3, GoalWeight4, and GoalWeight5 content controls, respectively.

Goal weights are numerical values, so we do not need to allow multiple paragraphs. We just need to prevent users from deleting these content controls. To modify the properties of the GoalWeight content controls, use the following steps:

1. Click the GoalWeight1 content control in the document.
2. Click the Developer tab in the ribbon.
3. In the Controls group, click Properties.

4. In the Content Control Properties dialog box, in the Locking section, select the Content control cannot be deleted check box.

5. Click OK.

6. Repeat steps 1–5 for the GoalWeight2, GoalWeight3, GoalWeight4, and GoalWeight5 content controls.

For each GoalWeight content control, if users type a value less than 0 or greater than 1, a red-dashed border will appear around the content control. This is the result of the minimum (0) and maximum (100) values you specified when creating the site columns, with those values being converted to percentages.

GoalScore

The five content controls that correspond to the Score table header are mapped to the GoalScore site columns of our content type. Each of these site columns is defined as a Number data type, thus making them bound to plain text content controls in the document. To add the GoalScore content controls, use the following steps:

1. Place the cursor in the first empty cell below the Score header in the document.

2. Click the Insert tab on the ribbon.

3. In the Text group, from the Quick Parts menu, click the Document Property submenu and then click GoalScore1.

4. Repeat steps 1–3 for the other four empty cells below the Score header, making sure to add the GoalScore2, GoalScore3, GoalScore4, and GoalScore5 content controls, respectively.

Goal scores are also numerical values, so we do not need to allow multiple paragraphs. We just need to prevent users from deleting these content controls. To modify the properties of the GoalScore content controls, do the following:

1. Click the GoalScore1 content control in the document.

2. Click the Developer tab in the ribbon.

3. In the Controls group, click Properties.

4. In the Content Control Properties dialog box, in the Locking section, select the Content control cannot be deleted check box.

5. Click OK.

6. Repeat steps 1–5 for the GoalScore2, GoalScore3, GoalScore4, and GoalScore5 content controls.

For each GoalScore content control, if users type a value less than 0 or greater than 5, a red-dashed border will appear around the content control. This is the result of the minimum and maximum values you specified when creating the site columns.

WeightTotal

At the bottom of the Weight column, we will insert the content control that maps to the WeightTotal site column of our content type. This site column is defined as a Number data type, thus making it bound to a plain text content control in the document. To add the WeightTotal content control, use these steps:

1. Place the cursor in the empty cell at the bottom of the Weight column (in the Totals area).
2. Click the Insert tab on the ribbon.
3. In the Text group, from the Quick Parts menu, click the Document Property submenu and then click WeightTotal. Figure 4.11 shows the WeightTotal content control added to the Totals area of the document.

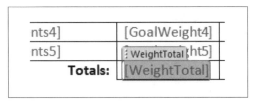

FIGURE 4.11 Add the WeightTotal content control to the document.

The weight total is a numerical value, so we do not need to allow multiple paragraphs. However, this content control will calculate the sum of the GoalWeight values, and we want to prevent users from editing its contents. The functionality that calculates the sum of the GoalWeight values will be discussed when we customize the Document Information Panel in the next chapter. To modify the properties of the WeightTotal content control, use the following steps:

1. Click the WeightTotal content control in the document.
2. Click the Developer tab in the ribbon.
3. In the Controls group, click Properties.
4. In the Content Control Properties dialog box, in the Locking section, select the Content control cannot be deleted check box.

5. Select the Contents cannot be edited check box.

6. Click OK.

ScoreTotal

At the bottom of the Score column, we will insert the content control that maps to the ScoreTotal site column of our content type. This site column is defined as a Number data type, thus making it bound to a plain text content control in the document. To add the ScoreTotal content control:

1. Place the cursor in the empty cell at the bottom of the Score column (in the Totals area).

2. Click the Insert tab on the ribbon.

3. In the Text group, from the Quick Parts menu, click the Document Property submenu and then click ScoreTotal.

The score total is a numerical value, so we do not need to allow multiple paragraphs. However, this content control will calculate the sum of the Goal-WeightedScore values, and we want to prevent users from editing its contents. The GoalWeightedScore content controls will not appear in the document template, and the functionality that calculates the sum of those values will be discussed when we customize the Document Information Panel in the next chapter. To modify the properties of the ScoreTotal content control, do the following:

1. Click the ScoreTotal content control in the document.

2. Click the Developer tab in the ribbon.

3. In the Controls group, click Properties.

4. In the Content Control Properties dialog box, in the Locking section, select the Content control cannot be deleted check box.

5. Select the Contents cannot be edited check box.

6. Click OK.

EmployeeOverallComments

Below the Goals table, we will insert the content control that maps to the Employee-OverallComments site column of our content type. This site column is defined as a Multiple lines of text data type, thus making it bound to a plain text content control in the document.

To add the EmployeeOverallComments content control, do the following:

1. Place the cursor to the right of the Employee Comments header in the document.
2. Click the Insert tab on the ribbon.
3. In the Text group, from the Quick Parts menu, click the Document Property submenu and then click EmployeeOverallComments.

Employee comments can be verbose, so multiple paragraphs are allowed, which is the default setting for plain text content controls that are mapped to Multiple lines of text data types. We just need to prevent users from deleting the content control. To modify the properties of the EmployeeOverallComments content control, do the following:

1. Click the EmployeeOverallComments content control in the document.
2. Click the Developer tab in the ribbon.
3. In the Controls group, click Properties.
4. In the Content Control Properties dialog box, in the Locking section, select the Content control cannot be deleted check box.
5. Click OK.

AppraiserOverallComments

Below the EmployeeOverallComments content control, we will insert the content control that maps to the AppraiserOverallComments site column of our content type, the last content control that needs to be added. This site column is defined as a Multiple lines of text data type, thus making it bound to a plain text content control in the document. To add the AppraiserOverallComments content control, use the following steps:

1. Place the cursor to the right of the Reviewer Comments header in the document.
2. Click the Insert tab on the ribbon.
3. In the Text group, from the Quick Parts menu, click the Document Property submenu and then click AppraiserOverallComments.

Appraiser comments can also be verbose, so multiple paragraphs are allowed, which is the default setting for plain text content controls that are mapped to

Multiple lines of text data types. We just need to prevent users from deleting the content control. To modify the properties of the AppraiserOverallComments content control:

1. Click the AppraiserOverallComments content control in the document.
2. Click the Developer tab in the ribbon.
3. In the Controls group, click Properties.
4. In the Content Control Properties dialog box, in the Locking section, select the Content control cannot be deleted check box.
5. Click OK.

Your document template should now appear as shown in Figure 4.12.

Performance Appraisal

Employee:	[EmployeeName]	Period Start:	[AppraisalPeriodStart]
Reviewer:	[AppraiserName]	Period End:	[AppraisalPeriodEnd]
Date of Appraisal:	[AppraisalDate]		

Goals

Description	Metric	Comments	Weight	Score
[GoalDescription1]	[GoalMetric1]	[GoalComments1]	[GoalWeight1]	[GoalScore1]
[GoalDescription2]	[GoalMetric2]	[GoalComments2]	[GoalWeight2]	[GoalScore2]
[GoalDescription3]	[GoalMetric3]	[GoalComments3]	[GoalWeight3]	[GoalScore3]
[GoalDescription4]	[GoalMetric4]	[GoalComments4]	[GoalWeight4]	[GoalScore4]
[GoalDescription5]	[GoalMetric5]	[GoalComments5]	[GoalWeight5]	[GoalScore5]
			Totals: [WeightTotal]	[ScoreTotal]

Employee Comments:	[EmployeeOverallComments]
Reviewer Comments	[AppraiserOverallComments]

FIGURE 4.12 Review the document template with the content controls.

Placeholder Text

If you want to change the placeholder text for a content control, you will need to click the Developer tab and then, in the Controls group, click Design Mode. Then you can edit the placeholder text accordingly.

NOTE

DEFINE A NAMING CONVENTION

On an initial save of a document, Office Word 2007 will use the first line of text it sees in the file name. If you were to save the document template right now, you would see that the "Performance Appraisal" text at the top is the default file name. To make the default file-naming convention dynamic, you can use content controls at the top of the document template. For our scenario, we will add side-by-side EmployeeName and AppraisalDate content controls, which will concatenate the two corresponding values into a default file name.

To add the two content controls to the document, do the following:

1. Place the cursor to the left of the "Performance Appraisal" text, at the top of the document, and press Enter.

2. Place the cursor on the empty line above the "Performance Appraisal" text.

3. Click the Insert tab on the ribbon.

4. In the Text group, from the Quick Parts menu, click the Document Property submenu and then click EmployeeName.

5. Place the cursor to the right of the EmployeeName content control.

6. Click the Insert tab on the ribbon.

7. In the Text group, from the Quick Parts menu, click the Document Property submenu and then click AppraisalDate. Figure 4.13 shows the content controls side-by-side at the top of the document.

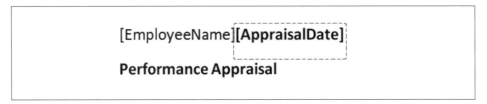

FIGURE 4.13 Add content controls for the naming convention.

It should be noted that when identifying the first line of text in a document, Office Word 2007 stops when it encounters a character that is not a space or alphanumeric (for example, comma, dash, slash, and so on). So when adding the AppraisalDate content control at the top of the document, you will need to select a date format that contains only alphanumeric or space characters.

To modify the date format properties of the AppraisalDate content control, do the following:

1. Click the AppraisalDate content control at the top of the document.
2. Click the Developer tab in the ribbon.
3. In the Controls group, click Properties.
4. In the Date Picker Properties section, click the date format that displays "d MMMM yyyy" in the Display the date like this box, as shown in Figure 4.14.
5. Click OK.

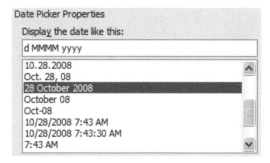

FIGURE 4.14 Select the date format for the naming convention.

If you want to "hide" these content controls from end users, there is a simple formatting trick to employ. Just change the font color to match that of the background color and the font size to a minuscule amount. You cannot remove the content controls, but you can change their properties so that they seem invisible. To modify the font properties of a content control, you must ensure that the Contents cannot be edited check box is not selected. To modify the font color and size for these controls, use the following steps:

1. Click the EmployeeName content control at the top of the document.
2. Click the Developer tab in the ribbon.
3. In the Controls group, click Properties.
4. In the Content Control Properties dialog box, in the Locking section, clear the Contents cannot be edited check box.
5. Click OK.

6. Select the first line of the document, which includes the EmployeeName and AppraisalDate content controls.

7. Click the Home tab in the ribbon.

8. In the Font group, select the font size, type **1**, and press Enter. Figure 4.15 shows how to modify the font size in the ribbon.

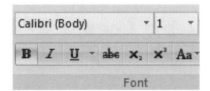

FIGURE 4.15 Change the font size.

9. Click the Font Color command and click the color that matches the background color of the document template (for example, white). Figure 4.16 shows how to modify the font color in the ribbon.

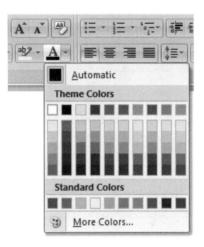

FIGURE 4.16 Change the font color.

We also do not want users deleting the content controls or editing their contents, so we will lock down both of them. To modify the properties of these controls, follow these steps:

1. Click the EmployeeName content control at the top of the document.

2. Click the Developer tab in the ribbon.

3. In the Controls group, click Properties.

4. In the Content Control Properties dialog box, in the Locking section, select the Content control cannot be deleted check box.

5. Select the Contents cannot be edited check box.

6. Click OK.

7. Click the AppraisalDate content control at the top of the document.

8. Click the Developer tab in the ribbon.

9. In the Controls group, click Properties.

10. In the Content Control Properties dialog box, in the Locking section, select the Content control cannot be deleted check box.

11. Select the Contents cannot be edited check box.

12. Click OK.

GROUP THE DOCUMENT

After all content controls have been added, you can group the document to prevent users from changing any of the document headers. Essentially, you want anyone with access to the performance appraisal document to use only the content controls (or the Document Information Panel) to modify content. This will make the document template act more like a form than a word-processing application and limit edits to the site column data. To group the entire document, do the following:

1. Place the cursor anywhere in the document and press Ctrl+A.

2. Click the Developer tab in the ribbon.

3. In the Controls group, from the Group menu, click Group.

To confirm that the document has been grouped, try to change the Performance Appraisal header at the top of the document to something else. When you attempt an edit, the status bar at the bottom displays a message indicating that the selection is locked, as shown in Figure 4.17.

NOTE

Ungroup the Document

To ungroup the document template, select the entire document by pressing Ctrl+A, click the Developer tab in the ribbon, and then click Ungroup from the Group menu.

FIGURE 4.17 Group the document template.

UPDATE THE CONTENT TYPE

When you are finished with all edits in Office Word 2007, you can then update the Performance Appraisal content type to use the new template. First, save the document to a shared location by following these steps:

1. Press Ctrl+S.
2. In the Save As dialog box, navigate to a location from which you can upload the document to SharePoint, type a name in the File name box, and then click Save.
3. Close Office Word 2007.

To upload the new document template, you must navigate to the Site Content Type Advanced Settings page for the Performance Appraisal content type, as shown in these steps:

1. In the browser, navigate to the site collection home page.
2. From the Site Actions menu, click Site Settings | Modify All Site Settings.
3. In the Galleries section, click Site content types.
4. In the Human Resources section, click Performance Appraisal.

5. In the Settings section, click Advanced settings.

6. On the Site Content Type Advanced Settings page, in the Document Template section, click Upload a new document template and then click Browse.

7. In the Choose file dialog box, navigate to the location of your new Office Word 2007 document and double-click it.

8. Click OK.

Uploading the new document template updates all content types inheriting from the site collection level. So, when you navigate back to the appraiser document library and start a performance appraisal in Office Word 2007, the new document template will be used.

Two Uploads

Why did we upload the document template twice in this chapter? The first upload was simply to associate the document template with the Performance Appraisal content type, thus allowing the site columns to appear within the Quick Parts menu in the ribbon of Office Word 2007. The second upload was necessary to update the content type document template so that it included the content controls.

5 Document Information Panel

T he Document Information Panel is an Office InfoPath 2007 form template that is embedded in the Office Word 2007 template for the content type. It is displayed at the top of the document template and contains data source nodes for all of the content type site columns, which also map to content controls used in the document template. With Office InfoPath 2007, you also get a rich, declarative rules engine that allows you to add data validation, calculated fields, and other functionality to the document template, without having to write code. In this chapter, we will create a new custom form template for the out-of-the-box performance appraisal solution.

NEW PERFORMANCE APPRAISAL FORM TEMPLATE

At the moment, the Performance Appraisal content type uses a default form template for the Document Information Panel. As you may recall from the previous chapter, the default form template exposes all of the site columns in our content type. Having all these controls at the top of the document template expends a lot of vertical space and is rather inefficient, especially since many of the site columns are also mapped to content controls in the document template. So, in this chapter, we will create a new custom form template that displays only a subset of site columns:

- EmployeeName
- AppraiserName
- AppraisalPeriodStart
- AppraisalPeriodEnd
- AppraisalStatus

NOTE

Install Office InfoPath 2007

To create a custom Document Information Panel, Office InfoPath 2007 must be installed on your machine.

To create a new custom form template, you must navigate to the Document Information Panel Settings page for the content type, as follows:

1. In the browser, navigate to the site collection home page.
2. From the Site Actions menu, click Site Settings | Modify All Site Settings.
3. In the Galleries section, click Site content types.
4. In the Human Resources section, click Performance Appraisal.
5. In the Settings section, click Document Information Panel settings.
6. In the Document Information Panel Template section, click Create a new custom template, as shown in Figure 5.1.
7. In Office InfoPath 2007, in the Data Source Wizard dialog box, click Finish.

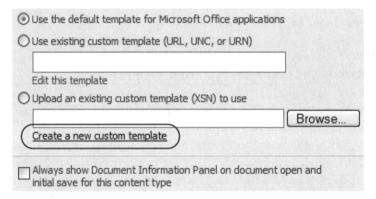

FIGURE 5.1 Create a new custom form template.

FORM TEMPLATE LAYOUT

When your new custom template starts in Office InfoPath 2007, all of the site columns are mapped to controls in the form view. Each of the site column controls is contained within its own horizontal region control. In addition, each site column control has a corresponding expression box that displays a header, which by default is the site column name.

For the Performance Appraisal content type, we will simplify the Document Information Panel. First, we will delete all of the horizontal region controls except for the ones containing our aforementioned subset of site columns:

1. Click the horizontal region control containing the Title header and corresponding text box.
2. Press Delete.
3. Repeat the previous two steps for all horizontal region controls except the ones containing AppraisalPeriodEnd, AppraisalPeriodStart, AppraisalStatus, AppraiserName, and EmployeeName. The form view should appear as shown in Figure 5.2.

FIGURE 5.2 Delete horizontal region controls.

When horizontal regions are used as they currently are, the controls will wrap in the Document Information Panel if they do not fit across the width of the Office Word 2007 document template. To ensure that wrapping will not occur in the Document Information Panel, and thus preserve vertical space in the document template, you can place the controls and corresponding headers into a layout table with a single row. To create the layout table for the Document Information Panel, use the following steps:

1. Place the cursor on the empty line below the horizontal regions.
2. From the Table menu, click Insert | Layout Table.
3. In the Insert Table dialog box, change the Number of columns value to 5 and then change the Number of rows value to 1.
4. Click OK. Figure 5.3 shows the layout table below the horizontal regions.

In the subsections that follow, we will move the controls from the horizontal regions to the layout table.

FIGURE 5.3 Insert a layout table.

EmployeeName

In the Office Word 2007 document template, the EmployeeName site column, defined as a Person or Group data type, was bound to a plain text content control. We then modified the settings of that content control so that it could not be edited. This was done to re-direct users of this solution to the Document Information Panel, where they could use a people picker control instead. The people picker has address book functionality and allows you to select from a list of authenticated users in your SharePoint site collection. When you select a user in the people picker, the display name will get added to the corresponding plain text control in the Office Word 2007 document template. To move the EmployeeName people picker and header into the layout table, follow these steps:

1. Select the EmployeeName header, which is an expression box control, and the corresponding people picker control. Press Ctrl to multiselect.
2. Drag the selected controls into the first cell of the layout table.
3. To modify the header text, double-click the expression box, change the Text box value to "Employee Name:" (space added), and then click OK.
4. Delete the empty horizontal region.
5. Adjust the width of the first cell accordingly.

NOTE

InfoPath People Picker Control

The people picker is not available as a standard control in Office InfoPath 2007 and is added to the form view when a new Document Information Panel is created. If you delete the people picker from the form view, to get it back into the form, you may need to use the Add or Remove Custom Controls dialog box. For more information about adding the people picker control to an InfoPath form template, go to http://blogs.msdn.com/infopath/archive/2007/02/28/using-the-contact-selector-control.aspx.

AppraiserName

As is the case with the EmployeeName site column, the AppraiserName site column is defined as a Person or Group data type and is bound to a plain text content control in the Office Word 2007 document template. Likewise, the content control in the document template cannot be edited. So, once again users of this solution will turn to the people picker in the Document Information Panel to identify the appraiser's name. To move the AppraiserName people picker and header into the layout table, do the following:

1. Select the AppraiserName header, which is an expression box control, and the corresponding people picker control.
2. Drag the selected controls into the second cell of the layout table.
3. To modify the header text, double-click the expression box, change the Text box value to "Appraiser Name:" (space added), and then click OK.
4. Delete the empty horizontal region.
5. Adjust the width of the second cell accordingly.

AppraisalPeriodStart

The AppraisalPeriodStart site column is bound to a date picker in both the Office Word 2007 document template and Document Information Panel. Users of this solution can modify the appraisal period start date with either control. Later in this chapter, we will add a default value and some data validation for this site column. To move the AppraisalPeriodStart date picker and header into the layout table, use these steps:

1. Select the AppraisalPeriodStart header, which is an expression box control, and the corresponding date picker control.
2. Drag the selected controls into the third cell of the layout table.
3. To modify the header text, double-click the expression box, change the Text box value to "Appraisal Period Start:" (spaces added), and then click OK.
4. Delete the empty horizontal region.
5. Adjust the width of the third cell accordingly.

AppraisalPeriodEnd

The AppraisalPeriodEnd site column is also bound to a date picker in both the Office Word 2007 document template and Document Information Panel. Users of this solution can modify the appraisal period end date with either control. Later in this chapter, we will add a default value and some data validation for this site column as well. To move the AppraisalPeriodEnd date picker and header into the layout table, follow these steps:

1. Select the AppraisalPeriodEnd header, which is an expression box control, and the corresponding date picker control.

2. Drag the selected controls into the fourth cell of the layout table.

3. To modify the header text, double-click the expression box, change the Text box value to "Appraisal Period End:" (spaces added), and then click OK.

4. Delete the empty horizontal region.

5. Adjust the width of the fourth cell accordingly.

AppraisalStatus

The AppraisalStatus site column is defined as a Choice data type and is not displayed in the Office Word 2007 document template. In the Document Information Panel, this site column is bound to a drop-down list box control, which offers five options. Each option represents a particular stage in the performance appraisal solution. When users change the value of the drop-down list box control and save the document template, a specific workflow is triggered. In the next chapter, we will discuss workflow configuration in greater detail. To move the AppraisalStatus drop-down list box and header into the layout table, follow these steps:

1. Select the AppraisalStatus header, which is an expression box control, and the corresponding drop-down list box control.

2. Drag the selected controls into the fifth cell of the layout table.

3. To modify the header text, double-click the expression box, change the Text box value to "Appraisal Status:" (space added), and then click OK.

4. Delete the empty horizontal region.

5. Adjust the width of the fifth cell accordingly. The form view should now appear, as shown in Figure 5.4.

FIGURE 5.4 Complete the layout table.

DEFAULT VALUES

We had the option of identifying default values for site columns in Chapter 3. However, Office InfoPath 2007 offers more advanced declarative logic for setting values, especially with respect to columns defined as Date and Time data types. So, we will identify default values for the AppraisalPeriodStart, AppraisalPeriodEnd, and AppraisalDate site columns in the Document Information Panel.

AppraisalPeriodStart

The appraisal period start date by default should be the date on which the appraiser first starts the performance appraisal solution for a particular employee. For example, if the appraiser kicks off the Office Word 2007 document template for one of his direct reports on July 1, 2009, then the AppraisalPeriodStart value should be set to that date. However, if the AppraisalPeriodStart value has already been set when a user starts the Office Word 2007 document template, then the value will not be changed. If users of this solution need to modify the AppraisalPeriodStart value afterward, they can still do so in the document template or the Document Information Panel.

To set the default value for the AppraisalPeriodStart site column in the Document Information Panel, use the following steps:

1. From the Tools menu, click Form Options.
2. In the Form Options dialog box, for the Open and Save category, click Rules.
3. In the Rules for Opening Forms dialog box, click Add.
4. In the Rule dialog box, in the Name box, type **Set AppraisalPeriodStart** and then click Set Condition.
5. Click the list on the left and then click Select a field or group.
6. In the Select a Field or Group dialog box, expand the p:properties group and then expand the :documentManagement group.
7. Double-click the ns2:AppraisalPeriodStart node.
8. In the Condition dialog box, click the middle list and then click "is blank." Figure 5.5 shows how the Condition dialog box should appear.

FIGURE 5.5 Set the condition for the AppraisalPeriodStart default value.

9. Click OK.

10. In the Rule dialog box, click Add Action.

11. In the Action dialog box, click the Action list and then click Set a field's value.

12. Click the Select a Field or Group button, located to the right of the Field box.

13. In the Select a Field or Group dialog box, expand the p:properties group and then expand the :documentManagement group.

14. Double-click the ns2:AppraisalPeriodStart node.

15. In the Action dialog box, click the Insert Formula button, located to the right of the Value box.

16. In the Insert Formula dialog box, click Insert Function.

17. In the Insert Function dialog box, click the Date and Time category and then double-click the now function.

18. In the Insert Formula dialog box, click OK. The Action dialog box should appear, as shown in Figure 5.6.

19. In the Action dialog box, click OK.

20. In the Rule dialog box, click OK.

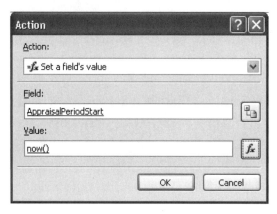

FIGURE 5.6 Set the AppraisalPeriodStart default value.

AppraisalPeriodEnd

The AppraisalPeriodEnd value represents the last day of the appraisal period. The default value for this site column can be determined based on the value entered for the AppraisalPeriodStart site column. In our implementation of the solution, performance appraisals are done annually, so the AppraisalPeriodEnd value can be determined by adding 364 days (or 365 in a leap year) to the AppraisalPeriodStart value. However, if the AppraisalPeriodEnd value has already been set when a user starts the Office Word 2007 document template, then the value will not be changed. Of course, you can adjust the number of days in the appraisal period accordingly, depending on the frequency of appraisals in your organization.

To set the default value for the AppraisalPeriodEnd site column in the Document Information Panel, do the following:

1. In the Rules for Opening Forms dialog box, click Add.
2. In the Rule dialog box, in the Name box, type **Set AppraisalPeriodEnd** and then click Set Condition.
3. Click the list on the left and then click Select a field or group.
4. In the Select a Field or Group dialog box, expand the p:properties group and then expand the :documentManagement group.
5. Double-click the ns2:AppraisalPeriodEnd node.
6. In the Condition dialog box, click the middle list and then click "is blank."
7. Click OK.
8. In the Rule dialog box, click Add Action.
9. In the Action dialog box, click the Action list and then click Set a field's value.
10. Click the Select a Field or Group button, located to the right of the Field box.
11. In the Select a Field or Group dialog box, expand the p:properties group and then expand the :documentManagement group.
12. Double-click the ns2:AppraisalPeriodEnd node.
13. In the Action dialog box, click the Insert Formula button, located to the right of the Value box.
14. In the Insert Formula dialog box, click Insert Function.
15. In the Insert Function dialog box, click the Date and Time category and then double-click the addDays function.
16. In the Insert Formula dialog box, double-click the first double click to insert field prompt, as shown in Figure 5.7.

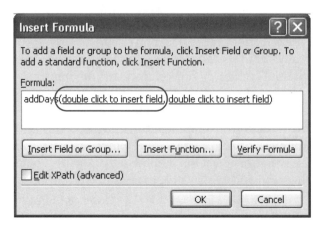

FIGURE 5.7 Identify the node to which days are added.

17. In the Select a Field or Group dialog box, expand the p:properties group and then expand the :documentManagement group.

18. Double-click the ns2:AppraisalPeriodStart node.

19. In the Insert Formula dialog box, replace the other double click to insert field prompt with 364. The Insert Formula dialog box should now appear, as shown in Figure 5.8.

20. In the Insert Formula dialog box, click OK.

21. In the Action dialog box, click OK.

22. In the Rule dialog box, click OK.

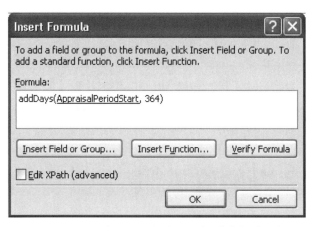

FIGURE 5.8 Set the AppraisalPeriodEnd default value.

AppraisalDate

The AppraisalDate value represents the date of the face-to-face meeting that occurs between the employee and appraiser. We removed the date picker in the Document Information Panel, but you can still use declarative logic to set the site column value, which will be displayed in the plain text content control in the document template. The default value for this site column can be determined based on the value entered for the AppraisalPeriodEnd site column. In our implementation of the solution, face-to-face meetings occur two weeks after the conclusion of the appraisal period, so the AppraisalDate value can be determined by adding 13 days to the AppraisalPeriodEnd value. However, if the AppraisalDate value has already been set when a user starts the Office Word 2007 document template, then the value will not be changed. Again, you can adjust the number of days accordingly, depending on when face-to-face meetings actually take place.

To set the default value for the AppraisalDate site column in the Document Information Panel, follow these steps:

1. In the Rules for Opening Forms dialog box, click Add.
2. In the Rule dialog box, in the Name box, type **Set AppraisalDate** and then click Set Condition.
3. Click the list on the left and then click Select a field or group.
4. In the Select a Field or Group dialog box, expand the p:properties group and then expand the :documentManagement group.
5. Double-click the ns2:AppraisalDate node.
6. In the Condition dialog box, click the middle list and then click "is blank."
7. Click OK.
8. In the Rule dialog box, click Add Action.
9. In the Action dialog box, click the Action list and then click Set a field's value.
10. Click the Select a Field or Group button, located to the right of the Field box.
11. In the Select a Field or Group dialog box, expand the p:properties group and then expand the :documentManagement group.
12. Double-click the ns2:AppraisalDate node.
13. In the Action dialog box, click the Insert Formula button, located to the right of the Value box.
14. In the Insert Formula dialog box, click Insert Function.

15. In the Insert Function dialog box, click the Date and Time category and then double-click the addDays function.

16. In the Insert Formula dialog box, double-click the first double click to insert field prompt.

17. In the Select a Field or Group dialog box, expand the p:properties group and then expand the :documentManagement group.

18. Double-click the ns2:AppraisalPeriodEnd node.

19. In the Insert Formula dialog box, replace the other double click to insert field prompt with 13. The Insert Formula dialog box should now appear, as shown in Figure 5.9.

20. Click OK until all dialog boxes have been closed.

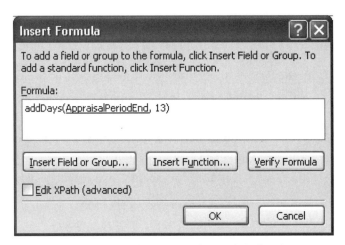

FIGURE 5.9 Set the AppraisalDate default value.

DATA VALIDATION

Adding data validation to the Document Information Panel ensures that users do not violate certain business logic in your solution. For example, you should not be able to specify an appraisal period end date that precedes the start date. Moreover, the appraisal date should occur sometime after the appraisal period end date. Currently, in our solution, users can modify these dates however they prefer, without any check to determine that dates are in a logical time sequence. We will add data validation to the Document Information Panel to remedy that issue.

AppraisalPeriodEnd

The appraisal period end date cannot precede the appraisal period start date. If we add data validation to support that logic, users of this solution will see a red-dashed border around the AppraisalPeriodEnd date pickers in the Document Information Panel and document template when they violate the rule. You must also specify a screen tip that will appear when users pause on the date picker control. Dialog box messages can also be displayed to provide additional information. To add data validation for the AppraisalPeriodEnd site column in the Document Information Panel, use the following steps:

1. In the Design Tasks task pane, click Data Source.

2. In the Data Source task pane, expand the p:properties group and the :documentManagement group and then double-click the ns2:AppraisalPeriodEnd node.

3. In the Field or Group Properties dialog box, click the Validation tab.

4. Click Add.

5. In the Data Validation (AppraisalPeriodEnd) dialog box, click the top-middle list and click is less than.

6. Click the top-right list and click Select a field or group.

7. In the Select a Field or Group dialog box, double-click the ns2:AppraisalPeriodStart node.

8. In the Data Validation (AppraisalPeriodEnd) dialog box, in the ScreenTip box, type **The end date cannot precede the start date.** Figure 5.10 shows how the Data Validation (AppraisalPeriodEnd) dialog box should appear.

9. Click OK until all dialog boxes have been closed.

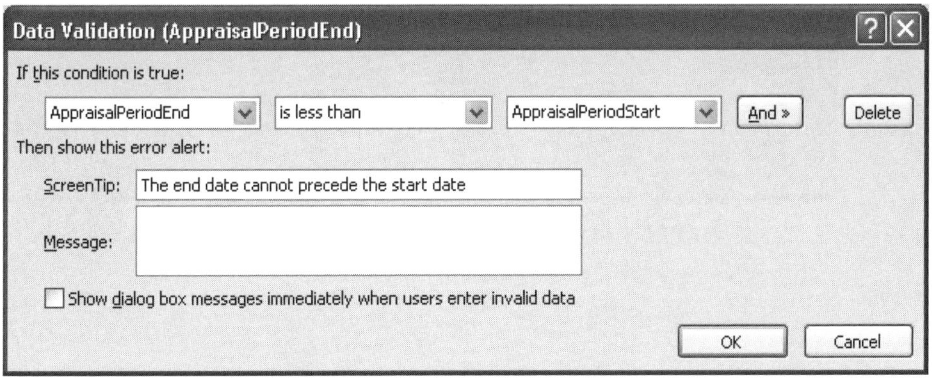

FIGURE 5.10 Set data validation for the AppraisalPeriodEnd site column.

AppraisalDate

The date of the face-to-face meeting between the employee and appraiser cannot precede the appraisal period end date. If we add data validation to support that logic, users will see a red-dashed border around the AppraisalDate date picker in the document template when they violate the rule. Again, you must also specify a screen tip. To add data validation for the AppraisalDate site column in the Document Information Panel, do the following:

1. In the Data Source task pane, double-click the ns2:AppraisalDate node.
2. In the Field or Group Properties dialog box, click the Validation tab.
3. Click Add.
4. In the Data Validation (AppraisalDate) dialog box, click the top-middle list and click is less than.
5. Click the top-right list and click Select a field or group.
6. In the Select a Field or Group dialog box, double-click the ns2:AppraisalPeriodEnd node.
7. In the Data Validation (AppraisalDate) dialog box, in the ScreenTip box, type **The appraisal date cannot precede the period end date.** Figure 5.11 shows how the Data Validation (AppraisalDate) dialog box should appear.
8. Click OK until all dialog boxes have been closed.

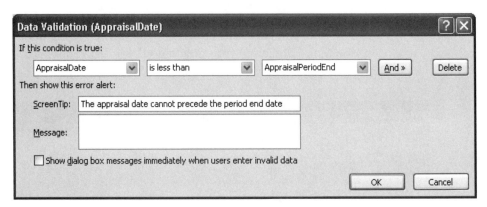

FIGURE 5.11 Set data validation for the AppraisalDate site column.

CALCULATED FIELDS

The Goals section of the Office Word 2007 document template contains a number of fields that need to be calculated. If you recall from Chapter 3, we elected not to use the Calculated data type when creating these columns. The reason for this was because Calculated columns do not have bound nodes in the Document Information Panel or bound content controls in the Office Word 2007 document template. As a result, we need to define calculated fields declaratively in the Document Information Panel.

GoalWeightedScore

The five GoalWeightedScore site columns, hidden in the Document Information Panel and Office Word 2007 document template, are calculated by taking the product of the corresponding GoalWeight and GoalScore columns. The GoalWeightedScore columns are then summed to get a score total, which we will describe in a later section. To set up each GoalWeightedScore column as a calculated field, do the following:

1. In the Data Source task pane, double-click the ns2:GoalWeightedScore1 node.
2. In the Field or Group Properties dialog box, click the Insert Formula button, located to the right of the Value box.
3. In the Insert Formula dialog box, click Insert Field or Group.
4. In the Select a Field or Group dialog box, double-click the ns2:GoalWeight1 node.
5. In the Insert Formula dialog box, in the Formula box, place the cursor to the right of GoalWeight1 and then type *.
6. Click Insert Field or Group.
7. In the Select a Field or Group dialog box, double-click the ns2:GoalScore1 node. Figure 5.12 shows how the Insert Formula dialog box should appear.

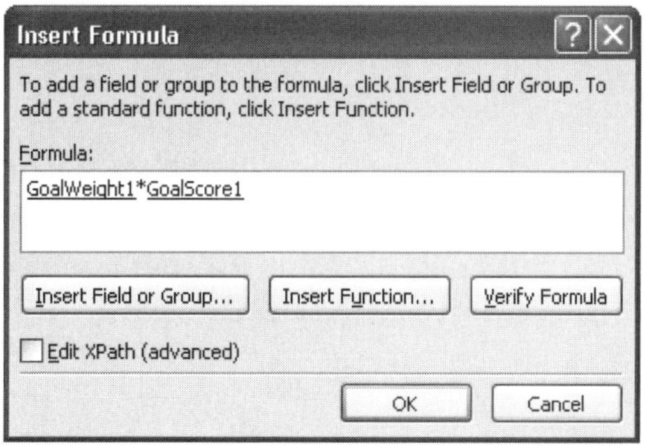

FIGURE 5.12 Set up the GoalWeightedScore columns as calculated fields.

8. Click OK until all dialog boxes have been closed.

9. Repeat steps 1-8 for the other four GoalWeightedScore nodes in the Data Source task pane.

Recalculated Values

By default, each GoalWeightedScore value will be recalculated each time either the corresponding GoalWeight or GoalScore value changes.

NOTE

WeightTotal

The WeightTotal site column is a sum of the five GoalWeight columns. The WeightTotal column is hidden in the Document Information Panel, but it is displayed in the Office Word 2007 document template, although the content control is not editable. To set up the WeightTotal column as a calculated field, use these steps:

1. In the Data Source task pane, double-click the ns2:WeightTotal node.

2. In the Field or Group Properties dialog box, click the Insert Formula button.

3. In the Insert Formula dialog box, click Insert Field or Group.

4. In the Select a Field or Group dialog box, double-click the ns2:GoalWeight1 node.

5. In the Insert Formula dialog box, in the Formula box, place the cursor to the right of GoalWeight1 and then type +.

6. Click Insert Field or Group.

7. In the Select a Field or Group dialog box, double-click the ns2:GoalWeight2 node.

8. In the Insert Formula dialog box, in the Formula box, place the cursor to the right of GoalWeight2 and then type +.

9. Click Insert Field or Group.

10. In the Select a Field or Group dialog box, double-click the ns2:GoalWeight3 node.

11. In the Insert Formula dialog box, in the Formula box, place the cursor to the right of GoalWeight3 and then type +.

12. Click Insert Field or Group.

13. In the Select a Field or Group dialog box, double-click the ns2:GoalWeight4 node.

14. In the Insert Formula dialog box, in the Formula box, place the cursor to the right of GoalWeight4 and then type +.

15. Click Insert Field or Group.

16. In the Select a Field or Group dialog box, double-click the ns2:GoalWeight5 node. Figure 5.13 shows how the Insert Formula dialog box should appear.

17. Click OK until all dialog boxes have been closed.

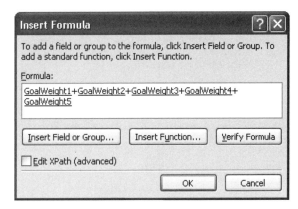

FIGURE 5.13 Set up the WeightTotal column as a calculated field.

Recalculated Value

By default, the WeightTotal value will be recalculated each time any of the Goal-Weight values are updated.

ScoreTotal

The ScoreTotal site column is a sum of the five GoalWeightedScore columns. As with the WeightTotal column, the ScoreTotal column is hidden in the Document Information Panel, but it is displayed in the Office Word 2007 document template, with the content control not editable. To set up the ScoreTotal column as a calculated field, do the following:

1. In the Data Source task pane, double-click the ns2:ScoreTotal node.

2. In the Field or Group Properties dialog box, click the Insert Formula button.

3. In the Insert Formula dialog box, click Insert Field or Group.

4. In the Select a Field or Group dialog box, double-click the ns2:GoalWeightedScore1 node.

5. In the Insert Formula dialog box, in the Formula box, place the cursor to the right of GoalWeightedScore1 and then type +.

6. Click Insert Field or Group.

7. In the Select a Field or Group dialog box, double-click the ns2:GoalWeightedScore2 node.

8. In the Insert Formula dialog box, in the Formula box, place the cursor to the right of GoalWeightedScore2 and then type +.

9. Click Insert Field or Group.

10. In the Select a Field or Group dialog box, double-click the ns2:GoalWeightedScore3 node.

11. In the Insert Formula dialog box, in the Formula box, place the cursor to the right of GoalWeightedScore3 and then type +.

12. Click Insert Field or Group.

13. In the Select a Field or Group dialog box, double-click the ns2:GoalWeightedScore4 node.

14. In the Insert Formula dialog box, in the Formula box, place the cursor to the right of GoalWeightedScore4 and then type +.

15. Click Insert Field or Group.

16. In the Select a Field or Group dialog box, double-click the ns2:GoalWeightedScore5 node. Figure 5.14 shows how the Insert Formula dialog box should appear.

17. Click OK until all dialog boxes have been closed.

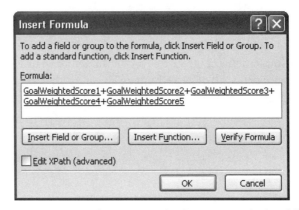

FIGURE 5.14 Set up the ScoreTotal column as a calculated field.

Recalculated Value

By default, the ScoreTotal value will be recalculated each time any of the Goal-WeightedScore values are updated.

NOTE

CONDITIONAL FORMATTING

You can add logic to the Document Information Panel that changes the formatting of controls based on certain conditions. In our solution, the AppraisalPeriodStart and AppraisalPeriodEnd date pickers should be disabled once the appraisal advances past the 1 - Goals Draft stage, defined by the AppraisalStatus column. We will add conditional formatting to both date pickers that disable the controls when the AppraisalStatus value does not equal 1 - Goals Draft. To add conditional formatting for these controls, use these steps:

1. In the form view, double-click the AppraisalPeriodStart date picker.
2. In the Date Picker Properties dialog box, click the Display tab.
3. Click Conditional Formatting.
4. In the Conditional Formatting dialog box, click Add.
5. In the Conditional Format dialog box, click the top-left list and then click AppraisalStatus.
6. Click the top-middle list and click is not equal to.
7. Click the top-right list and click "1 - Goals Draft."
8. Select the Read-only check box. Figure 5.15 shows how the Conditional Format dialog box should appear.

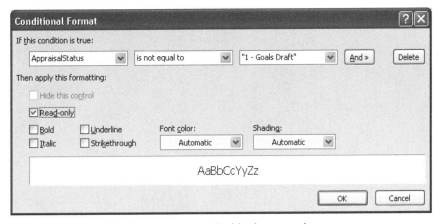

FIGURE 5.15 Disable the control.

9. Click OK until all dialog boxes have been closed.

10. Repeat steps 1-9 for the AppraisalPeriodEnd date picker.

NOTE

Disabling the Date Pickers

Disabling the date pickers in the Document Information Panel does not disable the corresponding content controls in the Office Word 2007 document template. The appraiser would need to manually override the content control settings to disable those date pickers.

PUBLISH THE FORM TEMPLATE

After all changes have been made to the Document Information Panel, it can be published as a template for a SharePoint site content type, overwriting the default template. Once you publish the new form template, users will see the updated Document Information Panel when they start a new performance appraisal in Office Word 2007. To publish the new form template, use these steps:

1. From the File menu, click Publish.

2. In the Save As dialog box, navigate to any location on your local machine, type a name in the File name box, and then click Save.

3. In the first page of the Publishing Wizard, ensure that the As a Document Information Panel template for a SharePoint site content type or list content type (recommended) option is selected, as shown in Figure 5.16.

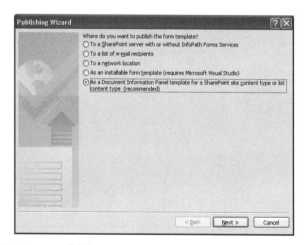

FIGURE 5.16 Publish as a Document Information Panel template.

4. Click Next.

5. In the next page of the Publishing Wizard, click Publish.

6. In the last page, click Close.

7. Close Office InfoPath 2007.

DOCUMENT INFORMATION PANEL SETTINGS

Before closing the book on the Document Information Panel, we will quickly discuss some of its settings. In the browser session from which you started Office InfoPath 2007, the Creating Custom Template: Performance Appraisal page is visible. Click Go back to the Document Information Panel settings page to review these settings.

USING THE DEFAULT TEMPLATE

When you create a content type, the default option in the Document Information Panel Template section is to use the default InfoPath form template. The default template has controls (and headers) for all the site columns in the content type. If you want to revert to the default template, click Use the default template for Microsoft Office applications.

USING THE EXISTING CUSTOM TEMPLATE

The custom form template you just published can be edited from the Document Information Panel Settings: Performance Appraisal page. If you click Edit this template, below the Use existing custom template (URL, UNC, or URN) box, the custom template will start in the Office InfoPath 2007 designer. You can make changes accordingly and then follow the steps in the Publish the Form Template section to update the Document Information Panel for the content type.

UPLOADING AN EXISTING CUSTOM TEMPLATE

If you already have a custom form template to use, you can upload it by clicking Browse, located to the right of the Upload an existing custom template (XSN) to use box. In our scenario, the form template that we saved locally when publishing could first be modified in the Office InfoPath 2007 designer and then uploaded with this option. If you want to start over and create a new custom form template, which will again have controls and headers for all the site columns in the content type, click Create a new custom template.

SHOWING THE DOCUMENT INFORMATION PANEL

In the Show Always section, the default option is to not automatically display the Document Information Panel when starting the Office Word 2007 document. Even with this option cleared, the Document Information Panel will always appear when you start a new Office Word 2007 document template for the content type. If you select the Always show Document Information Panel on document open and initial save for this content type check box, the Document Information Panel will appear every time you open the document, both before and after the initial save.

In Office Word 2007, users can make the Document Information Panel appear/disappear from the Office button (File menu). To illustrate this point, try these steps:

1. In the browser, navigate to the appraiser document library that you created in the previous chapter.

2. From the New menu, click Performance Appraisal.

3. If a Windows Internet Explorer message box appears asking for confirmation to open the file, click OK to continue.

4. Click the X at the top-right of the Document Information Panel to close it, as shown in Figure 5.17.

FIGURE 5.17 Close the Document Information Panel.

5. To re-open the Document Information Panel, click the Office button (File menu) and click Prepare | Properties.

6. Close Office Word 2007 without saving changes.

6 Workflows

Out-of-the-box, SharePoint workflows allow you to leverage existing templates to route task assignments to various users in your organization. With Office SharePoint Designer 2007, you can also create rules-based workflow logic for any SharePoint list and perform actions such as sending an email message, pausing until a specific date, or updating a list item. In this chapter, we will walk through the out-of-the-box templates and Office SharePoint Designer 2007 capabilities and then configure some workflow logic for the performance appraisal solution.

OUT-OF-THE-BOX TEMPLATES

Out-of-the-box workflows can be configured for content types at the site collection, site, or list levels. You can also create out-of-the-box workflows for all items in a particular SharePoint list, regardless of whether content types are used in that list or not. Workflows can be started manually by users with at least Edit Items permissions, or they can be started automatically when a new item is created or an item is changed. The four out-of-the-box templates are the following:

- Approval
- Collect Feedback
- Collect Signatures
- Disposition Approval

One major drawback of using the out-of-the-box templates is the fact that conditional logic is not supported. In other words, if you wanted a workflow to start automatically when a document's AppraisalStatus value changed to "2 - Goals Finalized," you could not achieve that functionality with any of the out-of-the-box templates. Instead, you would need either an Office SharePoint Designer 2007 workflow or a Visual Studio workflow. We will discuss the capabilities of Office SharePoint Designer 2007 workflows later in this chapter. In Chapters 9 and 10, we will explore some of the more advanced workflow capabilities using custom code in Visual Studio 2008.

In the performance appraisal solution, except for the Disposition Approval template, the out-of-the-box workflow templates would not be practical at the site collection or site levels. Because you cannot look up site column data with these templates, there are no means to route tasks automatically to the employee or to specific peer reviewers, unless you use an Office SharePoint Designer 2007 or Visual Studio workflow. However, at the SharePoint list level, appraisers can create certain workflows using the templates and then start them manually at different stages of the appraisal cycle. The following subsections describe the out-of-the-box templates and show examples of how they can be used in the performance appraisal solution.

Approval Template

The Approval workflow template routes a document to specified users for approval. In the performance appraisal solution, depending on your organizational structure, the appraiser's manager or a department head may need to sign off on the appraisal before it is considered final.

At the SharePoint list level, the appraiser can create an Approval workflow for the content type that assigns a task to different users, asking them to review and approve the appraisal document. The approvers can be set at design time or at runtime, and the workflow can be started for any appraisals within the appraiser document library. To create an Approval workflow for the performance appraisal solution, follow these steps:

1. In the browser, navigate to the appraiser document library.
2. From the Settings menu, click Document Library Settings.
3. In the Content Types section, click Performance Appraisal.
4. In the Settings section, click Workflow settings.
5. On the Change Workflow Settings: Performance Appraisal page, click Add a workflow.
6. On the Add a Workflow: Performance Appraisal page, in the Workflow section, select the Approval workflow template.
7. In the Name section, type a unique name for the workflow.
8. Select a task list and history list in the Task List and History List sections, respectively.

9. In the Start Options section, note the different workflow start options and ensure that the Allow this workflow to be manually started by an authenticated user with Edit Items Permissions check box is selected. Figure 6.1 shows how the Add a Workflow: Performance Appraisal page should appear.

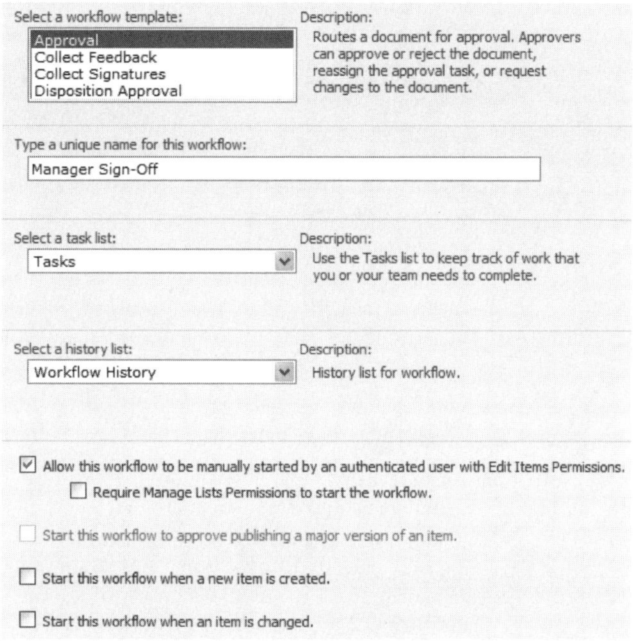

Select a workflow template:
Approval
Collect Feedback
Collect Signatures
Disposition Approval

Description:
Routes a document for approval. Approvers can approve or reject the document, reassign the approval task, or request changes to the document.

Type a unique name for this workflow:
Manager Sign-Off

Select a task list:
Tasks

Description:
Use the Tasks list to keep track of work that you or your team needs to complete.

Select a history list:
Workflow History

Description:
History list for workflow.

☑ Allow this workflow to be manually started by an authenticated user with Edit Items Permissions.
☐ Require Manage Lists Permissions to start the workflow.

☐ Start this workflow to approve publishing a major version of an item.

☐ Start this workflow when a new item is created.

☐ Start this workflow when an item is changed.

FIGURE 6.1 Set up an Approval workflow.

10. Click Next.

11. In the Workflow Tasks section, note the choice to assign tasks serially or in parallel and additional options to allow task reassignment and to request a change before completing a task.

12. In the Default Workflow Start Values section, in the Approvers box, type the name of the appropriate approver(s) and click the Check Names button control (or press Ctrl+K). Multiple names must be separated with a semicolon.

13. If tasks are assigned serially, type the number of day(s) or week(s) to give each person to finish his or her task. If tasks are assigned in parallel, specify the date on which tasks must be completed. Figure 6.2 shows how the Customize Workflow page should appear.

14. Click OK.

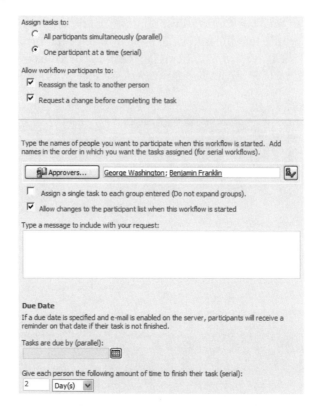

FIGURE 6.2 Customize the Approval workflow.

The Customize Workflow page has some additional options for Approval workflows that are worth mentioning. In the Complete the Workflow section, you can choose to have the workflow canceled when the document is rejected or changed. By default, these options are cleared, meaning that the workflow will complete when all approvers have finished their tasks. In the Default Workflow Start Values section, you can also type a custom message to include with your request. This message will appear in the body of the email message that is sent to the approver when the task is assigned.

Workflow Email Messages

Regardless of whether you define a custom message or not, the email message that is sent to approvers will still contain instructions on how to complete the approval tasks and will have a link to the appraisal document.

If you recall from Chapter 4, we modified the permissions of the appraiser document library so that only the appraiser had access. If you want approvers to have access as well, you will need to modify permissions, either at the SharePoint list level or at the document level. In the case of the performance appraisal solution, if the approvers are always the same for a given appraiser, it would make sense to modify permissions at the list level. To modify permissions so that approvers have access to appraisal documents, do the following:

1. On the Change Workflow Settings: Performance Appraisal page, in the breadcrumb trail, click Settings.

2. In the Permissions and Management section, click Permissions for this document library.

3. On the Permissions page, from the New menu, click Add Users.

4. In the Users/Groups box, type the name of the appropriate approver(s) and click the Check Names button control (or press Ctrl+K). Multiple names must be separated with a semicolon.

5. In the Give Permission section, select the Approve - Can edit and approve pages, list items, and documents check box. Figure 6.3 shows how the Add Users page should appear.

6. Click OK.

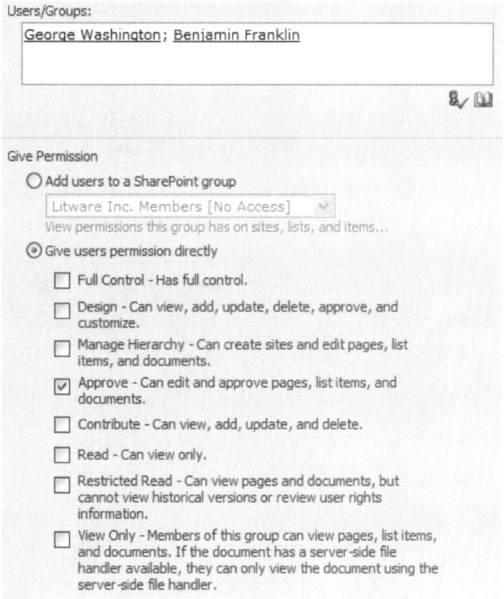

FIGURE 6.3 Provide approvers with access to the appraiser document library.

COLLECT FEEDBACK TEMPLATE

The Collect Feedback workflow template routes a document to specified users for review. In the performance appraisal solution, reviewers can provide feedback during the "3 - Collect Feedback" stage.

At the SharePoint list level, the appraiser can create a Collect Feedback workflow that assigns a task to different users, asking them for feedback about the appraisal. As with the approvers in the Approval template, reviewers in the Collect Feedback template can be set at design time or at runtime, and the workflow can be started for any appraisals within the appraiser document library. To create a Collect Feedback workflow for the performance appraisal solution, do the following:

1. On the Permissions page, in the breadcrumb trail, click Settings.
2. In the Content Types section, click Performance Appraisal.
3. In the Settings section, click Workflow settings.
4. On the Change Workflow Settings: Performance Appraisal page, click Add a workflow.
5. On the Add a Workflow: Performance Appraisal page, in the Workflow section, select the Collect Feedback workflow template.
6. In the Name section, type a unique name for the workflow.
7. Select a task list and history list in the Task List and History List sections, respectively.
8. In the Start Options section, note the different workflow start options and ensure that the Allow this workflow to be manually started by an authenticated user with Edit Items Permissions check box is selected. Figure 6.4 shows how the Add a Workflow: Performance Appraisal page should appear.
9. Click Next.
10. In the Workflow Tasks section, note the choice to assign tasks serially or in parallel and additional options to allow task reassignment and to request a change before completing a task.
11. In the Default Workflow Start Values section, in the Reviewers box, type the name of the appropriate reviewer(s) and click the Check Names button control (or press Ctrl+K). Multiple names must be separated with a semicolon.
12. If tasks are assigned in parallel, specify the date on which tasks must be completed. If tasks are assigned serially, type the number of day(s) or week(s) to give each person to finish his task. Figure 6.5 shows how the Customize Workflow page should appear.
13. Click OK.

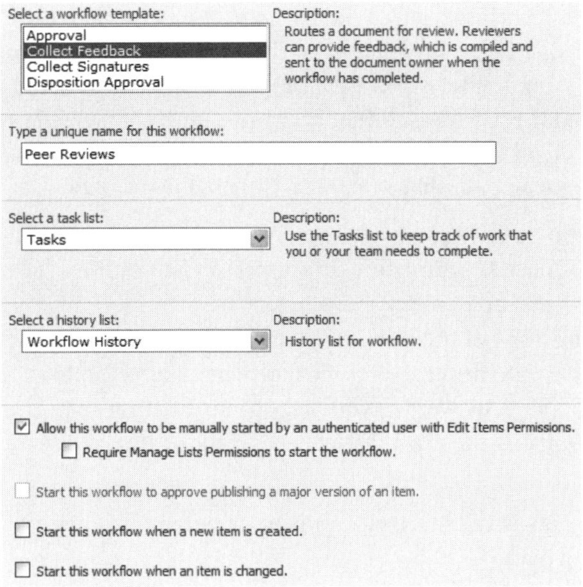

FIGURE 6.4 Set up a Collect Feedback workflow.

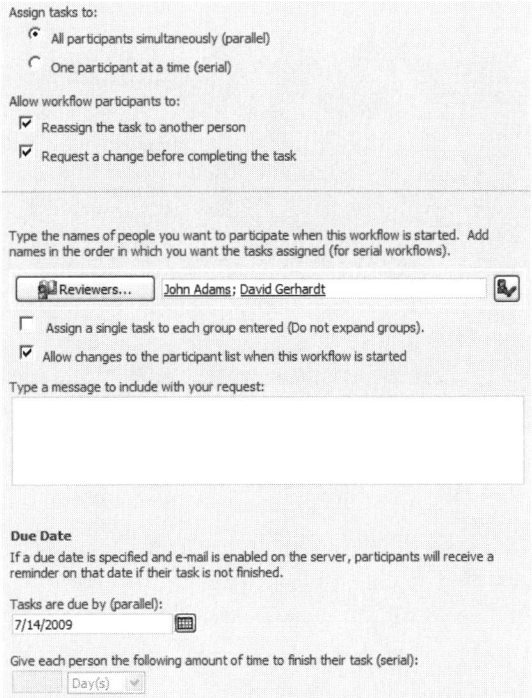

FIGURE 6.5 Customize the Collect Feedback workflow.

On the Customize Workflow page, the Complete the Workflow section for the Collect Feedback template is slightly different from the Approval template. You can choose to have the workflow completed when a specific number of review tasks have been finished. Also, the option to cancel the workflow on rejection is disabled. By default, all the options in this section are cleared, meaning that the workflow will complete when all reviewers have finished their tasks.

In the performance appraisal solution, reviewers will vary for each employee being appraised. At runtime, the appraiser can modify the list of reviewers when the Collect Feedback workflow is manually started. Access to appraisals, however, should be done at the document level, not the list level. This will prevent reviewers from viewing/editing appraisals that are not applicable to them. To modify permissions so that reviewers have access to an existing appraisal in the appraiser document library, do the following:

1. Navigate back to the appraiser document library.

2. Click the context menu for an existing document and then click Manage Permissions, as shown in Figure 6.6. If there is no document in the appraiser document library, you can create one from the New menu.

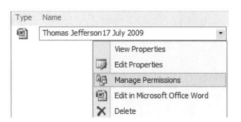

FIGURE 6.6 Manage permissions for a document.

3. On the Permissions page, from the Actions menu, click Edit Permissions.

4. In the Windows Internet Explorer message box, click OK to create unique permissions for the document.

5. On the Permissions page, from the New menu, click Add Users.

6. In the Users/Groups box, type the name of the appropriate reviewer(s) and click the Check Names button control (or press Ctrl+K). Multiple names must be separated with a semicolon.

7. In the Give Permission section, select the Contribute - Can view, add, update, and delete check box.

8. Click OK.

COLLECT SIGNATURES TEMPLATE

The Collect Signatures workflow template gathers signatures needed to complete a document. In the performance appraisal solution, the end-to-end process may not be considered complete until both the employee and appraiser sign off on the appraisal.

At the SharePoint list level, the appraiser can create a Collect Signatures workflow that gathers the required signatures, and that workflow can be started for any appraisals within the document library. Unlike the other templates, though, the Collect Signatures workflow can be started only from within an Office client application. To create a Collect Signatures workflow for the performance appraisal solution, follow these steps:

1. Navigate back to the appraiser document library.
2. From the Settings menu, click Document Library Settings.
3. In the Content Types section, click Performance Appraisal.
4. In the Settings section, click Workflow settings.
5. On the Change Workflow Settings: Performance Appraisal page, click Add a workflow.
6. On the Add a Workflow page, in the Workflow section, select the Collect Signatures workflow template.
7. In the Name section, type a unique name for the workflow.
8. Select a task list and history list in the Task List and History List sections, respectively.
9. In the Start Options section, ensure that the Allow this workflow to be manually started by an authenticated user with Edit Items Permissions check box is selected. Figure 6.7 shows how the Add a Workflow: Performance Appraisal page should appear.
10. Click OK.

Collect Signatures Start Options

On the Add a Workflow page, in the Start Options section, the automatic start options for the Collect Signatures template are disabled.

NOTE

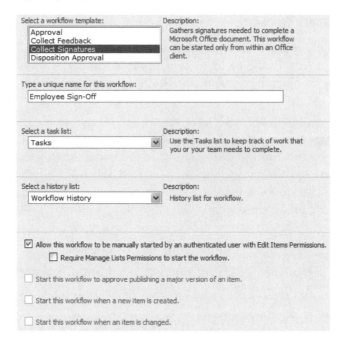

FIGURE 6.7 Set up a Collect Signatures workflow.

The appraisal must also contain Microsoft Office signature lines to allow multiple parties to sign the document. To add a signature line, follow these steps:

1. Start an existing appraisal document in Office Word 2007 (or modify the existing document template for the content type).

NOTE

Grouped Document

Because you grouped the performance appraisal template in Chapter 4 to prevent users from making modifications outside of the content controls, you will need to ungroup the document so that you can insert a signature line. To ungroup the document template, select the entire document by pressing Ctrl+A, click the Developer tab in the ribbon, and then click Ungroup from the Group menu.

2. Place the cursor where you want the signature line to display.

3. Click the Insert tab on the ribbon.

4. In the Text group, click the Signature Line command.

5. In the Microsoft Office Word dialog box, click OK after reading the disclaimer about Microsoft Office digital signatures.

6. In the Signature Setup dialog box, enter the applicable signing information. Figure 6.8 shows how the Signature Setup dialog box should appear.

FIGURE 6.8 Add a Microsoft Office signature line.

7. Click OK.

8. Save the appraisal document back to the document library and close Office Word 2007.

The employee will need edit permissions in order to sign the appraisal document. As with the Collect Feedback workflow, access to appraisals for the Collect Signatures workflow should be done at the document level, not the list level. This will prevent employees from viewing/editing appraisals that are not applicable to them. To modify permissions so that the employee has access to an existing appraisal in the appraiser document library, follow these steps:

1. Navigate back to the appraiser document library.

2. Click the context menu for an existing document and then click Manage Permissions. If there is no document in the appraiser document library, you can create one from the New menu.

3. On the Permissions page, from the New menu, click Add Users.

4. In the Users/Groups box, type the name of the employee and click the Check Names button control (or press Ctrl+K).

5. In the Give Permission section, select the Contribute - Can view, add, update, and delete check box.

6. Click OK.

DISPOSITION APPROVAL TEMPLATE

The Disposition Approval template manages document expiration and retention by allowing participants to decide whether to retain or delete expired documents. When an appraisal process has been completed and the appraisal document subsequently reaches its expiration date, it might be necessary to delete the document from the appraiser document library.

A retention policy might be in place for your entire organization, so it would be practical in that case to define a workflow for the content type at the site collection level. This workflow could then get started for any appraisal document within the site collection. To create a Disposition Approval workflow for the performance appraisal solution, use these steps:

1. Navigate to the site collection home page.
2. From the Site Actions menu, click Site Settings | Modify All Site Settings.
3. In the Galleries section, click Site content types.
4. In the Human Resources section, click Performance Appraisal.
5. In the Settings section, click Workflow settings.
6. On the Change Workflow Settings: Performance Appraisal page, click Add a workflow.
7. On the Add a Workflow page, in the Workflow section, select the Disposition Approval workflow template.
8. In the Name section, type a unique name for the workflow.
9. Type a task list name and history list name in the Task List and History List sections, respectively.
10. In the Start Options section, note the different workflow start options and ensure that the Allow this workflow to be manually started by an authenticated user with Edit Items Permissions check box is selected.
11. In the Update List and Site Content Types section, note the option to Add this workflow to all content types that inherit from this content type. Figure 6.9 shows how the Add a Workflow: Performance Appraisal page should appear.
12. Click OK.

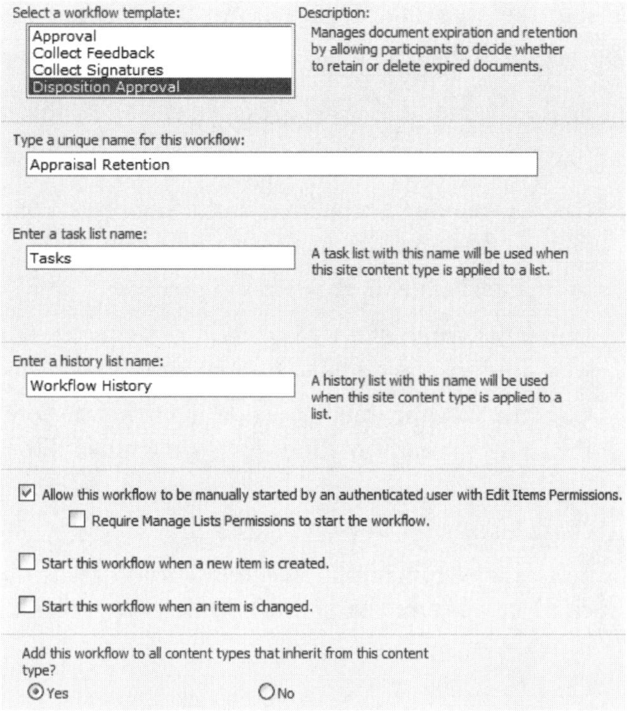

Select a workflow template: Description:
Approval   Manages document expiration and retention
Collect Feedback   by allowing participants to decide whether
Collect Signatures   to retain or delete expired documents.
Disposition Approval

Type a unique name for this workflow:

Appraisal Retention

Enter a task list name:

Tasks   A task list with this name will be used when
                                        this site content type is applied to a list.

Enter a history list name:

Workflow History   A history list with this name will be used
                                        when this site content type is applied to a
                                        list.

☑ Allow this workflow to be manually started by an authenticated user with Edit Items Permissions.
    ☐ Require Manage Lists Permissions to start the workflow.

☐ Start this workflow when a new item is created.

☐ Start this workflow when an item is changed.

Add this workflow to all content types that inherit from this content
type?
   ⦿ Yes   ○ No

FIGURE 6.9 Set up a Disposition Approval workflow.

SHAREPOINT DESIGNER WORKFLOW

Office SharePoint Designer 2007 allows you to write workflow logic that is more advanced than anything you get from the out-of-the-box templates. Within the Workflow Designer, you can look up site column values and then conditionally perform actions based on those values. The one major drawback of using Office SharePoint Designer 2007 workflows is that they cannot be defined for content types. Instead, each Office SharePoint Designer 2007 workflow must be attached to a specific list, which means you do not have the same reuse capabilities that exist for out-of-the-box templates.

We will define a workflow that gets triggered every time an appraisal in the appraiser document library is modified. The AppraisalStatus column will be evaluated each time to determine the actions to perform.

To start the Workflow Designer and attach it to your appraiser document library, use the following steps:

1. Start Office SharePoint Designer 2007.

2. From the File menu, click Open Site.

3. In the Open Site dialog box, in the Site name box, type the URL for the Human Resources site and then click Open.

4. From the File menu, click New | Workflow.

5. In the first page of the Workflow Designer, in the Give a name to this workflow box, type a unique name for the workflow.

6. Click the What SharePoint list should this workflow be attached to list and then click the name of the appraiser document library.

7. Select the Automatically start this workflow when a new item is created check box.

8. Select the Automatically start this workflow whenever an item is changed check box. Figure 6.10 shows how the first page of the Workflow Designer should appear.

9. Click Next.

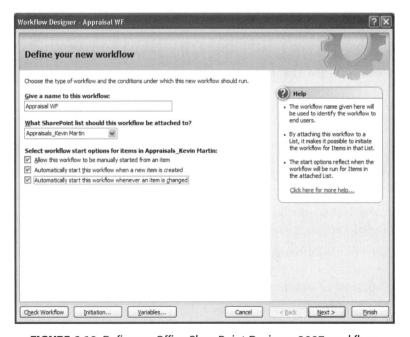

FIGURE 6.10 Define an Office SharePoint Designer 2007 workflow.

An Office SharePoint Designer 2007 workflow is composed of steps, which are composed of sets of conditions and actions. Each workflow step is processed in the order listed in the Workflow Steps task pane. Sets of conditions and actions are also processed in the order listed within each step. Processing within a step stops when one set of conditions evaluates to true. For this workflow, we will create a single step that has conditions for each of the five AppraisalStatus values.

1 - GOALS DRAFT

When a new performance appraisal document is created by the appraiser, the initial value for the AppraisalStatus column is "1 - Goals Draft." During this stage of the appraisal process, the employee will review the goals that have been defined by the appraiser. At this early stage, the appraiser might not want to give the employee edit permissions to the document. Instead, an email message can be sent to the employee listing the goals defined in the appraisal. The employee can then review the goals and respond to the appraiser with suggested changes, which can be incorporated by the appraiser into the appraisal document. Each time the appraisal document is modified and the AppraisalStatus value is set to "1 - Goals Draft," an email message containing the goals will be sent to the employee. To create the condition for this stage of the workflow, do the following:

1. Click the Conditions list and then click the Compare {Appraiser List Name} field option (likely the top option), as shown in Figure 6.11.

FIGURE 6.11 Compare an appraiser list field.

2. Click the field link and then click AppraisalStatus.
3. Click the value link and then click 1 - Goals Draft.

If you want the Subject line for your email message to have a combination of static and dynamic text, you need to use the Build Dynamic String option, which will create a workflow variable that you can reference for your lookup. You can change the name of the variable to something more intuitive after building the dynamic string. To create the action to build a dynamic string for the Subject line, use the following steps:

1. Click the Actions list and then click Build Dynamic String. If the Build Dynamic String option does not appear in the list, click More Actions from the Actions list and then, in the Workflow Actions dialog box, double-click Build Dynamic String.

2. Click the dynamic string link.

3. In the String Builder dialog box, in the Name box, type **Review goals from**.

4. Add a space and then click Add Lookup.

5. In the Define Workflow Lookup dialog box, click the Field list and then click AppraiserName.

6. Click OK. Figure 6.12 shows how the String Builder dialog box should appear.

FIGURE 6.12 Build a dynamic subject string for the employee.

7. In the String Builder dialog box, click OK.

8. Click the Variables button at the bottom of the Workflow Designer.

9. In the Workflow Local Variables dialog box, click the variable named "variable" and then click Modify.

10. In the Edit Variable dialog box, in the Name box, change the value to Stage1Subject.

11. Click OK until all dialog boxes have been closed.

12. In the Workflow Designer, click Variable: variable and then click Variable: Stage1Subject, as shown in Figure 6.13.

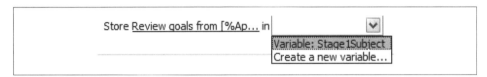

FIGURE 6.13 Change the variable in which to store the dynamic string.

When defining the email message, you can perform lookups for the To, CC, and Subject lines and in the message body. You can also use HTML tags in the message body to modify the formatting. For our solution, we will use bold formatting for the goal "headers" and then add lookups for each goal metric. To define the email message that is sent to the employee, use the following steps:

1. Click the Actions list and then click Send an Email. If the Send an Email option does not appear in the list, click More Actions from the Actions list and then, in the Workflow Actions dialog box, double-click Send an Email.

2. Click the "this message" link.

3. In the Define E-mail Message dialog box, click the Select Users button that is located to the right of the To box.

4. In the Select Users dialog box, double-click Workflow Lookup.

5. In the Define Workflow Lookup dialog box, click the Field list and then click EmployeeName.

6. Click OK.

7. In the Select Users dialog box, click OK.

8. In the Define E-mail Message dialog box, click the Define Workflow Lookup button located to the right of the Subject box.

9. In the Define Workflow Lookup dialog box, click the Source list and then click Workflow Data.

10. Click the Field list and then click Variable: Stage1Subject. Figure 6.14 shows how the Define Workflow Lookup dialog box should appear.

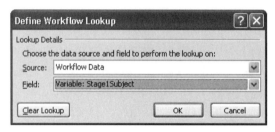

FIGURE 6.14 Look up the subject variable.

11. Click OK.

12. In the Define E-mail Message dialog box, click Add Lookup to Body.

13. In the Define Workflow Lookup dialog box, click the Field list and then click EmployeeName.

14. Click OK.

15. In the message body, after the EmployeeName lookup, type a colon, type some lead-in text for the goals, and then press Enter, as shown in Figure 6.15.

[%Appraisals_Kevin Martin:EmployeeName%]:

The following goals have been defined for your next appraisal period…

FIGURE 6.15 Modify the message body for the employee.

16. Press Enter and type Goal 1 - .

17. Click Add Lookup to Body.

18. In the Define Workflow Lookup dialog box, click the Field list and then click GoalMetric1.

19. Click OK.

20. Repeat steps 16–19 for the other four GoalMetric columns. Figure 6.16 shows the updated message body.

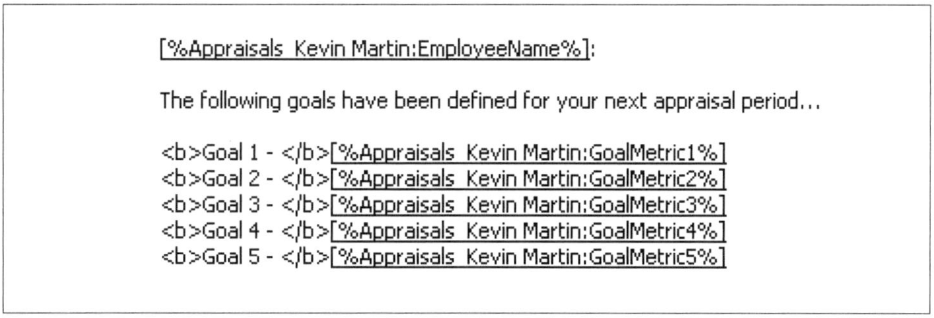

[%Appraisals Kevin Martin:EmployeeName%]:
The following goals have been defined for your next appraisal period...
<b>Goal 1 - </b>[%Appraisals Kevin Martin:GoalMetric1%]
<b>Goal 2 - </b>[%Appraisals Kevin Martin:GoalMetric2%]
<b>Goal 3 - </b>[%Appraisals Kevin Martin:GoalMetric3%]
<b>Goal 4 - </b>[%Appraisals Kevin Martin:GoalMetric4%]
<b>Goal 5 - </b>[%Appraisals Kevin Martin:GoalMetric5%]

FIGURE 6.16 Add the metrics to the message body.

21. Press Enter and then type some closing text for the email message, as shown in Figure 6.17.

Define E-mail Message
To:
Appraisals_Kevin Martin:EmployeeName
CC:
Subject:
Variable: Stage1Subject
[%Appraisals Kevin Martin:EmployeeName%]:
The following goals have been defined for your next appraisal period...
<b>Goal 1 - </b>[%Appraisals Kevin Martin:GoalMetric1%]
<b>Goal 2 - </b>[%Appraisals Kevin Martin:GoalMetric2%]
<b>Goal 3 - </b>[%Appraisals Kevin Martin:GoalMetric3%]
<b>Goal 4 - </b>[%Appraisals Kevin Martin:GoalMetric4%]
<b>Goal 5 - </b>[%Appraisals Kevin Martin:GoalMetric5%]
If you have any questions or comments regarding these goals, please contact the appraiser identified in the subject of this message.
Regards,
Human Resources
Add Lookup to Body
OK
Cancel

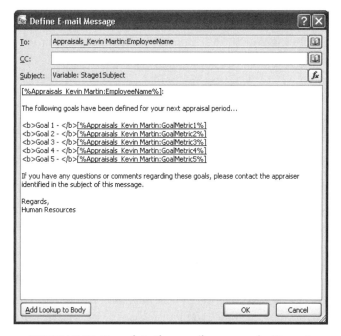

FIGURE 6.17 Complete the email message for Stage 1.

22. Click OK. Figure 6.18 shows the set of conditions and actions for Stage 1.

FIGURE 6.18 Complete the set of conditions and actions for Stage 1.

 Goal Metric Headers
With the email message that we defined, the goal "headers" will be displayed, regardless of whether the GoalMetric columns contain text or not.

2 - Goals Finalized

After the employee and appraiser come to an agreement on the goals for an appraisal period, the appraiser sets the AppraisalStatus column to "2 - Goals Finalized." The appraisal process enters a "waiting" period during this stage, with a reminder email message being sent once the appraisal period ends about filling out the appraisal document. To create the condition for this stage of the workflow, use the following steps:

1. In the Workflow Designer, click Add 'Else If' Conditional Branch.
2. Click the new Conditions list and then click the Compare {Appraiser List Name} field option.
3. Click the field link and then click AppraisalStatus.
4. Click the value link and then click 2 - Goals Finalized.

When the AppraisalStatus value is changed to "2 - Goals Finalized," the workflow will pause until the date value specified in the AppraisalPeriodEnd column. Here, you will need to use the Pause Until Date action, which will prevent actions that follow from being triggered until the date specified occurs. To create the action to pause until the date specified in the AppraisalPeriodEnd column, use the following steps:

1. Click the new Actions list and then click Pause Until Date. If the Pause Until Date option does not appear in the list, click More Actions from the Actions list and then, in the Workflow Actions dialog box, double-click Pause Until Date.

2. Click the "this time" link and then click the Display data binding button, located to the far right of the action, as shown in Figure 6.19.

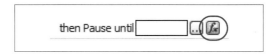

FIGURE 6.19 Bind the Pause Until Date action to a site column.

3. In the Define Workflow Lookup dialog box, click the Field list and then click AppraisalPeriodEnd.

4. Click OK.

Again, if you want the Subject line for your email message to have a combination of static and dynamic text, you need to use the Build Dynamic String option. To create the action to build a dynamic string for the Subject line, use the following steps:

1. Click the second Actions list and then click Build Dynamic String.

2. Click the dynamic string link.

3. In the String Builder dialog box, in the Name box, type **Appraisal period is up for**.

4. Add a space and then click Add Lookup.

5. In the Define Workflow Lookup dialog box, click the Field list and then click EmployeeName.

6. Click OK. Figure 6.20 shows how the String Builder dialog box should appear.

7. In the String Builder dialog box, click OK.

8. Click the Variables button.

9. In the Workflow Local Variables dialog box, click the variable named "variable" and then click Modify.

10. In the Edit Variable dialog box, in the Name box, change the value to Stage2Subject.

11. Click OK until all dialog boxes have been closed.

12. In the Workflow Designer, click Variable: variable and then click Variable: Stage2Subject.

FIGURE 6.20 Build a dynamic subject string for the appraiser.

After the appraisal period concludes, an email message is sent to the appraiser, reminding him that the appraisal process needs to move to the next stage. The message can contain a hard-coded link to the appraisal document for quick reference. To define the email message that is sent to the appraiser, use the following steps:

1. Click the second Actions list and then click Send an Email.
2. Click the "this message" link.
3. In the Define E-mail Message dialog box, click the Select Users button that is located to the right of the To box.
4. In the Select Users dialog box, double-click Workflow Lookup.
5. In the Define Workflow Lookup dialog box, click the Field list and then click AppraiserName.
6. Click OK.
7. In the Select Users dialog box, click OK.
8. In the Define E-mail Message dialog box, click the Define Workflow Lookup button located to the right of the Subject box.
9. In the Define Workflow Lookup dialog box, click the Source list and then click Workflow Data.

10. Click the Field list and then click Variable: Stage2Subject.

11. Click OK.

12. In the Define E-mail Message dialog box, click Add Lookup to Body.

13. In the Define Workflow Lookup dialog box, click the Field list and then click AppraiserName.

14. Click OK.

15. In the message body, after the AppraiserName lookup, type a colon and some text to remind the appraiser about the review process, including a hard-coded URL for the appraiser document library (in our example, http://moss.litwareinc.com/hr/Appraisals_Kevin%20Martin). Figure 6.21 shows how the Define E-mail Message dialog box should appear.

FIGURE 6.21 Modify the message body for the appraiser.

16. Add some closing text for the email message, which should now appear, as shown in Figure 6.22.

17. Click OK.

FIGURE 6.22 Complete the email message for Stage 2.

3 - COLLECT FEEDBACK

For the "3 - Collect Feedback" stage, you can leverage the out-of-the-box workflow that was created earlier in this chapter. An email message can be sent to the appraiser to have that workflow manually started, and a reminder can be included to have permissions for the appraisal document updated for the peer reviewers. To create the condition for this stage of the workflow, use these steps:

1. In the Workflow Designer, click Add 'Else If' Conditional Branch.
2. Click the new Conditions list and then click the Compare {Appraiser List Name} field option.
3. Click the field link and then click AppraisalStatus.
4. Click the value link and then click 3 - Collect Feedback.

You need to use the Build Dynamic String option if you want the Subject line for your email message to have a combination of static and dynamic text. To create the action to build a dynamic string for the Subject line, use the following:

1. Click the new Actions list and then click Build Dynamic String.

2. Click the dynamic string link.

3. In the String Builder dialog box, in the Name box, type **Collect feedback for the appraisal of**.

4. Add a space and then click Add Lookup.

5. In the Define Workflow Lookup dialog box, click the Field list and then click EmployeeName.

6. Click OK.

7. In the String Builder dialog box, click OK.

8. Click the Variables button.

9. In the Workflow Local Variables dialog box, click the variable named "variable" and then click Modify.

10. In the Edit Variable dialog box, in the Name box, change the value to Stage3Subject.

11. Click OK until all dialog boxes have been closed.

12. In the Workflow Designer, click Variable: variable and then click Variable: Stage3Subject.

The appraiser should enable change tracking in the document before starting the Collect Feedback workflow. The email message sent to the appraiser is a reminder of this and the fact that this step is optional. Once all feedback is received, the appraiser can add ratings and additional comments and then change the AppraisalStatus value to "4 - Appraisal Draft." To define the email message that is sent to the appraiser, use these steps:

1. Click the third Actions list and then click Send an Email.

2. Click the "this message" link.

3. In the Define E-mail Message dialog box, click the Select Users button that is located to the right of the To box.

4. In the Select Users dialog box, double-click Workflow Lookup.

5. In the Define Workflow Lookup dialog box, click the Field list and then click AppraiserName.

6. Click OK.

7. In the Select Users dialog box, click OK.

8. In the Define E-mail Message dialog box, click the Define Workflow Lookup button located to the right of the Subject box.

9. In the Define Workflow Lookup dialog box, click the Source list and then click Workflow Data.

10. Click the Field list and then click Variable: Stage3Subject.

11. Click OK.

12. In the Define E-mail Message dialog box, click Add Lookup to Body.

13. In the Define Workflow Lookup dialog box, click the Field list and then click AppraiserName.

14. Click OK.

15. In the message body, after the AppraiserName lookup, type a colon, some text to remind the appraiser about the Collect Feedback workflow, and some instructions after collecting all feedback. Figure 6.23 shows how the Define E-mail Message dialog box should appear.

16. Click OK.

FIGURE 6.23 Complete the email message for Stage 3.

4 - Appraisal Draft

The "4 - Appraisal Draft" stage refers to the face-to-face meeting between the employee and manager, and any modifications made afterward to the appraisal document. The face-to-face meeting occurs on the date specified by the AppraisalDate column. To create the condition for this stage of the workflow, use these steps:

1. In the Workflow Designer, click Add 'Else If ' Conditional Branch.
2. Click the new Conditions list and then click the Compare {Appraiser List Name} field option.
3. Click the field link and then click AppraisalStatus.
4. Click the value link and then click 4 - Appraisal Draft.

Again, use the Build Dynamic String option if you want the Subject line for your email message to have a combination of static and dynamic text. To create the action to build a dynamic string for the Subject line, do the following:

1. Click the new Actions list and then click Build Dynamic String.
2. Click the dynamic string link.
3. In the String Builder dialog box, in the Name box, type **Schedule the appraisal meeting for**.
4. Add a space and then click Add Lookup.
5. In the Define Workflow Lookup dialog box, click the Field list and then click EmployeeName.
6. Click OK.
7. In the String Builder dialog box, click OK.
8. Click the Variables button.
9. In the Workflow Local Variables dialog box, click the variable named "variable" and then click Modify.
10. In the Edit Variable dialog box, in the Name box, change the value to Stage4Subject.
11. Click OK until all dialog boxes have been closed.
12. In the Workflow Designer, click Variable: variable and then click Variable: Stage4Subject.

The appraiser should disable change tracking in the document and then schedule the face-to-face meeting with the employee. For the meeting, the appraiser can print out the appraisal document so that he and the employee can review ratings and comments. After the face-to-face meeting, the appraiser can incorporate changes to the document as needed and then change the AppraisalStatus value to "5 - Appraisal Finalized." To define the email message that is sent to the appraiser:

1. Click the fourth Actions list and then click Send an Email.
2. Click the "this message" link.
3. In the Define E-mail Message dialog box, click the Select Users button that is located to the right of the To box.
4. In the Select Users dialog box, double-click Workflow Lookup.
5. In the Define Workflow Lookup dialog box, click the Field list and then click AppraiserName.
6. Click OK.
7. In the Select Users dialog box, click OK.
8. In the Define E-mail Message dialog box, click the Define Workflow Lookup button located to the right of the Subject box.
9. In the Define Workflow Lookup dialog box, click the Source list and then click Workflow Data.
10. Click the Field list and then click Variable: Stage4Subject.
11. Click OK.
12. In the Define E-mail Message dialog box, click Add Lookup to Body.
13. In the Define Workflow Lookup dialog box, click the Field list and then click AppraiserName.
14. Click OK.
15. In the message body, after the AppraiserName lookup, type a colon, some instructions about scheduling the face-to-face meeting, and steps to finalize the appraisal document. Figure 6.24 shows how the Define E-mail Message dialog box should appear.
16. Click OK.

FIGURE 6.24 Complete the email message for Stage 4.

5 - APPRAISAL FINALIZED

For the "5 - Appraisal Finalized" stage, you can leverage the out-of-the-box Collect Signatures workflow that was created earlier in this chapter. An email message can be sent to the appraiser to have that workflow manually started, and a reminder can be included to have permissions for the appraisal document updated for the employee. To create the condition for this stage of the workflow, use these steps:

1. In the Workflow Designer, click Add 'Else If' Conditional Branch.
2. Click the new Conditions list and then click the Compare {Appraiser List Name} field option.
3. Click the field link and then click AppraisalStatus.
4. Click the value link and then click 5 - Appraisal Finalized.

As with the other stages of the workflow, use the Build Dynamic String option if you want the Subject line for your email message to have a combination of static and dynamic text.

To create the action to build a dynamic string for the Subject line, follow these steps:

1. Click the new Actions list and then click Build Dynamic String.
2. Click the dynamic string link.
3. In the String Builder dialog box, in the Name box, type **Collect signatures for the appraisal of**.
4. Add a space and then click Add Lookup.
5. In the Define Workflow Lookup dialog box, click the Field list and then click EmployeeName.
6. Click OK.
7. In the String Builder dialog box, click OK.
8. Click the Variables button.
9. In the Workflow Local Variables dialog box, click the variable named "variable" and then click Modify.
10. In the Edit Variable dialog box, in the Name box, change the value to Stage5Subject.
11. Click OK until all dialog boxes have been closed.
12. In the Workflow Designer, click Variable: variable and then click Variable: Stage5Subject.

The email message should remind the appraiser to start the Collect Signatures workflow and ensure that the employee has edit permissions to the appraisal document. To define the email message that is sent to the appraiser and thus finish the workflow, follow these steps:

1. Click the fifth Actions list and then click Send an Email.
2. Click the "this message" link.
3. In the Define E-mail Message dialog box, click the Select Users button that is located to the right of the To box.
4. In the Select Users dialog box, double-click Workflow Lookup.
5. In the Define Workflow Lookup dialog box, click the Field list and then click AppraiserName.
6. Click OK.
7. In the Select Users dialog box, click OK.

8. In the Define E-mail Message dialog box, click the Define Workflow Lookup button located to the right of the Subject box.

9. In the Define Workflow Lookup dialog box, click the Source list and then click Workflow Data.

10. Click the Field list and then click Variable: Stage5Subject.

11. Click OK.

12. In the Define E-mail Message dialog box, click Add Lookup to Body.

13. In the Define Workflow Lookup dialog box, click the Field list and then click AppraiserName.

14. Click OK.

15. In the message body, after the AppraiserName lookup, type a colon and some text to remind the appraiser about the Collect Signatures workflow. Figure 6.25 shows how the Define E-mail Message dialog box should appear.

16. Click OK.

17. In the Workflow Designer, click Finish.

18. Close Office SharePoint Designer 2007.

FIGURE 6.25 Complete the email message for Stage 5.

ASSIGN A TO-DO ITEM ACTION

In the Office SharePoint Designer 2007 workflow that we built in this chapter, each "else if" condition contains a Send an Email action that notifies either the employee or appraiser of the appraisal document's status. Alternatively, you could have used the Assign a To-do Item action, which assigns a SharePoint task to a specified user. When a SharePoint task is assigned, the user receives an email message with instructions on how to complete the task, with a link to the corresponding document.

One drawback to using the Assign a To-do Item action is the inability to add lookups at design time for either the SharePoint task name or description. Instead, these values must be hard-coded, which is different from the dynamic capabilities offered for the subject and message body in the Send an Email action.

For more information about the Assign a To-do Item action, go to http://office. microsoft.com/en-us/sharepointdesigner/HA102336231033.aspx.

7 Information Management Policies and Document Conversions

U p to this point, you have built a document content type that includes a data model (site columns), presentation layer (Office Word 2007 template), business logic (Document Information Panel), and automated business processes (workflows). There are additional optional elements that you could use to enhance the overall functionality of the performance appraisal solution, namely information management policies and document conversions. Information management policies allow you to manage content types to ensure that documents are in compliance with company policy in terms of usage and retention. With document conversions, you can convert Office Word 2007 documents into Web pages.

Unfortunately, we are emphasizing that these features should be optional when building your solution. During the testing phase for this solution, we found that some of the functionality described in this chapter did not work as advertised. Specifically, when we created information management policies for labels and barcodes, there were errors that prevented the Document Information Panel from loading when starting the Office Word 2007 document. The error created by the label policy, for example, is shown in Figure 7.1. These errors may be corrected in a subsequent service pack of Office SharePoint Server 2007, but you should still use caution when implementing information management policies and document conversions on your SharePoint server. We have always found it helpful to use a virtual machine first as a development environment. That way, if critical errors occur, you can always use the undo disks feature to restore a previous version of the environment.

In this chapter, we will review how information management policies and document conversions can be configured for a content type, but we will also point out the errors that were found during testing. In the next chapter, when we do a full walk-through of the out-of-the-box performance appraisal solution, we will not discuss any of the features described in this chapter.

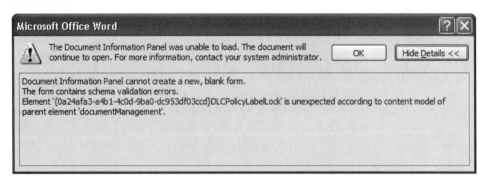

FIGURE 7.1 Document Information Panel error with the label policy.

Information Management Policies

Do not implement the information management policies described in this chapter for the performance appraisal content type, because the label and barcode policies will likely prevent the Document Information Panel from loading in the Office Word 2007 document. The steps listed in the Information Management Policies section are for information only. You can, however, implement an auditing or expiration policy on a different content type.

INFORMATION MANAGEMENT POLICIES

Information management policies provide the means to build a unified infrastructure for managing documents. With content types, you can define a combination of policies centrally that assign labels, identify auditing events, schedule content disposition when a document expires, or insert barcodes into documents. In the following subsections, we will describe each of the policy types and show examples of how they can be used in document content types.

LABELS

Labels can ensure that important information is included in documents. With labels you can specify a combination of static and dynamic text and prompt users to have labels inserted before documents are saved or printed. You can also prevent changes to labels after they are added to documents.

During our testing of the performance appraisal solution, the label policy caused an error that prevented the Document Information Panel from loading, so we could not implement the policy. If you decide to create a different content type solution and the Document Information Panel is integral, note that it might not load in your document template if you have defined a label policy. That said, the remainder of this section will identify how to set up a label policy for your content type.

For a content type solution, you might consider a label that expresses the confidential nature of the document. When specifying the label format, you can reference site columns and use the "\n" character sequence to add multiple lines to your label. You can reference a site column by using the "{SiteColumnName}" label format, which will display the value of the site column when the document is opened. To create a label that references a site column and contains a line break, perform the following steps:

1. Navigate to the settings page for your content type.

2. In the Settings section, click Information management policy settings.

3. On the Information Management Policy Settings page, click Define a policy and then click OK.

4. To display a policy description for list managers when they are configuring policies on a list or content type, type a description in the Administrative Description box.

5. To display a policy statement for end users when they open items subject to this policy, type a statement in the Policy Statement box.

6. In the Labels section, select the Enable Labels check box.

7. Select the Prompt users to insert a label before saving or printing check box.

8. If you want to keep users from updating labels in documents, select the Prevent changes to labels after they are added check box.

9. In the Label format box, type **Confidential\n** and then type a header for the site column that you will be referencing.

10. After the header, type the site column name using the "{SiteColumnName}" format.

11. Update the formatting for the label in the Appearance and Label Size areas accordingly. Figure 7.2 shows the label settings for the policy. Do not click OK here, as we will make a policy change on this page in the next section.

Preview Labels

You can preview how labels will appear at the top of documents in the Preview area of the Labels section. Click Refresh to see how the current settings apply to your label. If you reference a site column, the corresponding value will not appear in the Preview area.

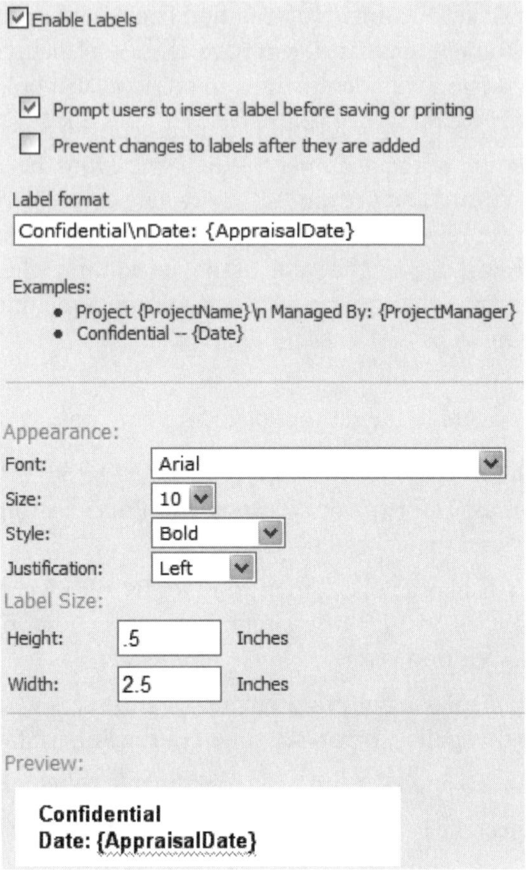

FIGURE 7.2 Set up the label policy.

AUDITING

By enabling auditing for a content type, you can create a record of events, tracking what users have done to documents. You can specify the following events to audit with an information management policy:

- Opening or downloading documents, viewing items in lists, or viewing item properties
- Editing items
- Checking out or checking in items
- Moving or copying items to another location in the site
- Deleting or restoring items

For your content type solution, you might need a policy that identifies when documents have been edited, moved, copied, or deleted. With the auditing feature, you can specify multiple events to track for your documents. To modify your content type solution to include auditing for documents that have been edited, moved, copied, or deleted, follow these steps:

1. Continuing on the Edit Policy page, in the Auditing section, select the Enable Auditing check box.

2. Select the Editing items check box.

3. Select the Moving or copying items to another location in the site check box.

4. Select the Deleting or restoring items check box. Figure 7.3 shows the auditing settings for the policy.

5. Click OK.

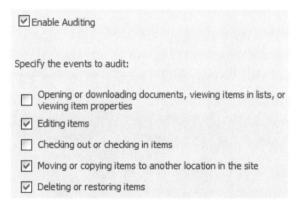

FIGURE 7.3 Set up the auditing policy.

As the content type solution gets used within your organization, events will be recorded in reports that can be accessed from the site collection's View Auditing Reports page. To view a report that collects audit log data for a site collection, do the following:

1. Navigate to the site collection home page.

2. From the Site Actions menu, click Site Settings | Modify All Site Settings.

3. In the Site Collection Administration section, click Audit log reports.

4. On the View Auditing Reports page, click one of the report links to view audit log data associated with a particular event.

Auditing Report Contains No Data

If a particular event has not occurred for any of the content type documents, you will see the error message shown in Figure 7.4 when clicking the corresponding report link on the View Auditing Reports page.

FIGURE 7.4 Run an auditing report that contains no data.

5. In the File Download dialog box, click Open to start the report in Office Excel 2007. Figure 7.5 shows an example of the Content modifications report, which tracks all events that modified content within the site collection.

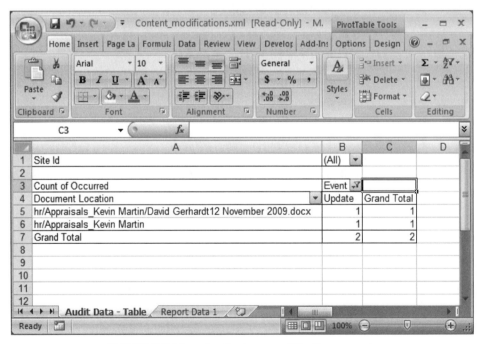

FIGURE 7.5 View the Content modifications report.

6. In Office Excel 2007, click the Report Data 1 tab to view individual events.

7. When you are done reviewing the report data, close Office Excel 2007 without saving any changes.

EXPIRATION

An expiration policy allows you to schedule content disposition by specifying a retention period for documents and then performing a certain action at the end of that period. The retention period can be identified by using a system date property for a document (for example, the modified date) or a custom site column defined as a Date and Time data type (for example, in the performance appraisal solution, the AppraisalDate column). When the document expires, you can choose to have it deleted or start a workflow that is associated with the content type. To create a policy that deletes expired documents, use the following steps:

1. Navigate to the settings page for your content type.

2. In the Settings section, click Information management policy settings.

3. On the Information Management Policy Settings page, click Define a policy and then click OK.

4. On the Edit Policy page, in the Expiration section, select the Enable Expiration check box.

5. Click A time period based on the item's properties.

6. Change the property list value from Created to some other date value.

7. Type **2** in the box to the right of the property list to specify the number of years for the retention period.

8. In the When the item expires area, note that workflows associated with the content type are options in the Start this workflow list.

9. Click Perform this action and ensure that Delete is selected. Figure 7.6 shows the settings for the expiration policy. Do not click OK here, as we will make a policy change on this page in the next section.

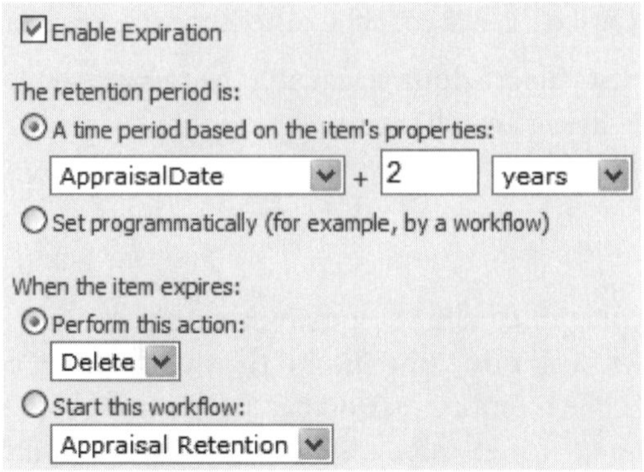

☑ Enable Expiration

The retention period is:
  ◉ A time period based on the item's properties:
    [AppraisalDate ▾] + [2] [years ▾]
  ○ Set programmatically (for example, by a workflow)

When the item expires:
  ◉ Perform this action:
    [Delete ▾]
  ○ Start this workflow:
    [Appraisal Retention ▾]

FIGURE 7.6 Set up the expiration policy.

BARCODES

Like labels, barcodes can be inserted into content type documents. They share another thing in common with labels: the corresponding policy caused an error for us during our testing of the performance appraisal solution. The error prevented the Document Information Panel from loading, so we did not implement the policy. So, again, if the Document Information Panel is an integral part of your content type solution, note that it might not load in your document template if you have defined a barcode policy. That said, the remainder of this section will identify how to set up a barcode policy for your content type.

Barcodes are automatically generated on the SharePoint server for documents when they are uploaded or modified in a library. Additionally, you can configure the policy to prompt users to insert a barcode before saving or printing a document. To create a policy that assigns barcodes to documents and prompts users to insert a barcode before saving or printing, do the following:

1. Continuing on the Edit Policy page, in the Barcodes section, select the Enable Barcodes check box.

2. Select the Prompt users to insert a barcode before saving or printing check box. Figure 7.7 shows the barcode settings for the policy.

3. Click OK.

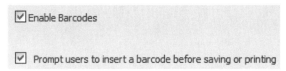

☑ Enable Barcodes

☑ Prompt users to insert a barcode before saving or printing

FIGURE 7.7 Set up the barcode policy.

Document Conversions

At the conclusion of any end-to-end content type process, it might be a requirement that certain users access documents in the browser, without needing the Office Word 2007 client and without having the ability to edit the site column data. Document conversions offer the ability to create read-only Web pages from content type documents.

When configuring conversions for a content type, you can specify the layout for new pages, similar to how layouts are defined when creating new pages at the SharePoint site collection or site level. You can also set the default location for converted pages and indicate whether pages should be created one at a time or in the background.

Converters can be configured for four different content types:

- From InfoPath Form to Web Page
- From Word Document to Web Page
- From Word Document with Macros to Web Page
- From XML to Web Page

Since the performance appraisal solution is an Office Word 2007 document content type, we will provide an example of how to configure the From Word Document to Web Page converter. In our example, because we will be creating Web pages on the Human Resources site, we must first ensure that the Office SharePoint Server Publishing Infrastructure feature is activated on the site collection and that the Office SharePoint Server Publishing feature is activated on the site. To activate these features, use the following steps:

1. Navigate to the site collection home page.
2. From the Site Actions menu, click Site Settings | Modify All Site Settings.
3. In the Site Collection Administration section, click Site collection features.
4. On the Site Collection Features page, find the Office SharePoint Server Publishing Infrastructure feature. If the Status is not Active, click the Activate button for that feature, as shown in Figure 7.8.
5. Navigate to the Human Resources site home page.
6. From the Site Actions menu, click Site Settings.
7. In the Site Administration section, click Site features.

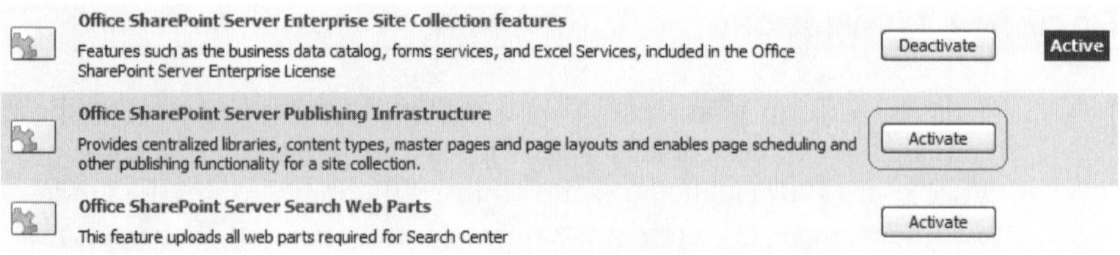

FIGURE 7.8 Activate the Office SharePoint Server Publishing Infrastructure feature.

8. On the Site Features page, find the Office SharePoint Server Publishing feature. If the Status is not Active, click the Activate button for that feature, as shown in Figure 7.9.

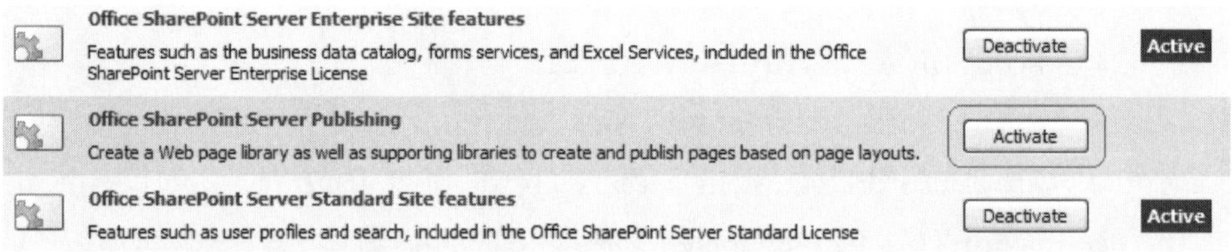

FIGURE 7.9 Activate the Office SharePoint Server Publishing feature.

Once the Office SharePoint Server Publishing feature is activated for the Human Resources site, you can modify the content type settings to define a converter that automatically creates pages on that site. To configure a From Word Document to a Web Page converter for the performance appraisal solution, perform the following:

1. Navigate to the site collection home page.

2. From the Site Actions menu, click Site Settings | Modify All Site Settings.

3. In the Galleries section, click Site content types.

4. In the Human Resources section, click Performance Appraisal.

5. In the Settings section, click Manage document conversion for this content type.

6. On the Manage Document Conversion for Performance Appraisal page, ensure that the From Word Document to Web Page check box is selected and then click the corresponding Configure link, as shown in Figure 7.10.

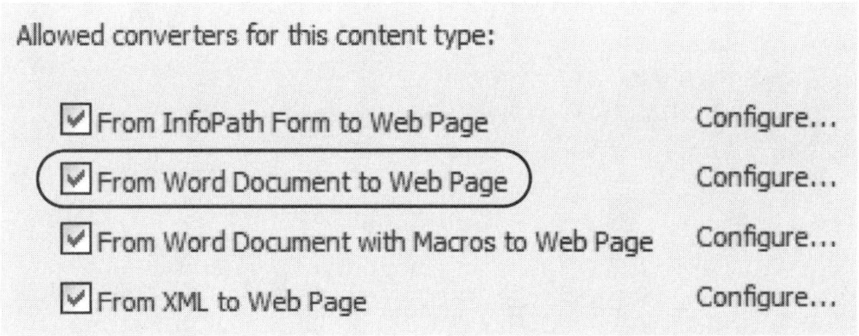

Allowed converters for this content type:

- ☑ From InfoPath Form to Web Page   Configure...
- ☑ From Word Document to Web Page   Configure...
- ☑ From Word Document with Macros to Web Page   Configure...
- ☑ From XML to Web Page   Configure...

FIGURE 7.10 Configure the From Word Document to Web Page converter.

7. In the Inheritance section, click Define unique settings for this content type.

8. In the Page Layout section, click the Page layout list and then click (Article Page) Article page with body only. This option will probably suffice for the performance appraisal content type, since there are no images or links to display.

9. In the Location section, select the Set a default site for creating pages check box.

10. In the Site URL area, click Browse.

11. In the Choose site dialog box, click Human Resources and then click OK. Figure 7.11 shows the page layout and location settings for the converter.

12. In the Processing section, choose whether to create pages one at a time or in the background. With the one-at-a-time option, users are taken to the page as soon as it is created. If you opt for creating pages in the background, users are returned to the document library while the conversion is in process.

13. Click OK.

In our example, we did not make any additional changes to the converter, but it is worth noting some of the other options. In the Page Layout section, you can specify a field on the Web page for converted content. The options for the Field for converted document contents list are Page Content (the default), Image Caption, and Style Definitions. You can also choose to remove the CSS <styles> section from the converted Web page or store that section in one of the aforementioned field options. In addition, in the Location and Processing sections, you can prevent users from changing the corresponding settings when pages are created.

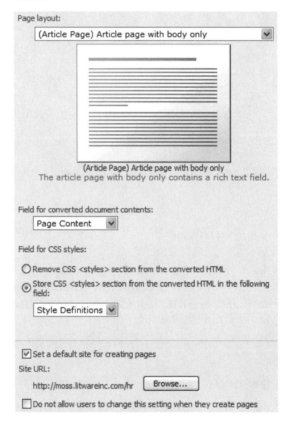

FIGURE 7.11 Set up the converter page layout and location settings.

Documents Not Converted

Although the converter configured in this section did not cause an error like the label and barcode policies, we were still unable to convert performance appraisal documents into Web pages during our testing of the solution.

8 Out-of-the-Box Solution Walkthrough

Now that the out-of-the-box performance appraisal solution has been completed, it is time to enjoy the fruits of your labor. In this chapter, we will walk through an end-to-end scenario with the book authors and two of the Founding Fathers of the United States playing different user roles. Table 8.1 identifies who will be the participants of our sample process.

Table 8.1 User Roles for the Sample Walkthrough

User Name	Role
Thomas Jefferson	Employee
Kevin Martin	Appraiser
John Adams	Peer Reviewer
David Gerhardt	Peer Reviewer

There will be different users in your environment, but this walkthrough serves mainly to offer context for the content type that we developed together. We also understand that there are time elements involved in the process. For example, during the "2 - Goals Finalized" stage, an email message is not sent to the appraiser until the appraisal period ends. Obviously, we do not expect for you to wait up to a year to complete this walkthrough. So we will take shortcuts as necessary to get you through each of the process stages in a reasonable timeframe.

1 - Goals Draft

The end-to-end process kicks off with Kevin, who will start the Office Word 2007 document template at the beginning of the appraisal period. Kevin will identify the employee, appraiser, appraisal period start and end dates, and a tentative appraisal date, which may change as we near the end of the appraisal period. In addition, Kevin lists one or more goals for the employee, with each goal having a description, metric, and weight. The sum of the goal weight values should equal 1. To start the appraisal process, Kevin would use the following steps:

1. In the browser, navigate to the appraiser document library.
2. From the New menu, click Performance Appraisal.
3. If a Windows Internet Explorer message box appears asking for confirmation to open the file, click OK to continue.
4. In the Document Information Panel of the Office Word 2007 document, in the Employee Name people picker, type the name of the employee and click the Check Names button (or press Ctrl+K).
5. In the Appraiser Name people picker, type the name of the appraiser and click the Check Names button (or press Ctrl+K).
6. Change the Appraisal Period Start and Appraisal Period End values as needed. We recommend setting the Appraisal Period End date to tomorrow, in order to speed up this sample process.
7. In the document template, modify the Date of Appraisal content control value accordingly.
8. In the Goals table, fill in the Description, Metric, and Weight columns for a few goals. Figure 8.1 shows an example of how the draft appraisal might appear.
9. Press Ctrl+S.
10. In the Save As dialog box, note the default filename and then click Save to save the appraisal to the appraiser document library.
11. Close Office Word 2007.

GoalWeight Values

If you recall from when we created the site columns in Chapter 3, the individual GoalWeight column values must be from 0–1.

NOTE

FIGURE 8.1 Create draft goals for the appraisal.

Saving the appraisal to the document library triggers the Office SharePoint Designer 2007 workflow that we created in Chapter 6. The workflow recognizes that the AppraisalStatus value is "1 - Goals Draft" and thus sends an email message to Thomas, indicating the goals for the upcoming appraisal period. Figure 8.2 shows the email message that Thomas receives.

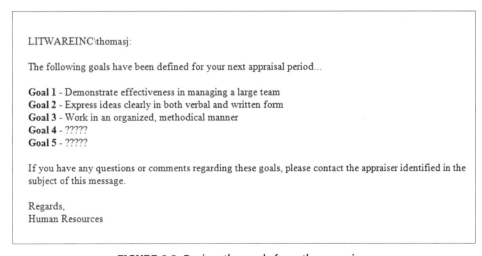

FIGURE 8.2 Review the goals from the appraiser.

Empty GoalMetric Values

An empty GoalMetric value in the appraisal document will result in a corresponding "?????" string in the email message that is sent to the employee.

Thomas will review the goals in this email message and then forward any comments to Kevin. If any comments result in a change to the goals, Kevin would need to modify the appraisal in the document library, which would again trigger the Office SharePoint Designer 2007 workflow and send another email message to Thomas identifying the goals. This back-and-forth process would continue until the two agreed upon the goals. Then Kevin would update the AppraisalStatus value in the appraisal document, which can be done as follows:

1. In the browser, navigate to the appraiser document library.

2. From the context menu for the appraisal document, click Edit in Microsoft Office Word, as shown in Figure 8.3.

3. If a Windows Internet Explorer message box appears asking for confirmation to open the file, click OK to continue.

4. To display the Document Information Panel, click the Office button (File menu) and then click Properties from the Prepare menu.

5. Click the Appraisal Status list and then click 2 - Goals Finalized.

6. Press Ctrl+S.

7. Close Office Word 2007.

FIGURE 8.3 Edit the appraisal document.

2 - GOALS FINALIZED

In a typical scenario, months would pass before the appraiser would get an email message indicating that the appraisal period had ended. However, in our test case, Kevin will receive an email message tomorrow, with a reminder that the AppraisalStatus value needs to be changed to "3 - Collect Feedback" and a link to the appraiser document library. Figure 8.4 shows the email message that Kevin receives at the end of the appraisal period. To move forward with the appraisal process, Kevin would use the following steps:

LITWAREINC\kevinm:

This message is a reminder that it is time to proceed with the appraisal for the employee identified in the subject line. Please open the appraisal document, change the **Status** value to "3 - Collect Feedback", and save the document back to the library...

http://moss.litwareinc.com/hr/Appraisals_Kevin%20Martin

Regards,
Human Resources

FIGURE 8.4 Receive notification that the appraisal period has ended.

1. In the email message indicating that the appraisal period has ended, click the link to the appraisal document library.
2. From the context menu for the appraisal document, click Edit in Microsoft Office Word.
3. If a Windows Internet Explorer message box appears asking for confirmation to open the file, click OK to continue.
4. To display the Document Information Panel, click the Office button (File menu) and then click Properties from the Prepare menu.
5. Click the Appraisal Status list and then click 3 - Collect Feedback.
6. Press Ctrl+S.
7. Close Office Word 2007.

3 - COLLECT FEEDBACK

When the appraisal moves into the "3 - Collect Feedback" stage, the appraiser will receive an email message indicating that he can collect feedback from peer reviewers as needed. Figure 8.5 shows the email message that Kevin receives at this point. The message reminds him to enable change tracking in the document and modify user permissions accordingly. To enable change tracking in the appraisal document, Kevin would do the following:

LITWAREINC\kevinm:

If you wish to receive feedback from other users about the employee identified in the subject line, start the **Peer Reviews** workflow. Make sure to enable change tracking in the document and to modify user permissions accordingly before starting the workflow.

After receiving all feedback, accept/reject changes from the reviewers as needed, add comments of your own, and add ratings for each of the goals. Then, change the **Status** value to "4 - Appraisal Draft".

Regards,
Human Resources

FIGURE 8.5 Receive notification about collecting feedback from peers.

1. In the appraiser document library, from the context menu for the appraisal document, click Edit in Microsoft Office Word.

2. If a Windows Internet Explorer message box appears asking for confirmation to open the file, click OK to continue.

3. In Office Word 2007, click the Review tab on the ribbon.

4. In the Tracking group, click the Track Changes command.

5. Press Ctrl+S.

6. Close Office Word 2007.

Duplicate Email Message

After Kevin enables change tracking and saves the appraisal back to the document library, he receives a duplicate email message about collecting feedback from peers. In essence, the Office SharePoint Designer 2007 workflow will send out an email message every time the appraisal document is updated, regardless of whether the AppraisalStatus value is updated or not.

REDUCE DUPLICATE EMAIL MESSAGES

The duplicate email messages for this stage and later stages can get rather annoying. One way to reduce these duplicates is to add a site column that identifies whether the stage has been started or not. In the Document Information Panel, you can add a rule that sets the site column accordingly, and then the Office SharePoint Designer 2007 workflow can be modified to send an email message only when the stage has not been started. For example, to add a site column that identifies whether the "3 - Collect Feedback" stage has started, do the following:

1. In the browser, navigate to the site collection home page.
2. From the Site Actions menu, click Site Settings | Modify All Site Settings.
3. In the Galleries section, click Site content types.
4. In the Human Resources section, click Performance Appraisal.
5. In the Columns section, click Add from new site column.
6. In the Column name box, type **Stage3Started**.
7. Click Yes/No (check box).
8. In the Group section, click the Existing group list and then click Human Resources.
9. In the Additional Column Settings section, click the Default value list and then click No.
10. Click OK.

Once the new site column is added, you can update the Document Information Panel with a rule that updates this column. The rule will change the column value to true when the Document Information Panel is opened and the AppraisalStatus value is equal to "3 – Collect Feedback." To add the rule, perform the following steps:

1. In the Settings section, click Document Information Panel settings.
2. In the Document Information Panel Template section, click Edit this template.
3. In the Microsoft Office InfoPath dialog box, click Yes to update the form template.
4. In the Data Source Wizard, click Yes to update the data source.
5. Click Tools | Form Options.
6. In the Open and Save category, click Rules.
7. In the Rules for Opening Forms dialog box, click Add.
8. In the Name box, type **Set Stage 3 Flag** and then click Set Condition.
9. In the Condition dialog box, click the first list on the left and then click Select a field or group.
10. In the Select a Field or Group dialog box, expand p:properties and then expand :documentManagement.
11. Double-click ns2:AppraisalStatus.
12. In the Condition dialog box, click the third list from the left and then click "3 - Collect Feedback".

13. Click OK.

14. In the Rule dialog box, click Add Action.

15. In the Action dialog box, click the Action list and then click Set a field's value.

16. Click the Select a Field or Group button, located to the right of the Field box.

17. In the Select a Field or Group dialog box, expand p:properties and then expand :documentManagement.

18. Double-click ns2:Stage3Started.

19. In the Action dialog box, in the Value box, type **true**.

20. Click OK until all dialog boxes have been closed.

21. Click File | Publish.

22. In the Save As dialog box, navigate to any location on your local machine, type a name in the File name box, and then click Save.

23. In the first page of the Publishing Wizard, ensure that the As a Document Information Panel template for a SharePoint site content type or list content type (recommended) option is selected and then click Next.

24. In the next page of the Publishing Wizard, click Publish.

25. In the Microsoft Office InfoPath dialog box, click OK to replace the existing template.

26. In the last page, click Close.

27. Close Office InfoPath 2007.

After adding the rule to the Document Information Panel, the last step is to update the Stage 3 condition in the Office SharePoint Designer 2007 workflow. To modify the workflow, do the following:

1. Start Office SharePoint Designer 2007.

2. From the File menu, click Open Site.

3. In the Open Site dialog box, in the Site name box, type the URL for the Human Resources site and then click Open.

4. In the Folder List task pane, expand Workflows and then expand Appraisal WF (or whatever you named the workflow in Chapter 6).

5. Double-click Appraisal WF.xoml.

6. Click the third conditions list and then click the Compare {Appraiser List Name} field option.

7. Click the field link and then click Stage3Started.

8. Click the value link and then click No.

9. Click Finish.

10. Close Office SharePoint Designer 2007.

In Chapter 6, we walked through the steps for managing the permissions of an individual appraisal in the appraiser document library. Those steps will need to be repeated here in order for Kevin to grant peer reviewers write access to Thomas' appraisal document. To grant the reviewers write access to the document, Kevin would do the following:

1. In the appraiser document library, from the context menu for the appraisal document, click Manage Permissions.

2. On the Permissions page, from the Actions menu, click Edit Permissions.

3. In the Windows Internet Explorer message box, click OK to create unique permissions for the document.

4. On the Permissions page, from the New menu, click Add Users.

5. In the Users/Groups box, type the names of the reviewers and click the Check Names button control (or press Ctrl+K). Multiple names must be separated with a semicolon.

6. In the Give Permission section, select the Contribute - Can view, add, update, and delete check box.

7. In the Send E-Mail section, clear the Send welcome e-mail to the new users check box. Figure 8.6 shows how the Permissions page should appear.

8. Click OK.

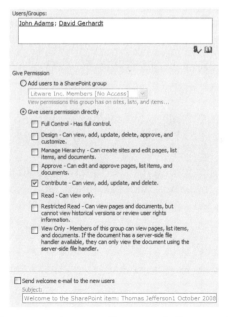

FIGURE 8.6 Give peer reviewers write access to the appraisal document.

NOTE

Email Message Regarding Write Access

In the previous set of steps, if the Send welcome e-mail to the new users check box were selected, an email message would have been sent to the reviewers about write access being granted. That message would have contained a link to the document's properties page, but not a link to the document itself.

Because the Send welcome e-mail to the new users check box was cleared in the previous set of steps, John and David will not receive an email message indicating that they have contribute (write) access to the appraisal document. However, Kevin will start the Peer Reviews workflow and identify them both as reviewers. This action will result in a SharePoint task being assigned to each of them, with an email message sent that contains a link to the appraisal document. To start the Peer Reviews workflow, Kevin would do the following:

1. Navigate to the appraiser document library.
2. From the context menu for the appraisal document, click Workflows.
3. On the Workflows page, in the Start a New Workflow section, click Peer Reviews (or whatever you named the Collect Feedback workflow in Chapter 6).
4. On the Start "Peer Reviews" page, in the Request Feedback section, update the list of peer reviewers in the Reviewers box and then click the Check Names button control (or press Ctrl+K). Multiple names must be separated with a semicolon.
5. In the Due Date section, modify the Tasks are due by date picker accordingly. Figure 8.7 shows how the Start "Peer Reviews" page should appear.
6. Click Start.

John and David will each receive an email message indicating that a review task has been assigned by Kevin, as shown in Figure 8.8. The message contains instructions on what the user must do to complete the task, and it contains a link to the appraisal document. John decides to take the lead in performing a peer review. To add comments to the appraisal document, John would do the following:

1. In the message indicating that a review task has been assigned, click the link to the appraisal document (in step 1).
2. In the File Download dialog box, click Open.
3. In Office Word 2007, at the top of the document, click Edit Document.

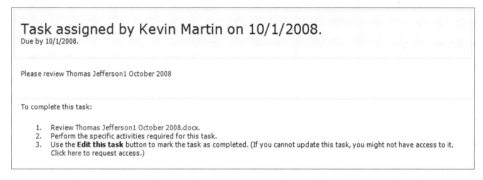

FIGURE 8.7 Start the Peer Reviews workflow.

Task assigned by Kevin Martin on 10/1/2008.
Due by 10/1/2008.

Please review Thomas Jefferson1 October 2008

To complete this task:

1. Review Thomas Jefferson1 October 2008.docx.
2. Perform the specific activities required for this task.
3. Use the **Edit this task** button to mark the task as completed. (If you cannot update this task, you might not have access to it. Click here to request access.)

FIGURE 8.8 Receive notification that a review task has been assigned.

4. Modify the Comments column for each of the goals, as shown in Figure 8.9.

5. At the top of the document, click Edit this task.

6. In the Please review dialog box, add general comments in the Type your feedback box, as shown in Figure 8.10.

7. Click Send Feedback, which will mark the SharePoint task as completed.

8. Press Ctrl+S.

9. Close Office Word 2007.

Goals

Description	Metric	Comments
Management	Demonstrate effectiveness in managing a large team	Thomas does not believe in micro-management, as evidenced by his resolutions against the Coercive Acts.
Communication	Express ideas clearly in both verbal and written form	His draft of the Declaration of Independence was a great read.
Organization	Work in an organized, methodical manner	Thomas has balanced time well between writing and legislative responsibilities.

FIGURE 8.9 Add reviewer comments to the appraisal document.

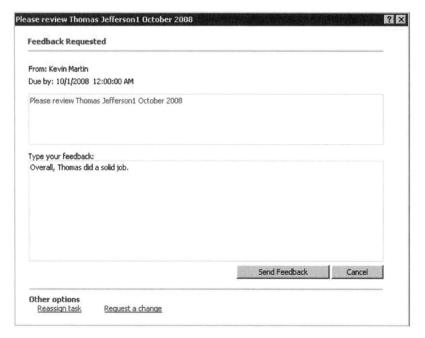

FIGURE 8.10 Send feedback about the appraisal.

Read-only Access

If another peer reviewer attempts to edit the appraisal document while it is in the process of being edited, a dialog box will be displayed indicating that the document is locked for editing. In that dialog box, the user can still open a read-only copy of the appraisal, create a local copy of the document and merge changes later, or receive notification when the document is available for editing.

For the peer reviews to be completed, David must also add his comments to the appraisal document. He can start his SharePoint review task after John unlocks (closes) the document. To add comments to the appraisal document, David would do the following:

1. In the message indicating that a review task has been assigned, click the link to the appraisal document (in step 1).

2. In the File Download dialog box, click Open.

3. In Office Word 2007, at the top of the document, click Edit Document.

4. Modify the Comments as needed, as shown in Figure 8.11.

5. At the top of the document, click Edit this task.

6. In the Please review dialog box, add general comments in the Type your feedback box and then click Send Feedback, which will mark the SharePoint task as completed.

7. Press Ctrl+S.

8. Close Office Word 2007.

Goals

Description	Metric	Comments	Weight	Score
Management	Demonstrate effectiveness in managing a large team	Thomas does not believe in micro-management, as evidenced by his resolutions against the Coercive Acts.	.5	[GoalScore1]
Communication	Express ideas clearly in both verbal and written form	His draft of the Declaration of Independence was a great read.	.25	[GoalScore2]
Organization	Work in an organized, methodical manner	~~Thomas has balanced time well between writing and legislative responsibilities.~~Thomas has balanced time well between writing and legislative responsibilities. He also finds time to practice law.	.25	[GoalScore3]

FIGURE 8.11 Add more reviewer comments to the appraisal document.

After John and David have added their comments, Kevin can review their feedback and update the appraisal document accordingly. In Office Word 2007, Kevin can approve or reject changes from the reviewers as needed and then disable change tracking in the document. He can then add his own comments and ratings for each of the goals. He completes the "3 - Collect Feedback" stage by changing the AppraisalStatus value to "4 - Appraisal Draft." To complete this stage, Kevin would do the following:

1. In the browser, navigate to the appraiser document library.

2. From the context menu for the appraisal document, click Edit in Microsoft Office Word.

3. If a Windows Internet Explorer message box appears asking for confirmation to open the file, click OK to continue.

4. In Office Word 2007, review comments from John and David and then click the Review tab on the ribbon.

5. In the Changes group, click Accept All Changes in Document from the Accept menu, as shown in Figure 8.12.

FIGURE 8.12 Accept all changes in the document.

6. In the Tracking group, click the Track Changes command to disable change tracking in the document.

7. Update comments as needed and then provide scores for each of the goals, as shown in Figure 8.13.

8. To display the Document Information Panel, click the Office button (File menu) and then click Properties from the Prepare menu.

Goals

Description	Metric	Comments	Weight	Score
Management	Demonstrate effectiveness in managing a large team	Thomas' resolutions against the Coercive Acts show that he can trust his staff to make sound decisions, and he fills in the gaps when needed.	.5	3
Communication	Express ideas clearly in both verbal and written form	Everyone enjoyed his draft of the Declaration of Independence.	.25	4.5
Organization	Work in an organized, methodical manner	Thomas has balanced time well between writing and legislative responsibilities. He also finds time to practice law.	.25	3.5
[GoalDescription4]	[GoalMetric4]	[GoalComments4]	[GoalWeight4]	[GoalScore4]
[GoalDescription5]	[GoalMetric5]	[GoalComments5]	[GoalWeight5]	[GoalScore5]
		Totals:	1	3.5

FIGURE 8.13 Update comments and provide scores.

9. Click the Appraisal Status list and then click 4 - Appraisal Draft.

10. Press Ctrl+S.

11. Close Office Word 2007.

NOTE

GoalScore Values

If you recall from earlier in the book, the individual GoalScore column values must be from 0–5.

4 - APPRAISAL DRAFT

When the appraisal moves into the "4 - Appraisal Draft" stage, the appraiser will receive an email message indicating that the face-to-face meeting needs to be scheduled with the employee, as shown in Figure 8.14. Kevin would print out the appraisal document, meet with Thomas to review the comments and scores for each of the goals, and then allow Thomas to add comments of his own. In a typical scenario, this stage might take roughly a week, but for testing purposes, we will expedite the process. Instead of printing out the document and scheduling a meeting, Kevin will just give Thomas write access to the appraisal, thus allowing Thomas to add comments directly to the document.

LITWAREINC\kevinm:

Please disable change tracking in the appraisal document for the employee identified in the subject line and schedule the face-to-face meeting. You can print out a copy of the document to review ratings and comments during the meeting.

After the meeting, make edits to the document as needed and then change the **Status** value to "5 - Appraisal Finalized".

Regards,
Human Resources

FIGURE 8.14 Receive notification to schedule the appraisal meeting.

To grant the employee write access to the document, Kevin would do the following:

1. Navigate to the appraiser document library.
2. From the context menu for the appraisal document, click Manage Permissions.
3. On the Permissions page, from the New menu, click Add Users.
4. In the Users/Groups box, type the name of the employee and click the Check Names button control (or press Ctrl+K).
5. In the Give Permission section, select the Contribute - Can view, add, update, and delete check box.
6. In the Send E-Mail section, ensure that the Send welcome e-mail to the new users check box is selected. Figure 8.15 shows how the Permissions page should appear.
7. Click OK.

NOTE

Peer Reviewer Permissions

Since the peer reviewers will no longer be involved in this appraisal process, now is a good time to remove their write access to the document. You can do this on the Permissions page by selecting the check boxes for the peer reviewers and then clicking Remove User Permissions from the Actions menu. In the corresponding Windows Internet Explorer dialog box, click OK to confirm the removal of permissions.

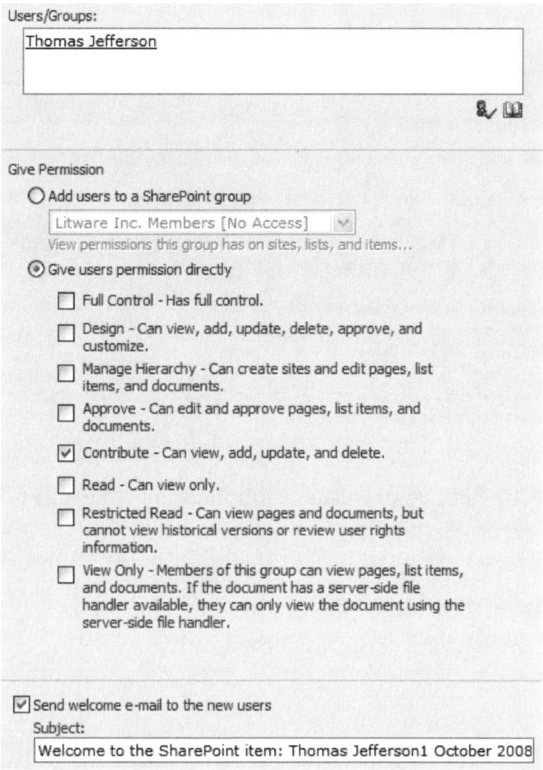

FIGURE 8.15 Give the employee write access to the appraisal document.

With the Send welcome e-mail to the new users check box selected in the previous set of steps, Thomas will receive an email message indicating that he has write access to the appraisal document, as shown in Figure 8.16. The link in the email message body is for the appraisal document's properties page, not the document itself. So Thomas will instead navigate to the appraiser document library, which he can infer from the link in the email message body. There, he can edit the document directly in Office Word 2007 and add general comments as needed. To update the appraisal document, Thomas would do the following:

1. Navigate to the appraiser document library.

2. From the context menu for the appraisal document, click Edit in Microsoft Office Word.

3. If a Windows Internet Explorer message box appears asking for confirmation to open the file, click OK to continue.

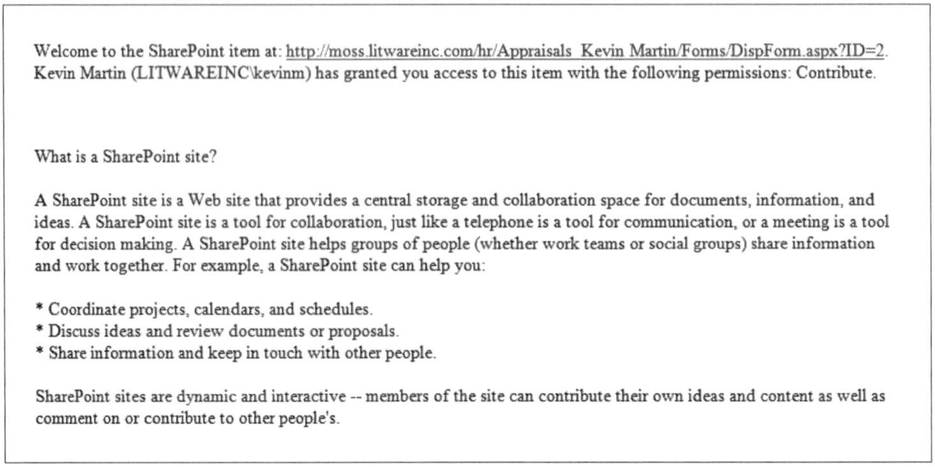

Welcome to the SharePoint item at: http://moss.litwareinc.com/hr/Appraisals_Kevin_Martin/Forms/DispForm.aspx?ID=2. Kevin Martin (LITWAREINC\kevinm) has granted you access to this item with the following permissions: Contribute.

What is a SharePoint site?

A SharePoint site is a Web site that provides a central storage and collaboration space for documents, information, and ideas. A SharePoint site is a tool for collaboration, just like a telephone is a tool for communication, or a meeting is a tool for decision making. A SharePoint site helps groups of people (whether work teams or social groups) share information and work together. For example, a SharePoint site can help you:

* Coordinate projects, calendars, and schedules.
* Discuss ideas and review documents or proposals.
* Share information and keep in touch with other people.

SharePoint sites are dynamic and interactive -- members of the site can contribute their own ideas and content as well as comment on or contribute to other people's.

FIGURE 8.16 Receive notification about having write access to the appraisal document.

4. At the bottom of the document, in the Employee Comments section, add general comments, as shown in Figure 8.17.

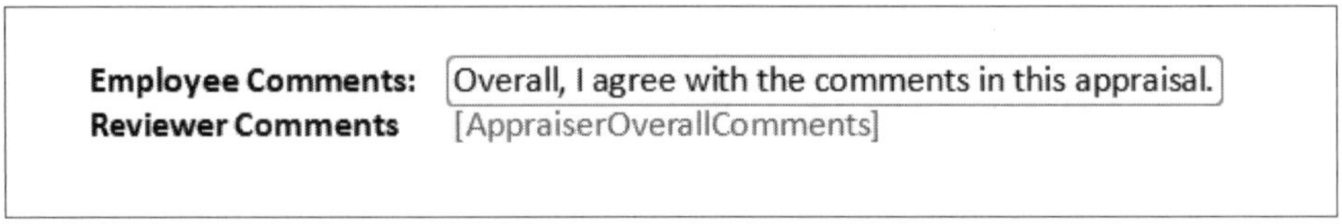

Employee Comments: Overall, I agree with the comments in this appraisal.
Reviewer Comments   [AppraiserOverallComments]

FIGURE 8.17 Update the Employee Comments section.

5. Press Ctrl+S.
6. Close Office Word 2007.

After the employee has provided his final comments, the appraiser can then advance the appraisal to the final stage. Kevin will navigate to the appraiser document library and start the appraisal document in Office Word 2007. At the bottom of the document, he can update the Reviewer Comments section. When he is done updating the document, he will change the AppraisalStatus value to "5 - Appraisal Finalized." To make these changes, Kevin would do the following:

1. Navigate to the appraiser document library.
2. From the context menu for the appraisal document, click Edit in Microsoft Office Word.

3. If a Windows Internet Explorer message box appears asking for confirmation to open the file, click OK to continue.

4. At the bottom of the document, in the Reviewer Comments section, add general comments, as shown in Figure 8.18.

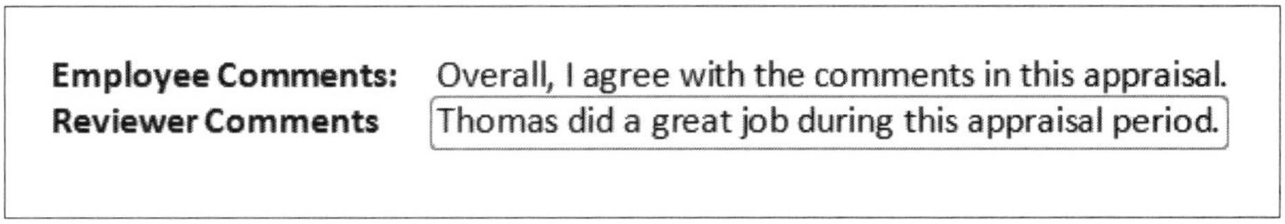

Employee Comments: Overall, I agree with the comments in this appraisal.
Reviewer Comments   Thomas did a great job during this appraisal period.

FIGURE 8.18 Update the Reviewer Comments section.

5. To display the Document Information Panel, click the Office button (File menu) and then click Properties from the Prepare menu.

6. Click the Appraisal Status list and then click 5 - Appraisal Finalized.

7. Press Ctrl+S.

8. Close Office Word 2007.

5 - Appraisal Finalized

When the appraisal enters the "5 - Appraisal Finalized" stage, the appraiser will receive an email message indicating that it is time to collect signatures for the appraisal document, as shown in Figure 8.19. Kevin would then insert a signature line into the document, allowing the employee to sign off on the appraisal. To insert a signature line, Kevin would do the following:

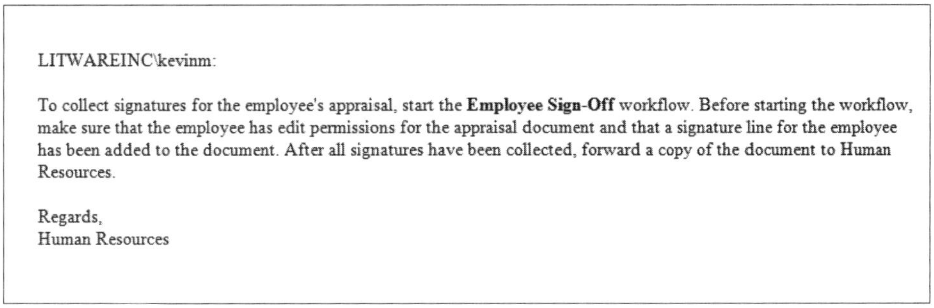

LITWAREINC\kevinm:

To collect signatures for the employee's appraisal, start the **Employee Sign-Off** workflow. Before starting the workflow, make sure that the employee has edit permissions for the appraisal document and that a signature line for the employee has been added to the document. After all signatures have been collected, forward a copy of the document to Human Resources.

Regards,
Human Resources

FIGURE 8.19 Receive notification about collecting signatures.

1. Navigate to the appraiser document library.

2. From the context menu for the appraisal document, click Edit in Microsoft Office Word.

3. If a Windows Internet Explorer message box appears asking for confirmation to open the file, click OK to continue.

NOTE

Grouped Document

Because you grouped the entire document in Chapter 4 to prevent users from making modifications outside of the content controls, you will need to ungroup the document so that you can insert a signature line.

4. Press Ctrl+A to select all content in the document.

5. Click the Developer tab on the ribbon.

6. In the Controls group, click Ungroup from the Group menu.

7. At the bottom of the document, place the cursor on the line below the Reviewer Comments section.

8. Click the Insert tab on the ribbon.

9. In the Text group, click Microsoft Office Signature Line from the Signature Line menu.

10. In the Microsoft Office Word dialog box, click OK after reading the disclaimer about Microsoft Office digital signatures.

11. In the Signature Setup dialog box, enter the applicable signing information, as shown in Figure 8.20.

FIGURE 8.20 Add the signing information for the employee.

12. Click OK. The bottom of the document should appear, as shown in Figure 8.21.

13. Press Ctrl+S.

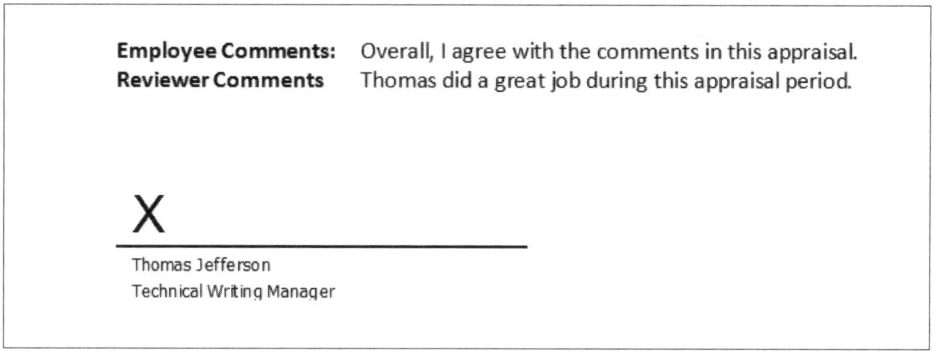

Employee Comments: Overall, I agree with the comments in this appraisal.
Reviewer Comments Thomas did a great job during this appraisal period.

X
_____

Thomas Jefferson
Technical Writing Manager

FIGURE 8.21 Add the signature line to the appraisal document.

With the signature line added to the document, Kevin can then start the Employee Sign-Off workflow. This will notify Thomas that a signature is needed before the appraisal is officially finalized. To start the Employee Sign-Off workflow, Kevin would do the following:

1. In Office Word 2007, click the Office button (File menu) and then click Workflows.

2. In the Workflows dialog box, click the Start button for the Employee Sign-Off workflow (or whatever you named the Collect Signatures workflow in Chapter 6).

3. In the Employee Sign-Off dialog box, in the Suggested signer box, type the name of the employee and then click the Check Names button. Figure 8.22 shows how the Employee Sign-Off dialog box would appear.

4. Click Start.

5. Close Office Word 2007.

After the workflow is started, Thomas will receive an email message indicating that the appraisal document requires his signature, as shown in Figure 8.23. The message contains instructions on how to complete the SharePoint signature task that is assigned and a link to the appraisal document.

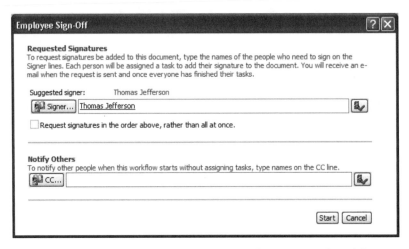

FIGURE 8.22 Identify the signer for the Employee Sign-Off workflow.

> **Task assigned by Kevin Martin on 10/1/2008.**
>
> This document requires your signature.
>
> To complete this task:
>
> 1. Review Thomas Jefferson1 October 2008.docx.
> 2. Perform the specific activities required for this task.
> 3. Use the **Edit this task** button to mark the task as completed. (If you cannot update this task, you might not have access to it. Click here to request access.)

FIGURE 8.23 Receive notification about having to sign the appraisal document.

To sign off on the document, Thomas would do the following:

1. In the message indicating that a signature task has been assigned, click the link to the appraisal document (in step 1).

2. In the File Download dialog box, click Open.

3. In Office Word 2007, at the top of the document, click Edit Document.

4. At the top of the document, click Sign.

5. In the Microsoft Office Word dialog box, click OK after reading the disclaimer about Microsoft Office digital signatures.

Digital Signature Authenticity

In the Get a Digital ID dialog box, the user has the option of getting a digital ID from a Microsoft partner or creating his own digital ID. In a typical scenario, you would probably choose the option of getting a digital ID from a Microsoft partner. However, you might not have verification software installed in your environment. So, for this scenario, you can instead choose the option to create your own digital ID. For more information about using digital IDs in the 2007 Microsoft Office system, go to http://office.microsoft.com/en-us/marketplace/EY100949011033.aspx.

6. In the Get a Digital ID dialog box, click Create your own digital ID, as shown in Figure 8.24.

FIGURE 8.24 Create your own digital ID.

7. Click OK.

8. In the Create a Digital ID dialog box, confirm the signing information and then click Create.

9. In the Sign dialog box, type the name of the employee next to the X and then click Sign.

10. In the Signature Confirmation message box, click OK. The bottom of the document should appear, as shown in Figure 8.25.

11. Close Office Word 2007.

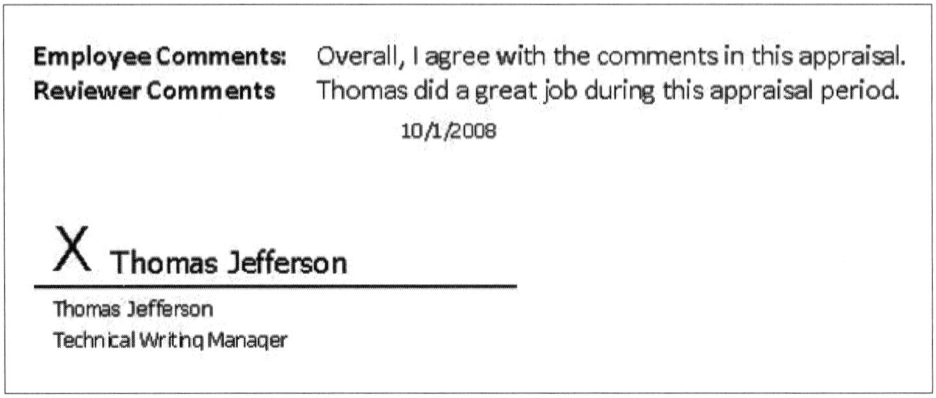

Employee Comments: Overall, I agree with the comments in this appraisal.
Reviewer Comments   Thomas did a great job during this appraisal period.

10/1/2008

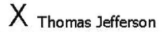 Thomas Jefferson

Thomas Jefferson
Technical Writing Manager

FIGURE 8.25 Sign the appraisal document.

You have now completed the end-to-end walkthrough of the out-of-the-box performance appraisal solution. In a typical scenario, the next step would have been to forward a signed copy of the appraisal document to Human Resources, but that is not necessary for testing purposes. You are now ready to start using Visual Studio 2008 to enhance the performance appraisal solution, which will be discussed in the next two chapters.

9 Automating the Performance Appraisal Solution

The solution at this point is complete and can be effectively deployed within an enterprise. However, the manager is required to perform a lot of manual steps as the performance appraisal moves through the different stages. These steps include setting the permissions on the appraisal document and gathering feedback information. In this and the next chapter, we will explore a custom workflow solution developed with Microsoft Visual Studio 2008 that will configure the security settings on the performance appraisal document, aggregate the peer review comments, and store the results in the performance appraisal document.

This chapter covers the new appraisal solution through the goals-finalized stage and automates the permissions settings. Chapter 10 describes the feedback process, as well as deploying the custom workflow.

PREREQUISITES

Within the solution, we'll need to enter some environment-specific values. For the next two chapters, the example code and steps will assume the following information:

- SharePoint site collection is located at "http://moss.litwareinc.com" and a site is located at "http://moss.litwareinc.com/hr."
- Document library within the site is named "Appraisals_Kevin Martin" with a URL of "http://moss.litwareinc.com/hr/Appraisals_Kevin Martin."
- Domain is named "litwareinc."

We'll do our development under the local administrator account. (You'll definitely want to test under a non-admin account.) The following domain accounts need to be created:

- benjaminf—Benjamin Franklin
- georgew—George Washington
- davidg—David Gerhardt
- kevinm—Kevin Martin

We need the specific accounts so the solution will be easier to understand when we start creating documents and assigning permissions.

As for the programming knowledge required, you'll need to have a background in the following areas:

- C#
- Visual Studio 2008 project and solution creation
- Adding references to a project in Visual Studio 2008
- Updating project properties in Visual Studio 2008
- Microsoft InfoPath 2007 Form Design

While you don't need to be an expert in any area, some basic steps may not be explained in as much detail as extreme novices would require. If you run into any of those basic steps (or problems) you don't understand, you can easily find the answers in Visual Studio Help, or you can refer back to the source code for the solution.

You can get the class listings as well as the resource image for the activity from the online source (at www.courseptr.com/downloads).

THE NEW PERFORMANCE APPRAISAL PROCESS

Our goal is to enhance the current appraisal process through automation. The manual steps are tedious by nature and are also prone to mistakes.

Reviewing the AppraisalStatus field from the Performance Appraisal Content Type from Chapter 3, we find the performance appraisal moves through five stages:

- Goals Draft
- Goals Finalized

- Collect Feedback
- Appraisal Draft
- Appraisal Finalized

The manager starts the appraisal process by drafting goals for the employee. When the manager first creates the appraisal document, the goals are empty. The manager is the only person with any access to the document. After drafting the goals and saving the document, the manager starts the workflow, and the appraisal document is unlocked for review by the employee.

The employee is reviewed over a certain amount of time, usually three, six, or twelve months. For the Litware appraisal process, the manager will be assigned a task to indicate when the evaluation period starts.

At the start of the evaluation period, the manager collects feedback from peer reviewers and the employee, and he incorporates that feedback into the final appraisal.

In this chapter, we'll be creating a Visual Studio 2008 workflow up to the point where the manager collects feedback. The rest of the process will be covered in the next chapter.

When finished with this chapter, you will be able to perform the following activities:

- Manually start the appraisal workflow.
- Assign read and edit permissions to the appraisal document with the workflow.
- Get the workflow ready for the evaluation process.

While the list may be short, we will be laying the groundwork to support the second half of the process. To get there, we will accomplish the following tasks:

- Create a workflow activity to set permissions on SharePoint list items.
- Create a sequential workflow.
- Create tasks and assign them to the appropriate people.
- Create forms for the tasks using Microsoft InfoPath.
- Utilize the custom activity to automatically set permissions on the appraisal document.

A CUSTOM ACTIVITY

Setting permissions with the out-of-the-box solution is tedious and error-prone. The Litware appraisal process contains only a few states and for the most part none of the information is too sensitive. That makes the appraiser's job relatively easy. However, if the process were to double the number of stages (such as collecting information on a project basis so people didn't lose track of progress over a six-month process), or if there were some extremely sensitive data (salary, bonus, human resource complaint, and so on), then a single mistake could cause embarrassment or worse, a law-suit. More bizarre things have happened.

To alleviate the tedium and ensure that only the people identified in the review process can read or edit an appraisal document, we're going to create an automated SharePoint list item permissions setting workflow activity, and we'll call it the SharePoint List Item Permissions Activity.

THE DESIGN OF THE ACTIVITY

The SharePoint List Item Permissions Activity was designed to allow a Workflow Designer to give designated users read-and-edit permissions on a specific list item. Normally, SharePoint items within a document library inherit permissions from the document library itself. This works great in most cases because usually documents in a given document library need similar protection. But having to maintain permissions on a document-by-document basis can complicate life considerably. Since the most common case is inherited security, the activity we're creating checks to make sure that the targeted item has unique permissions enabled. If not, the activity breaks the inherited security and enables unique permissions for the item.

Our activity exposes the following properties:

- `SiteId`. A GUID that identifies the SharePoint site that contains the list item being configured.
- `WebId`. A GUID that identifies the SharePoint Web that contains the list item being configured.
- `ListId`. A GUID that identifies the SharePoint list that contains the list item being configured.
- `ItemId`. An integer that identifies the SharePoint list item being configured.
- `Administrators`. A semicolon-separated list of user login names. The names represent users who are administrators of the item. We won't use this property, but it might be useful in another situation.

- `Editors.` A semicolon-separated list of user login names. The names represent users who can edit the item. We'll only allow the appraiser/manager to be an editor.

- `Readers.` A semicolon-separated list of user login names. The names represent users who can view the item. At different stages of the workflow, the employee and peer reviewers will be given read access to the appraisal document.

The properties can be set either in the Workflow Designer or through code using the object model. We'll be setting the properties in the Workflow Designer later on.

While the activity was designed specifically with the appraisal workflow in mind, it is also designed to be used in any SharePoint workflow. Our needs require us only to give read/view rights and edit rights to the item, but the activity includes the ability to assign administrative permissions, and it is also easily extensible should you require further permission settings.

The SharePoint list item is identified through the different ID properties. The workflow exposes the ID properties to us through the `workflowProperties` member.

Administrators, editors, and readers are set via properties. The properties are strings that require login names ("domain\username") separated by semicolons. For instance, to allow Benjamin Franklin and George Washington to have editor rights (how could we make George just a reader?), the property would be set to:

```
litwareinc\georgew;litwareinc\benjaminf
```

When the activity executes, all permissions are removed from the list item and then administrator, editor, and reader permissions are added to the item. If any of the user lists is empty, no users are added to the role for the item.

Basically, that's it for the design. We'll create the activity in the next section.

CREATING THE ACTIVITY

To simplify life, we'll only have one solution for this and the next chapter. The workflow is the main emphasis, so we'll create our solution with the workflow in mind. Just follow these steps.

Creating the Activity Project and Solution

We're going to create a blank solution and a Workflow Activity Library within Visual Studio 2008 using the following steps:

1. Open Visual Studio 2008. On the file menu, point to New and click Project.

2. In the New Project dialog (refer to Figure 9.1) under the Project Types list, expand Visual C# and choose Workflow. Under Templates, choose Workflow Activity Library.

3. Name the project SharePointItemPermissionActivity and name the solution PerformanceAppraisalWF Solution.

4. Make sure that the Create directory for solution option is checked.

5. Click OK to create the solution and project.

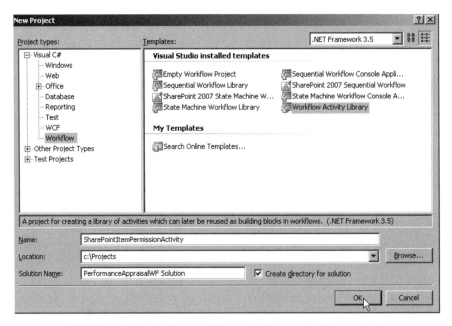

FIGURE 9.1 Create the workflow solution and activity project.

When you create an Activity Library, you need to create a strong name because the project will be deployed to the Global Assembly Cache (GAC) and the GAC requires all assemblies to be strong named. Add the strong name to the project by following these steps.

1. Right-click the project from within Solution Explorer and choose Properties.

2. Select the Signing tab.

3. Select Sign the assembly.

4. Expand the Choose a strong name key file drop-down and select <New>.

5. Enter **ActivityStrongName.snk** for the Key file name and make sure that Protect my key file with a password is unchecked.

6. Click OK to close the dialog.

7. Save your changes by clicking the File menu, Save All.

8. Close the Project Properties window.

Deploying the Activity to the GAC When Built

As mentioned in the previous section, the activity needs to be added to the GAC when deployed. While we will cover deployment in the next chapter, we need the assembly to be in the GAC to test the workflow. You'll find that `gacutil.exe` adds the assembly to the GAC.

We need to run `gacutil.exe` after every build of the activity. The utility is shipped with Software Development Kits (SDKs) and is not in a common folder on every machine. As such, you'll need to find a copy of `gacutil.exe` on your system. In our environment, `gacutil.exe` can be found in `c:\program files\microsoft sdks\windows\v6.0A\bin`.

1. Right-click the project from within Solution Explorer and choose Properties.

2. Select the Build Events tab and click Edit Post-build….

3. Enter text in the dialog box, as shown in Figure 9.2.

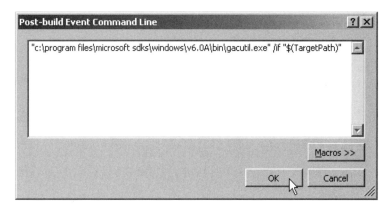

FIGURE 9.2 Set the Post-Build Event Command Line to add the activity to the GAC.

Post-build Event Command Line Macros and gacutil.exe

Visual Studio 2008 provides a number of macros that can be used within the build event command lines. The macros represent paths, file names, extensions, and so on, of files, paths, and configuration information for your project.

$TargetPath. represents the path to the built dll, regardless of the build environment (debug vs. retail), so we use that macro with the gacutil.exe command.

Speaking of gacutil.exe, make sure you change the path to gacutil.exe to point to the correct folder on your system. Also, notice the quotes around the path and around the $(TargetPath) macro. Both are necessary to allow for spaces in path names. Without the quotes, you'll get build errors. Also, make sure to include the "/if " parameters for gacutil.exe, as this will install (i) the assembly and force (f) the assembly to overwrite an existing dll if one already exists in the GAC. Without the force command, the dll won't be updated, and your hard work won't be reflected when you test your changes.

4. Click OK to close the dialog.

5. Save your changes by clicking the File menu, Save Selected Items.

6. Close the Project Properties window.

Finishing the Project Infrastructure

We are creating a custom SharePoint Workflow activity, and therefore need to rename our activity to a more representative name and add a reference to the SharePoint services dll. To finish the project infrastructure, let's set up the activity with the following steps:

1. Rename Activity1.cs to ItemPermissionsActivity.cs. When prompted to perform a rename in this project of all references, click Yes.

2. Add a project reference to Windows SharePoint Services by right-clicking the project in the Solution Explorer and choosing Add Reference. See Figure 9.3 for help.

3. Expand ItemPermissionsActivity.cs (if not already expanded) in Solution Explorer and open ItemPermissionsActivity.Designer.cs by double-clicking and modifying the InitializeComponent method so it contains the code in Listing 9.1.

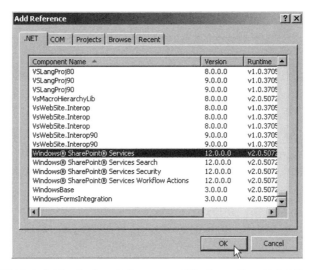

FIGURE 9.3 Add a Project Reference to Windows SharePoint Services.

LISTING 9.1   InitializeComponent Method in ItemPermissionsActivity.Designer.cs

```
private void InitializeComponent()
{
    this.Name = "ItemPermissionsActivity1";
}
```

Add Using Statement for SharePoint Services

Our activity requires us to add using statements to the namespaces that we'll be utilizing in our code. In the activity we'll be relying on both SharePoint services as well as the generic collections. To start the coding part of the process, follow these steps:

1. Open ItemPermissionsActivity.cs in code view by right-clicking ItemPermissionActivity.cs in the Solution Explorer and choosing View Code.

2. Add a using directive for SharePoint Services and generic collections, as shown in Listing 9.2.

| LISTING 9.2 | Using Statements |

```
using Microsoft.SharePoint;
using System.Collections.Generic;
```

Adding Custom Properties

The custom properties are implemented as `DependencyProperty` instances with very simple `get` and `set` methods. New dependency properties can be added by using code snippets, or they can be typed in directly.

To create the properties, open `ItemPermissionsActivity.cs` in code view and create the Activity Properties region directly after the class constructor. Listing 9.3 contains the entire code.

To use code snippets, create the region and from within the region right-click and choose Insert Snippet. Open the Other folder and within the workflow category, locate the snippet for inserting a dependency property. Once you have one defined, you can simply copy and paste to create the others. The Editors and Readers are especially easy since their return types are the same.

| LISTING 9.3 | Activity Properties |

```
#region Activity Properties
// DependencyProperty for ItemId
// This enables animation, styling, binding, etc...
public static readonly DependencyProperty ItemIdProperty =
    DependencyProperty.Register("ItemId", typeof(int),
        typeof(ItemPermissionsActivity));

 [Description("Id of item whose permissions are being assigned")]
public int ItemId
{
    get { return (int)GetValue(ItemIdProperty); }
    set { SetValue(ItemIdProperty, value); }
}
```

```
// DependencyProperty for ListId
// This enables animation, styling, binding, etc...
public static readonly DependencyProperty ListIdProperty =
   DependencyProperty.Register("ListId", typeof(Guid),
      typeof(ItemPermissionsActivity));


[Description("Id of list containing list item")]
public Guid ListId
{
   get { return (Guid)GetValue(ListIdProperty); }
   set { SetValue(ListIdProperty, value); }
}


// DependencyProperty for WebId
// This enables animation, styling, binding, etc...
public static readonly DependencyProperty WebIdProperty =
   DependencyProperty.Register("WebId", typeof(Guid),
      typeof(ItemPermissionsActivity));


[Description("Id of Web containing list item")]
public Guid WebId
{
   get { return (Guid)GetValue(WebIdProperty); }
   set { SetValue(WebIdProperty, value); }
}


// DependencyProperty for SiteId
// This enables animation, styling, binding, etc...
public static readonly DependencyProperty SiteIdProperty =
   DependencyProperty.Register("SiteId", typeof(Guid),
      typeof(ItemPermissionsActivity));


 [Description("Id of site containing list item")]
public Guid SiteId
```

```
{
    get { return (Guid)GetValue(SiteIdProperty); }
    set { SetValue(SiteIdProperty, value); }
}


// DependencyProperty for Editors.
// This enables animation, styling, binding, etc...
public static readonly DependencyProperty EditorsProperty =
    DependencyProperty.Register("Editors", typeof(string),
        typeof(ItemPermissionsActivity));


[Description("Users with edit permissions, separated by semicolons")]
public string Editors
{
    get { return (string)GetValue(EditorsProperty); }
    set { SetValue(EditorsProperty, value); }
}


// DependencyProperty for Readers.
// This enables animation, styling, binding, etc...
public static readonly DependencyProperty ReadersProperty =
    DependencyProperty.Register("Readers", typeof(string),
        typeof(ItemPermissionsActivity));


 [Description("Users with read permissions, separated by semicolons")]
public string Readers
{
    get { return (string)GetValue(ReadersProperty); }
    set { SetValue(ReadersProperty, value); }
}


// DependencyProperty for Administrators.
// This enables animation, styling, binding, etc...
```

```
public static readonly DependencyProperty AdministratorsProperty =

    DependencyProperty.Register("Administrators", typeof(string),

        typeof(ItemPermissionsActivity));


[Description("Users with admin permissions, separated by semicolons")]

public string Administrators

{

    get { return (string)GetValue(AdministratorsProperty); }

    set { SetValue(AdministratorsProperty, value); }

}

#endregion
```

Coding the Execute Method

Once the properties have been defined, we can implement the `Execute` method. The workflow engine looks for an `Execute` method within the activity to use as an entry point.

Where Are All the Comments?

The code shown has a minimal amount of commenting to save space and reduce the distractions. The online source code has all of the comments.

First, we'll create the Execute Routine region directly after the Activity Properties region. See Listing 9.4.

LISTING 9.4 Execute Region

```
#region Execute Routine



#endregion
```

The `Execute` method requires a number of supporting methods to be implemented before implementing `Execute` itself. We'll create the first helper function, `AddRoleAssignment`, which adds a role assignment to a list item. If you look at the method signature, you can see what the method's purpose is. We're going to take a user, a role, and give the user the role permissions for an item. The function doesn't return anything.

The SPRoleType enumeration contains five different role types, but we are only concerned with Reader and Contributor.

The method itself is contained in Listing 9.5 and should be added as the first function within the Execute Routine region.

LISTING 9.5 AddRoleAssignment Method

```
private void AddRoleAssignment(SPListItem listItem,
    SPUser user,
    SPRoleType roleType)
{
    // Create the role definition
    SPRoleDefinition roleDefinition =
        listItem.Web.RoleDefinitions.GetByType(roleType);


    // Create a new role assignment
    SPRoleAssignment roleAssignment = new SPRoleAssignment(user);


    // Bind the role assignment to the role definition
    roleAssignment.RoleDefinitionBindings.Add(roleDefinition);


    // Add the new role assignment to the list item
    listItem.RoleAssignments.Add(roleAssignment);
}
```

Building upon the previous function, we need to add a function that sets permissions for a list of users by calling AddRoleAssignment for each user in a list. The code (see Listing 9.6) is added as the last method within the Execute Routine region. The method first splits the user list string into an array of user strings. Each constituent string is turned into an SPUser instance. The list item is part of a list that is contained within a SharePoint Web (SPWeb). Users are associated and identified at the Web level. Luckily, the list item (represented by an SPItem instance) contains a direct link to the Web. The SPUser is found by using the login name indexer method of the Web. Once the user is instantiated, AddRoleAssignment is called.

An exception is thrown if any bad information is entered into the original user list string.

LISTING 9.6   `SetPermissions` Method

```
private void SetPermissions(SPListItem listItem,
    string users,
    SPRoleType roleType)
{
    List<SPUser> sharePointUsers = new List<SPUser>();

    string[] splitUsers = users.Split(new char[]{';'});

    SPUser user;

    try
    {
        foreach (string userName in splitUsers)
        {
            user = listItem.Web.AllUsers[userName];
            AddRoleAssignment(listItem, user, roleType);
        }
    }
    catch (Exception)
    {
        throw new ArgumentException(
            "Invalid user list for roleType - " + roleType.ToString());
    }
}
```

Since removing all existing permissions is the first permissions action taken every time, we'll add a method as the last method in the Execute Routine region to remove permissions from an item (see Listing 9.7). The method accepts a list item and simply walks through all of the role assignments for the list item and removes them. The code is added as the last method within the Execute Routine region.

LISTING 9.7   RemovePermissions Method

```
private void RemovePermissions(SPListItem listItem)
{
   // Walk the list of role assignments
   // and remove the last one until there
   // are no more items
   while (listItem.RoleAssignments.Count > 0)
   {
      listItem.RoleAssignments.Remove(
         listItem.RoleAssignments.Count - 1);
   }
}
```

The final piece of supporting code for our Execute method can be found in Listing 9.8. A reference to the SharePoint list item is created by walking down the SharePoint object tree from the site to the Web to the list to the item itself using the ID properties. Once again, the code is added as the last method within the Execute Routine region.

LISTING 9.8   GetConfiguredItem Method

```
private SPListItem GetConfiguredItem()
{
   SPListItem retValue = null;
   try
   {
      using (SPSite site = new SPSite(SiteId))
      {
         using (SPWeb web = site.AllWebs[WebId])
         {
            SPList list = web.Lists[ListId];
            retValue = list.GetItemById(ItemId);
         }
      }
```

```
    }
    catch (Exception)
    {
    }
    return retValue;
}
```

Finally, we get to add the `Execute` method itself. With all of the supporting code in place, `Execute` is very straight-forward and what you would expect. The code is added as the last method within the Execute Routine region. Reviewing Listing 9.9 reveals a few interesting points.

■ First, there is a check to make sure that the ID properties were set to a valid list item via a call to `GetConfiguredItem()`. If the properties don't result in a list item, the activity will throw an `ArgumentNullException`. This is important to know when building your workflows, as you will need to make sure you always set the ID properties. Adding a fault handler is also a good idea.

■ The second point of interest is to check to see if the item has unique role assignments. By default, list items inherit security from the list. This model is insufficient if you want to specify separate permissions for each item in a list. There's a good chance that the first time our activity is run against an item, the item will be inheriting security. We just call the Item's `BreakRoleInheritance` method to make the item security-managed independently from the list permissions. Since SharePoint workflows run under the System account, we don't need to elevate our permissions to complete this.

Listing 9.9   Execute Method

```
protected override ActivityExecutionStatus Execute(
    ActivityExecutionContext executionContext)
{
    // Assume success
    ActivityExecutionStatus retValue =
        ActivityExecutionStatus.Closed;

    SPListItem item = GetConfiguredItem();

    // Find the item that we need to set permissions for
    if (item != null)
```

```
        {
          // Make sure the item allows unique
          // permissions
          if (!item.HasUniqueRoleAssignments)
          {
            item.BreakRoleInheritance(true);
          }

          // Remove all permissions on the item
          RemovePermissions(item);

          // Set the admin permissions if any were indicated
          if (Administrators != null && Administrators.Trim().Length > 0)
          {
            SetPermissions(item, Administrators, SPRoleType.Administrator);
          }

          // Set the editor permissions if any were indicated
          if (Editors != null && Editors.Trim().Length > 0)
          {
            SetPermissions(item, Editors, SPRoleType.Contributor);
          }

          // Set the reader permissions if any were indicated
          if (Readers != null && Readers.Trim().Length > 0)
          {
            SetPermissions(item, Readers, SPRoleType.Reader);
          }
        }
        else
        {
          throw new ArgumentNullException("ListItem is null.");
        }

        return retValue;
    }
```

Save your changes and build the code.

VISUAL STUDIO 2008 DESIGNER SUPPORT

As it stands, our activity is completely functional but does not allow for configuration in the Visual Studio Workflow Designer. Designer support requires an `Activity Designer`-derived class to be implemented and a Designer attribute to be attached to the activity class. The `ActivityDesigner` class requires an `ActivityDesigner-Theme`-derived class to be implemented and added to the designer class as an attribute. The `ActivityDesigner` class is responsible for drawing the bounding rectangle for the activity as well as drawing the text box that sits below the bounding rectangle. The theme is responsible for setting the colors and styles of the graphic and the text for the activity.

Without the `ActivityDesigner` class, the Workflow Designer displays the custom activity as a standard Sequence activity and does not allow property values to be set from within the designer.

The implementation shown here is bare bones.

Creating the ActivityDesignerTheme Class

Make sure you have `ItemPermissionActivity.cs` open in code view and add the code in Listing 9.10 at the end of the namespace.

LISTING 9.10 The `ItemPermissionDesignerTheme` Class

```
#region ItemPermissionDesignerTheme
public class ItemPermissionDesignerTheme : ActivityDesignerTheme
{
    public ItemPermissionDesignerTheme(WorkflowTheme theme)
      :base(theme)
    {
        BackColorStart = Color.White;
        BackColorEnd = Color.LightSlateGray;
        BackgroundStyle =
            System.Drawing.Drawing2D.LinearGradientMode.Horizontal;
        ForeColor = Color.Black;
    }
}
#endregion
```

After the theme has been created, we can add the `ActivityDesigner` class implementation. The theme that was created in the last step is linked to the designer through the `ActivityDesignerTheme` attribute. The designer code overrides methods that handle the size of the activity in the Workflow Designer. Listing 9.11 shows the code.

LISTING 9.11 The `ItemPermissionActivityDesigner` Class

```
#region ItemPermissionActivityDesigner
[ActivityDesignerTheme(typeof(ItemPermissionDesignerTheme))]
public class ItemPermissionActivityDesigner : ActivityDesigner
{
    protected override Size OnLayoutSize(ActivityDesignerLayoutEventArgs e)
    {
        base.OnLayoutSize(e);
        return new Size(200, 45);
    }

    protected override Rectangle ImageRectangle
    {
        Rectangle rectActivity = this.Bounds;
        Size size = new Size(20,20);
        Rectangle rectImage = new Rectangle();
        rectImage.X = rectActivity.Left + 5;
        rectImage.Y = rectActivity.Top +
            ((rectActivity.Height - size.Height) / 2);
        rectImage.Width = size.Width;
        rectImage.Height = size.Height;
        return rectImage;
    }

    protected override Rectangle TextRectangle
    {
        Rectangle rectActivity = this.Bounds;
        Size size = new Size(170,40);
```

```
    Rectangle rectText = new Rectangle();

    rectText.X = this.ImageRectangle.Right + 5;

    rectText.Y = rectActivity.Top + 2;

    rectText.Width = size.Width;

    rectText.Size = size;

    return rectText;

    }

}
#endregion
```

The last step to make the `ItemPermissionsActivity` perform as expected in the Workflow Designer is to add the Designer attribute to the activity class, as shown in Listing 9.12. When this attribute is in place, the activity will be displayed correctly in the Workflow Designer. We'll see this when we add security to the custom workflow at the end of this chapter.

LISTING 9.12   Adding the Designer Attribute to the Activity Class

```
[Designer(typeof(ItemPermissionActivityDesigner))]

Public partial class ItemPermissionsActivity: SequenceActivity

...
```

Build the solution, close Visual Studio 2008, and then re-open Visual Studio 2008 and the workflow solution. This is required for the activity design changes to show up in the Workflow Designer.

DEPLOYMENT AND TESTING

Normally, we would jump into testing and deployment of the code. However, since a workflow is the normal testing environment for an activity, we'll test using the workflow we develop in the next section.

CREATING THE CUSTOM WORKFLOW

Now that the permissions activity has been created, it's time to build the workflow. As mentioned in the opening section of this chapter, we'll be implementing the first half of the business process. We'll add the workflow project to the existing solution and continue with the same project in the next chapter.

GOALS

The goals for the workflow for this chapter include the following:

■ Get the workflow up and running with task forms.

We will be adding a SharePoint Sequential Workflow project to the existing solution.

The task forms will be created in Microsoft InfoPath. We'll discuss the design high points and will show how to integrate the forms into our workflow.

■ Automate the security via our custom activity.

The List ItemPermissions Activity will be integrated into the workflow to keep the appraisal document's security permissions correct.

We will be deploying with Visual Studio in this chapter since debugging the project is faster and more convenient than trying to debug a production deployment. Deploying to a production server will be covered in Chapter 10.

CREATING THE WORKFLOW PROJECT

If Visual Studio 2008 or the solution isn't currently open, go ahead and open Visual Studio 2008 and open the `PerformanceAppraisalWF` solution.

1. On the file menu, point to New and click Project. Select the Workflow Project type and then SharePoint 2007 Sequential Workflow under Templates.

2. Name the project **PerformanceAppraisalWF**, as shown in Figure 9.4.

3. Click OK.

4. Keep the name of the workflow as `PerformanceAppraisalWF` and enter **http://moss.litwareinc.com/hr** as the local site.

5. Click Next.

6. Choose Appraisals_Kevin Martin as the list to run against. Keep the default task list and the history list entries.

Environment Settings

The steps require the specified environment listed in the Prerequisites section. If your environment is not set up the same, you'll need to choose the appropriate settings for your environment.

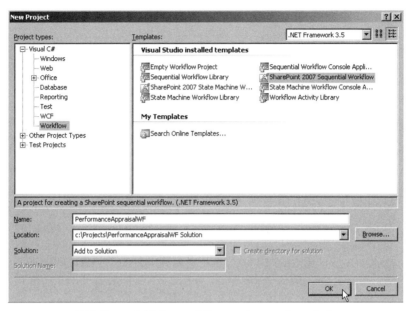

FIGURE 9.4 Add the workflow project to the solution.

7. Click Next.

8. Uncheck When an item is created. The manager will start the workflow after the draft goals are complete.

9. Click Finish.

Workflow Configuration

After the project has been created, we need to configure the workflow using the following steps:

1. Right-click `Workflow1.cs` in the Solution Explorer and then choose Rename.

2. Enter **AppraisalWorkflow.cs** for the new file name.

   Since we changed the name of the class, we need to update the `CodeBesideClass` property in `Workflow.xml` from `Workflow1` to `AppraisalWorkflow`, as shown in Listing 9.13.

3. Open `Workflow.xml` and change the value of the `CodeBesideClass` property to PerformanceAppraisalWF.AppraisalWorkflow.

LISTING 9.13	Updating the Workflow Properties Code Beside Class

```
<Workflow
    Name="PerformanceAppraisalWF"
    Description="My SharePoint Workflow"
    Id="69bb9b0a-bfc9-4143-96b6-a3972057910d"
    CodeBesideClass="PerformanceAppraisalWF.AppraisalWorkflow"
    ...
```

Workflow Activation

When a sequential workflow project is created, an `onWorkflowActivation` activity is created. This is the entry point for the workflow. Visual Studio doesn't configure the activity to the values we need so we'll need to update the activity by opening `AppraisalWorkflow.cs` in designer mode, selecting the `onWorkflowActivation` activity, and then setting properties (see Figure 9.5) as follows:

1. Expand the `CorrelationToken` property and change the OwnerActivityName to AppraisalWorkflow.

2. Update the binding name property.

3. Open `AppraisalWorkflow.designer.cs`, expand the Designer generated code region, and update `activitybind2.Name = Workflow1;` to `activitybind2.Name = AppraisalWorkflow;`.

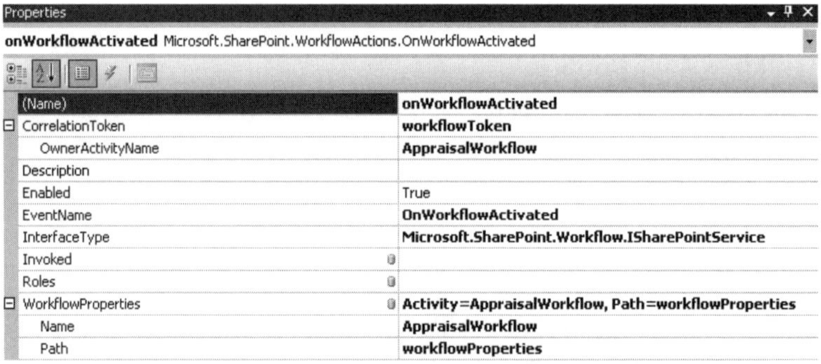

FIGURE 9.5 Set the workflow activated properties.

Now that setup is complete, we can create the code that will handle the appraisal process. Open `AppraisalWorkflow.cs` (right-click and choose View Code) from the Solution Explorer.

Let's add some code regions to help organize things a bit. The regions that need to be created are the following:

- Member Variables
- Properties
- Constructor

Add the code to the `AppraisalWorkflow` class, as shown in Listing 9.14.

LISTING 9.14 Code Regions

```
namespace PerformanceAppraisalWF
{
    public sealed partial class AppraisalWorkflow :
       SequentialWorkflowActivity
    {
        #region Member Variables
        #endregion

        #region Properties
        #endregion

        #region Constructor
        #endregion
    ...
```

Move the `workflowId` and `workflowProperties` lines into the Properties region and the constructor to the Constructor region, as shown in Listing 9.15.

LISTING 9.15 Initial Properties and Constructor

```
#region Properties
public Guid workflowId;
public SPWorkflowActivationProperties workflowProperties =
   new SPWorkflowActivationProperties();
#endregion
```

```
#region Constructor

Public AppraisalWorkflow()

{

   InitializeComponent();

}

#endregion
```

We need to add some member variables and properties to the code to represent the participants in the appraisal process. The participants will need to be assigned tasks and displayed in task forms, and we'll need their login names for task assignment and their full names for display.

The participants in the process include the employee, the manager (appraiser), and peer reviewers. We'll limit our focus to just the employee and manager right now and address the peer reviewers in the next chapter.

We're going to need a few more variables to store information about the review process and the workflow. For the review process, we're going to store the review period start and end dates to be used in task forms. We're also going to track the workflow duration and use that information when logging workflow history. The code for the member variables needs to be placed inside the Member Variables region and is shown in Listing 9.16.

LISTING 9.16   Member Variables Needed at Activation

```
// Employee Information

public string employeeFullName;

public string employeeLoginName;


// Manager/Appraiser Information

public string managerFullName;

public string managerLoginName;


// Appraisal Period Dates

public DateTime appraisalPeriodStart;

public DateTime appraisalPeriodEnd;
```

With the infrastructure out of the way, it's time to implement the code for the first activity of the workflow. Switch the active document in the editor to the Workflow Designer. If it isn't already open, open the file from the Solution Explorer. From the designer, click the onWorkflowActivated activity and enter **OnWorkflowActivated_Invoke** for the Invoked property value, as shown in Figure 9.6.

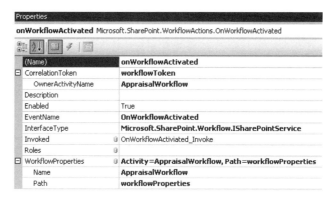

FIGURE 9.6 Set the workflow Invoked method.

Press Enter, and Visual Studio will take you to the code.

Viewing the code in Listing 9.17, you see that we can create a new workflow ID and save the workflow start time. Every workflow instance needs its own ID, and you'll want to create an activity in the activation code of every workflow you create.

The other functionality we need at start-up time is to retrieve the employee and appraiser information. Since the properties are part of the content type, we can retrieve them from the list item that represents the appraisal document. The item is part of the workflow properties so it's easy to retrieve.

First, we convert the information from the properties to SPUser objects and then retrieve the login and full names. I added the GetWebUserFromItemBasedOnPropertyName function to retrieve the information for each with the name of the property being the only different parameter.

GetWebUserFromItemBasedOnPropertyName walks through the list of users in the Web until a match is found. We search for a match using the user ID instead of the name because there might be more than one user with the same name. SharePoint user properties are stored in "id;#display name" format, so we just parse the ID from the string.

LISTING 9.17 OnWorkflowActivated_Invoke Method

```
#region Workflow Activation
private void OnWorkflowActivated_Invoke(object sender,
ExternalDataEventArgs e)
{
   // Create the workflow id
   workflowId = Guid.NewGuid();

   // Get the employee and manager from the appraisal document
   try
   {
      // Get the employee
      SPUser employee = GetWebUserFromItemBasedOnPropertyName(
                        workflowProperties.Web,
                        workflowProperties.Item, "EmployeeName");
      if(employee != null)
      {
         employeeFullName = employee.Name;
         employeeLoginName = employee.LoginName;
      }
      // Get the manager
      SPUser manager = GetWebUserFromItemBasedOnPropertyName(
                     workflowProperties.Web, workflowProperties.Item,
                     "AppraiserName");
      if(manager != null)
      {
         managerFullName = manager.Name;
         managerLoginName = manager.LoginName;
      }
      // Get the appraisal period dates
      appraisalPeriodStart = DateTime.Parse(
         workflowProperties.Item["AppraisalPeriodStart"].ToString());
      appraisalPeriodEnd = DateTime.Parse(
         workflowProperties.Item["AppraisalPeriodEnd"].ToString());
```

```
      }
      catch (IndexOutOfRangeException)
      {
         // This will be thrown when the property doesn't exist
         // in the list item. This could happen if the
         // employee or appraiser property in the content type
         // was modified. If values are simply missing no exception
         // will be thrown.
      }

      // Make sure the employee and manager are part
      // of the document. Otherwise the workflow will have to end
      if (employeeFullName.Length == 0 ||
          managerFullName.Length == 0)
      {
         throw new Exception("Bad employee or manager name in document");
      }

   }
   private SPUser GetWebUserFromItemBasedOnPropertyName(
      SPWeb web,
      SPListItem item,
      string propertyName)
   {
      // Assume the user doesn't exist
      SPUser retValue = null;

      // Get the property value from the item
      string propertyValue = item[propertyName] as string;

      // Make sure we have something to work with
      if (propertyValue != null && propertyValue.Length > 0)
      {
         int userId;
```

```
// See if we can get the id for the user from
// the input string. The string is expected to be
// in "id;#display name" format
if (int.TryParse(propertyValue.Substring(
        0, propertyValue.IndexOf(";")), out userId))
{
    // Walk through the users in web.Users
    // to find a match
    foreach (SPUser user in web.Users)
    {
        if (user.ID == userId)
        {
            retValue = user;
            break;
        }
    }
}


    return retValue;
}


#endregion
```

Now that we have the employee and manager information, we can finish the workflow. The strategy is to create the workflow infrastructure by adding task-related activities, then add task forms, and finally add in the custom permissions activity that we created earlier.

At the end of this chapter, we will be ready for the appraisal portion of the review cycle. To get there, we will need to add tasks to the workflow for both the employee and the manager. To start the appraisal process, the manager drafts goals and then discusses the goals with the employee to reach agreement. Once agreement is reached, the execution period begins. At the end of the review period, the manager will kick off the review portion of the appraisal process.

From the above description, we can see that we'll need to create a task for the employee to review the goals and indicate when the goals have been finalized. Once the goals are finalized, we'll need to wait for the execution period to pass. Under normal circumstances, the evaluation period would be based on a date. We are going to create a manual trigger for the manager to start that period. This will require us to create an additional task and assign that task to the manager.

Adding Workflow Task Activities

SharePoint tasks are created through activities. Most of the properties are set from the designer, but we'll need to add code to set the rest of them.

First, we create a task, wait for the person assigned to the task to indicate the task has been accomplished, and then mark the task complete.

We'll go through each of the steps for the Accept Goals task.

Creating Variables and Properties for the Workflow Tasks

To make our property settings easier when adding activities in the Workflow Designer, we'll add all of the properties that we'll need. By adding the properties to the code now, we'll just have to choose the property values in the Workflow Designer rather than having to create new variables in the designer.

The lines in Listing 9.18 are placed inside the Member Variables region.

LISTING 9.18   The Task Variables

```
public bool goalsAccepted = false;
public bool startEvaluation = false;
```

Next, we'll add the task properties, as shown in Listing 9.19. The code is placed inside the Properties region.

LISTING 9.19   The Task Properties

```
public Guid acceptGoalsTaskId;
public Guid startEvaluationTaskId;
public SPWorkflowTaskProperties acceptGoalsTaskProps =
    new SPWorkflowTaskProperties();
public SPWorkflowTaskProperties acceptGoalsTaskChanged_AfterProps =
```

```
      new SPWorkflowTaskProperties();
   public SPWorkflowTaskProperties acceptGoalsTaskChanged_BeforeProps =
      new SPWorkflowTaskProperties();
   public SPWorkflowTaskProperties startEvaluationTaskProps =
      new SPWorkflowTaskProperties();
   public SPWorkflowTaskProperties startEvaluationTaskChanged_AfterProps =
      new SPWorkflowTaskProperties();
   public SPWorkflowTaskProperties startEvaluationTaskChanged_BeforeProps =
      new SPWorkflowTaskProperties();
```

Although we'll cover the start evaluation task later in the chapter, we've added the properties for both tasks covered in this chapter.

Creating the Accept Goals Task

With our properties in place, we can design the Accept Goals task. Switch back (you will need to open the file if it was previously closed) to the workflow design and drag activities from the toolbox to the workflow so it looks like Figure 9.7. Don't worry about names and properties at the moment. We'll set each of them in the next sections. The activities to add, and the section of the toolbox in which the activity is located, are the following:

1. CreateTask Activity—SharePoint Workflow
2. While Activity—Windows Workflow v3.0
3. Sequence Activity—Windows Workflow v3.0
4. OnTaskChanged Activity—SharePoint Workflow
5. CompleteTask Activity—SharePoint Workflow

Click createTask1 to update the activity's properties using the following steps:

■ Name. Type **createAcceptGoalsTaskActivity** for the name of the activity.

■ CorrelationToken. Type **acceptGoalsTaskCorrelationToken** for the value of the Correlation Token. Next, you'll need to expand the Correlation Token, click in the OwnerActivityName property value, and choose AppraisalWorkflow from the drop-down.

■ `TaskId`. Click the ... button. When the Bind 'TaskId' to an activity's property dialog is displayed, choose acceptGoalsTaskId from the tree view, as shown in Figure 9.8.

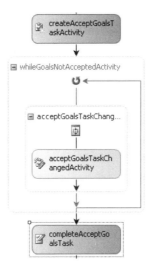

FIGURE 9.7 The acceptGoalsTaskActivity design.

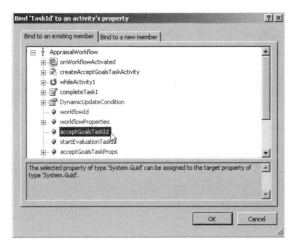

FIGURE 9.8 Set the `TaskId` property.

■ `TaskProperties`. Click the ... button. When the Bind 'TaskProperties' to an activity's property dialog is displayed, choose acceptGoalsTaskProps from the tree view (similar to the TaskId).

The property values for the activity should look like Figure 9.9.

Properties	▾ ╨ ×
createAcceptGoalsTaskActivity Microsoft.SharePoint.WorkflowActions.CreateTask	
(Name)	**createAcceptGoalsTaskActivity**
⊟ CorrelationToken	**acceptGoalsTaskCorrelationToken**
OwnerActivityName	**AppraisalWorkflow**
Description	
Enabled	True
InterfaceType	**Microsoft.SharePoint.Workflow.ITaskService**
ListItemId	-1
MethodInvoking	
MethodName	**CreateTask**
SpecialPermissions	
⊟ TaskId	**Activity=AppraisalWorkflow, Path=acceptGoalsTaskId**
Name	**AppraisalWorkflow**
Path	**acceptGoalsTaskId**
⊟ TaskProperties	**Activity=AppraisalWorkflow, Path=acceptGoalsTaskProps**
Name	**AppraisalWorkflow**
Path	**acceptGoalsTaskProps**

FIGURE 9.9 Set the `createAcceptGoalsTaskActivity` properties.

The last property that needs to be set is the `MethodInvoking`. `MethodInvoking` represents the method in the workflow code that will be called when the activity is executed. Enter `OnCreateAcceptGoalsTask` as the value for the `MethodInvoking` property. After entering the `MethodInvoking` value and pressing Enter, Visual Studio drops you into the code editor ready to add the source code. Listing 9.20 contains the code.

The first line creates an ID for the task. Similar to the workflow ID, each task needs a unique ID. After that we'll assign the task to the employee and set the title and description of the task.

The extended properties are set to communicate with the task form that we'll create in the next section.

You can see in the code that the extended properties communicate to the task form who the employee is, who the appraiser is, where the appraisal document can be found, and the review period (in string format, starting date–ending date)

LISTING 9.20 `OnCreateAcceptGoalsTask` Method

```
private void OnCreateAcceptGoalsTask(object sender, EventArgs e)
{
    // Create a new Id for the task
    acceptGoalsTaskId = Guid.NewGuid();
```

```
// Assign the task to the employee
acceptGoalsTaskProps.AssignedTo = employeeLoginName;


// Set the title and description with hard-coded strings. In a true
// production environment these strings would either be configurable
// or would at least be in resources
acceptGoalsTaskProps.Description =
   "Complete this task once the appraisal goals have been accepted.";
acceptGoalsTaskProps.Title = "Finalize Appraisal Goals";
acceptGoalsTaskProps.TaskType = 0;


// Set the information for the task form through
// the extended properties
acceptGoalsTaskProps.ExtendedProperties["tasktitle"] =
   "Accept Goals";
acceptGoalsTaskProps.ExtendedProperties["employee"] =
   employeeFullName;
acceptGoalsTaskProps.ExtendedProperties["appraiser"] =
   managerFullName;
acceptGoalsTaskProps.ExtendedProperties["reviewperiod"] =
   appraisalPeriodStart.ToShortDateString() + " - " +
   appraisalPeriodEnd.ToShortDateString();
acceptGoalsTaskProps.ExtendedProperties["itemtitle"] =
   "Appraisal Document";
acceptGoalsTaskProps.ExtendedProperties["itemlink"] =
   workflowProperties.WebUrl + "/" +
   workflowProperties.Item.File.Url;
acceptGoalsTaskProps.ExtendedProperties["iteminst"] =
   "Click on the link above to review the goals.";


acceptGoalsTaskProps.ExtendedProperties["inst1"] =
   "Please review the goals proposed by your manager.";
acceptGoalsTaskProps.ExtendedProperties["inst2"] =
   "Resolve all issues with your manager.";
```

```
acceptGoalsTaskProps.ExtendedProperties["inst3"] = "";

acceptGoalsTaskProps.ExtendedProperties["inst4"] =
    "Once the goals have been agreed upon, check the box below" +
    " and click \"Submit\" .";

acceptGoalsTaskProps.ExtendedProperties["completestatement"] =
    "I have reviewed and accept the goals for this review period";
}
```

Waiting for the Employee to Accept Goals

At this point, the workflow has created the task for the employee, and now we need to wait for the employee to accept the goals. If you look at the task form in Figure 9.10, you'll see a check box at the bottom that allows the employee to indicate the goals have been accepted. A SharePoint task can be modified in a number of ways. As a result, we can't just wait for the task to be changed, but need to see if the employee has actually accepted the goals each time the task has changed. If not, we need to wait until the task is changed again and do another check.

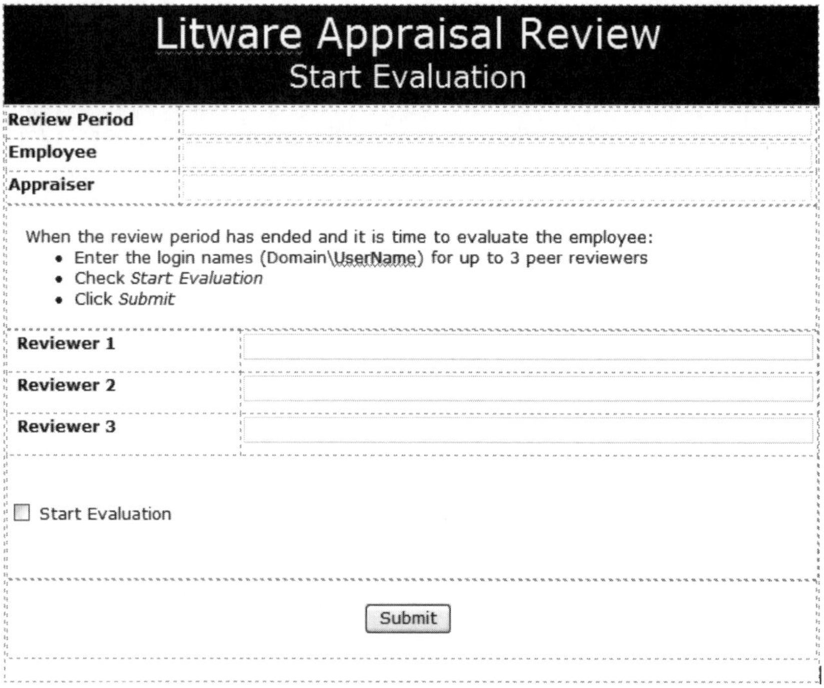

FIGURE 9.10 A blank Accept Goals task form.

The `While` Activity waits for the employee to accept the goals. Switch back to the Workflow Designer, click on the `While` Activity and set the properties as follows (see Figure 9.11 for help):

■   `Name`. Type **whileGoalsNotAcceptedActivity** for the value.

■   `Condition`. Choose Code Condition.

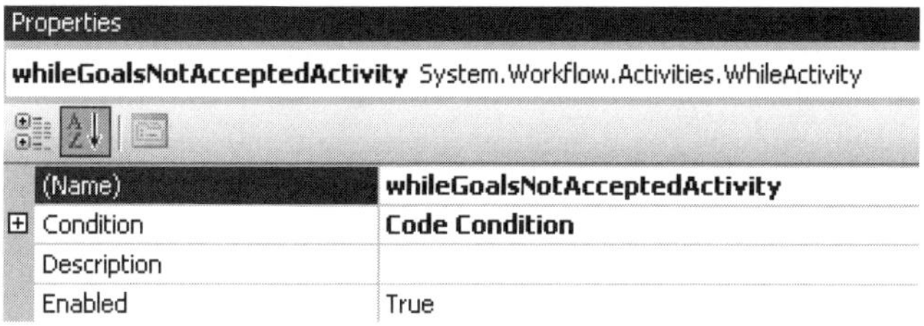

Properties	
whileGoalsNotAcceptedActivity System.Workflow.Activities.WhileActivity	
(Name)	**whileGoalsNotAcceptedActivity**
⊞ Condition	**Code Condition**
Description	
Enabled	True

FIGURE 9.11 Set `whileGoalsNotAcceptedActivity` properties.

Expand the `Condition` property and enter `GoalsNotAccepted` for the Condition subproperty value. When you press Enter, you'll be dropped into the code editor. The code for `GoalsNotAccepted` is in Listing 9.21.

LISTING 9.21   `GoalsNotAccepted` Method

```
private void GoalsNotAccepted(object sender, ConditionalEventArgs e)
{
    e.Result = !goalsAccepted;
}
```

Switch back to the Workflow Designer, click on the `Sequence` Activity, and enter `acceptGoalsTaskChangedSequenceActivity` as the activity name.

Handling the Accept Goals Task Change

To determine when the employee has accepted the appraisal goals, we need to check the results of the task form. We'll use the `OnTaskChanged` Activity. When the workflow encounters an `OnTaskChanged` Activity, the workflow is dehydrated, or has its state serialized to disk. When the task is modified, the workflow is rehydrated, or deserialized from disk, and the activity is run.

The biggest implication of the serialization/deserialization process is that the workflow class, and all of its members, must be serializable. If not, the workflow will simply stop and will be marked as completed, even though the workflow was not actually run to completion. All of our members are either base types or types that implement the `ISerializable` interface, and therefore that is not a concern for us with this workflow.

Click on the `onTaskChanged1` activity to update the activity's properties.

■ `Name`. Type **acceptGoalsTaskChangedActivity** for the name of the activity,

■ `AfterProperties`. Click the ... button. When the Bind 'AfterProperties' to an activity's property dialog is displayed, choose acceptGoalsTaskChanged_ AfterProps from the tree view.

■ `BeforeProperties`. Click the ... button. When the Bind 'BeforeProperties' to an activity's property dialog is displayed, choose acceptGoalsTaskChanged_ BeforeProps from the tree view.

■ `CorrelationToken`. Choose acceptGoalsTaskCorrelationToken from the drop-down.

■ `TaskId`. Click the ... button. When the Bind 'TaskId' to an activity's property dialog is displayed, choose acceptGoalsTaskId from the tree view.

The property values for the activity should look like Figure 9.12.

Properties	▼ ↴ ×
acceptGoalsTaskChangedActivity Microsoft.SharePoint.WorkflowActions.OnTaskChanged	

(Name)	acceptGoalsTaskChangedActivity
⊟ AfterProperties ⓘ	**Activity=AppraisalWorkflow, Path=acceptGoalsTaskChanged_AfterProps**
Name	**AppraisalWorkflow**
Path	**acceptGoalsTaskChanged_AfterProps**
⊟ BeforeProperties ⓘ	**Activity=AppraisalWorkflow, Path=acceptGoalsTaskChanged_BeforeProps**
Name	**AppraisalWorkflow**
Path	**acceptGoalsTaskChanged_BeforeProps**
⊟ CorrelationToken	**acceptGoalsTaskCorrelationToken**
OwnerActivityNa	**AppraisalWorkflow**
Description	
Enabled	True
EventName	**OnTaskChanged**
Executor ⓘ	
InterfaceType	**Microsoft.SharePoint.Workflow.ITaskService**
Invoked ⓘ	
Roles ⓘ	
⊟ TaskId ⓘ	**Activity=AppraisalWorkflow, Path=acceptGoalsTaskId**
Name	**AppraisalWorkflow**
Path	**acceptGoalsTaskId**

FIGURE 9.12 Set the `acceptGoalsTaskChangedActivity` properties.

The last property that needs to be set is the Invoked property. Invoked represents the method in the workflow code that will be called when the activity is executed. Enter OnAcceptGoalsTaskChanged as the value for the Invoked property. After entering the Invoked value and pressing Enter, Visual Studio drops you into the code editor ready to add your source code.

All that's left to do in the task changed activity is to set the goalsAccepted variable that the While Activity loop is checking. Listing 9.22 shows the code that we need to write to do just that.

SharePoint communication with task forms includes the task form being returned in the task after properties. The task form's data source has a Boolean field "TaskCompleted" that we need to extract from the after properties.

LISTING 9.22   Checking the Task Form Results

```
private void OnAcceptGoalsTaskChanged(object sender,
                ExternalDataEventArgs e)
{
// Check the task properties to see if the goals have been accepted
    string s = acceptGoalsTaskChanged_AfterProps.ExtendedProperties
["TaskCompleted"].ToString();

    bool result = false;

    if (bool.TryParse(s, out result))
    {
       goalsAccepted = result;
    }
    else
    {
       goalsAccepted = false;
    }
}
```

Once we have the value from the task form, we set goalsAccepted to that value. If goalsAccepted is false, the While Activity will wait until the task is changed and will run the check again. If goalsAccepted is true, the While Activity will drop out and move on to the next step in the workflow.

Completing the Accept Goals Task

When the employee has indicated in the task form that the goals have been accepted, we need to complete the task. SharePoint provides a `CompleteTask` Activity that we'll use to finish the goals accepted task.

Switch back to the Workflow Designer and click `completeTask1`. The properties will be set similarly to the other activities we've worked on. Use Figure 9.13 as a guide when setting the property values indicated below:

- `Name`. Enter **completeAcceptGoalsTask** for the name of the activity.

- `CorrelationToken`. Choose acceptGoalsTaskCorrelationToken from the drop-down.

- `TaskId`. Click the ... button. When the Bind 'TaskId' to an activity's property dialog is displayed, choose acceptGoalsTaskId from the tree view.

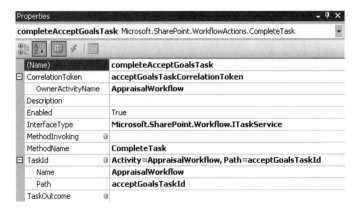

FIGURE 9.13 Set the `completeAcceptGoalsTask` property values.

Now we're done with the Accept Goals task. Since it's fresh in our minds, we'll create the Start Evaluation before discussing the task form design and integration.

Creating the Start Evaluation Task

For brevity's sake, we'll just cover the high points of the Start Evaluation Task. The task follows the same pattern as the Accept Goals task, except the manager is the actor instead of the employee.

We'll create the task, wait for the manager to set a status within the form, and then we will complete the task.

Switch back to the design mode and drag activities to the workflow just below the `completeAcceptGoalsTaskActivity` so it looks like Figure 9.14. Don't worry about names and properties at the moment. We'll set each of them in the next sections. The activities to add in order are:

1. `CreateTask` Activity
2. `While` Activity
3. `Sequence` Activity
4. `OnTaskChanged` Activity
5. `CompleteTask` Activity

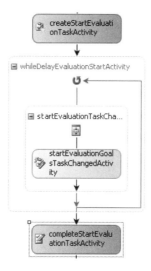

FIGURE 9.14 The Start Evaluation Task Activity design.

Setting Start Evaluation Create Task Properties

The properties for the Start Evaluation task are similar to the Accepted Goals task. Click `createTask1` and set properties as defined below (see Figure 9.15 for help).

■ `Name`. Type **createStartEvaluationTaskActivity** for the name of the activity.

■ `CorrelationToken`. Type **startEvaluationTaskCorrelationToken** for the value of the Correlation Token. Next, you'll need to expand the Correlation Token, click in the OwnerActivityName property value, and choose Appraisal Workflow from the drop-down.

- `TaskId`. Click the ... button. When the Bind 'TaskId' to an activity's property dialog is displayed, choose startEvaluationTaskId from the tree view.

- `TaskProperties`. Click the ... button. When the Bind 'TaskProperties' to an activity's property dialog is displayed, choose startEvaluationTaskProps from the tree view (similar to the TaskId).

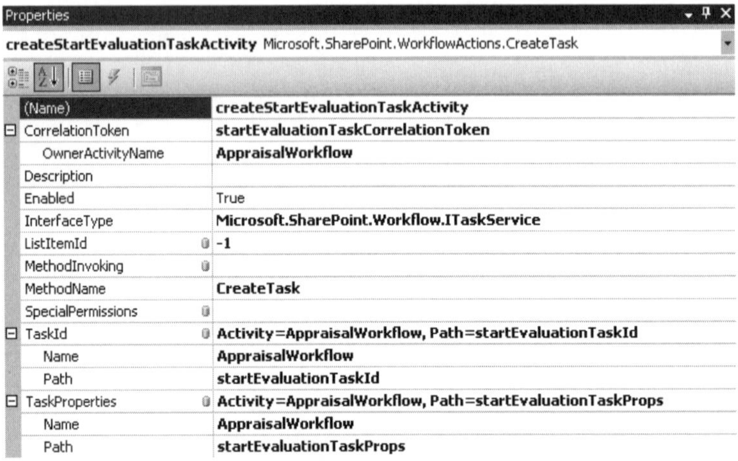

FIGURE 9.15 `createStartEvaluationTaskActivity` properties.

Enter **OnCreateStartEvaluationTask** as the value for the `MethodInvoking` property. After entering the `MethodInvoking` value and pressing Enter, Visual Studio drops you into the code editor ready to add your source code. We need to add code for task creation that is similar to the code for the `AcceptGoals` task.

The code for the task creation is shown in Listing 9.23.

LISTING 9.23   Creating the `StartEvaluation` Task

```
private void OnCreateStartEvaluationTask(object sender, EventArgs e)
{
    // Create a new Id for the task
    startEvaluationTaskId = Guid.NewGuid();

    // Assign the task to the manager
    startEvaluationTaskProps.AssignedTo = managerLoginName;
```

```
// Set the title and description with hard-coded strings. In a true
// production environment these strings would either be configurable
// or would at least be in resources
startEvaluationTaskProps.Title = "Start Evaluation";
startEvaluationTaskProps.Description =
   "Complete this task on the evaluation period start date";
startEvaluationTaskProps.TaskType = 1;


// Set the information for the task form through
// the extended properties
startEvaluationTaskProps.ExtendedProperties["employee"] =
   employeeFullName;
startEvaluationTaskProps.ExtendedProperties["appraiser"] =
   managerFullName;
startEvaluationTaskProps.ExtendedProperties["reviewperiod"] =
   appraisalPeriodStart.ToShortDateString() + " - " +
   appraisalPeriodEnd.ToShortDateString();
}
```

Looking at the code in Listing 9.23, you'll see three differences (beyond the title and description text):

1. The task is assigned to the manager instead of the employee.
2. Task Type is assigned 1.
3. The document link extended property is not used.

The first difference is obvious, and the third is inconsequential.

The task type is now set to 1 instead of 0. This will make more sense later when we discuss the integration of the task forms. For now, suffice it to say the `TaskType` is an integer property that indicates which form the task is associated with. We'll have three forms total, two in this chapter. The first in this chapter was the `CompleteTask` form (for the Accepted Goals task). The second is for the current task. The indexes are 0-based so the first form's task type is 0, and this form has a task type of 1. The default value is 0, so if you don't assign a value, you'll get the 0 form.

Waiting for the Manager to Start the Evaluation Period

Similar to the previous task, we need to wait for the manager to kick off the evaluation period. Waiting for the manager to start the evaluation period follows a familiar pattern. We have a while loop that waits for the manager to indicate the task is complete, and we have some code that checks whenever the task is updated to see if the manager has finished.

The `While` Activity waits for the manager to start the evaluation. Switch back to the Workflow Designer, click on the `While` Activity, and set the properties as follows (see Figure 9.16 for help):

- Name. Type **whileDelayEvaluationStartActivity** for the value.
- `Condition`. Choose Code Condition.

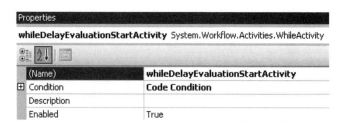

FIGURE 9.16 Set `whileDelayEvaluationStartActivity` properties.

Expand the `Condition` property and enter `DelayEvaluationStart` for the Condition subproperty value. When you press Enter, you'll be dropped into the code editor. The code for `DelayEvaluation` is in Listing 9.24.

LISTING 9.24 `DelayEvaluationStart` Method

```
private void DelayEvaluationStart(object sender, ConditionalEventArgs e)
{
    e.Result = !startEvaluation
}
```

Switch back to the Workflow Designer, click on the `Sequence` activity, and enter `startEvaluationTaskChangedSequenceActivity` as the activity name.

Handling the Start Evaluation Task Change

To determine when the manager has decided to start the evaluation process, we need to check the results of the task form. We'll use the `OnTaskChanged` Activity that was created earlier.

Click on the `onTaskChanged1` activity to update the activity's properties.

- `Name`. Type **startEvaluationGoalsTaskChangedActivity** for the name of the activity.

- `AfterProperties`. Click the ... button. When the Bind 'AfterProperties' to an activity's property dialog is displayed, choose startEvaluationTaskChanged_AfterProps from the tree view.

- `BeforeProperties`. Click the ... button. When the Bind 'BeforeProperties' to an activity's property dialog is displayed, choose startEvaluationTaskChanged_BeforeProps from the tree view.

- `CorrelationToken`. Choose startEvaluationTaskCorrelationToken from the drop-down.

- `TaskId`. Click the ... button. When the Bind 'TaskId' to an activity's property dialog is displayed, choose startEvaluationTaskId from the tree view.

The property values for the activity should look like Figure 9.17.

Properties	▾ ♯ ×
startEvaluationGoalsTaskChangedActivity Microsoft.SharePoint.WorkflowActions.OnTaskChanged	
(Name)	**startEvaluationGoalsTaskChangedActivity**
⊟ AfterProperties	**Activity=AppraisalWorkflow, Path=startEvaluationTaskChanged_AfterProps**
Name	**AppraisalWorkflow**
Path	**startEvaluationTaskChanged_AfterProps**
⊟ BeforeProperties	**Activity=AppraisalWorkflow, Path=startEvaluationTaskChanged_BeforeProps**
Name	**AppraisalWorkflow**
Path	**startEvaluationTaskChanged_BeforeProps**
⊟ CorrelationToken	**startEvaluationTaskCorrelationToken**
OwnerActivityName	**AppraisalWorkflow**
Description	
Enabled	True
EventName	**OnTaskChanged**
Executor	
InterfaceType	**Microsoft.SharePoint.Workflow.ITaskService**
Invoked	
Roles	
⊟ TaskId	**Activity=AppraisalWorkflow, Path=startEvaluationTaskId**
Name	**AppraisalWorkflow**
Path	**startEvaluationTaskId**

FIGURE 9.17 Set the `startEvaluationTaskChangedActivity` properties.

The last property that needs to be set is the Invoked property. Invoked represents the method in the workflow code that will be called when the activity is executed. Enter **OnStartEvaluationTaskChanged** as the value for the Invoked property. After entering the Invoked value, Visual Studio drops you into the code editor. Listing 9.25 contains the code.

LISTING 9.25   Checking the Task Form Results

```
private void OnStartEvaluationTaskChanged_Invoke(object sender,
            ExternalDataEventArgs e)
{
    // Check the task properties to see if it is time
    // to start the evaluation period
    string s = startEvaluationTaskChanged_AfterProps.ExtendedProperties[
        "TaskCompleted"].ToString();

    bool result = false;

    if (bool.TryParse(s, out result))
    {
        startEvaluation = result;
    }
    else
    {
        startEvaluation = false;
    }
}
```

Completing the Start Evaluation Task

When the manager has indicated in the task form that the evaluation period has begun, we need to complete the task.

Switch back to the Workflow Designer and click completeTask1 to set the following properties (see Figure 9.18 for help):

- `Name.` Enter **completeStartEvaluationTaskActivity** for the name of the activity.

- `CorrelationToken.` Choose startEvaluationTaskCorrelationToken from the drop-down menu.

- `TaskId.` Click the ... button. When the Bind 'TaskId' to an activity's property dialog is displayed, choose startEvaluationTaskId from the tree view.

FIGURE 9.18 `completeStartEvaluationTaskActivity` properties.

Now we're done with the workflow. Everything should work except that we haven't integrated the task forms into the solution. Once that's done, we'll be able to put the workflow through its paces.

The next section describes integrating task forms into our workflow solution.

TASK FORM INTEGRATION

The solution contains three task forms: Start Evaluation, Employee Self-Evaluation, and Complete Task. The Start Evaluation form is used to indicate when the evaluation period has started. The Employee Self-Evaluation form is for the employee to indicate when he has completed the self-evaluation portion.

The Complete Task form is a more generic form that is used in various situations:

- Goal acceptance from the employee
- Getting feedback from the reviewers
- Getting feedback from the employee
- Finalizing the review form by the manager

Since we are running inside of Microsoft Office SharePoint Server (MOSS), we'll be using Microsoft InfoPath 2007 to create the task forms. InfoPath is part of the Microsoft Office platform and can be used as a stand-alone form editor, as well as integrated with SharePoint. When integrated with SharePoint, InfoPath can be used as a client application that allows you to edit files similarly to how Microsoft Word documents can be edited within SharePoint. SharePoint also has a forms service that is included with MOSS and is available as an add-on for WSS (Windows SharePoint Services). The forms service allows the InfoPath forms to be run on the server and shows up in the user's browser instead of requiring the InfoPath client to be installed on each client machine. Forms service, or browser-compatible, InfoPath forms can be used as task forms inside workflows, which is the feature we'll be utilizing in our solution.

Task Form Design

While this book is not a book on InfoPath form design, there are some basic concepts that need to be known for our forms. All of our forms are very simple forms with just a few fields that are part of the main document. Since our forms are task forms, we won't be saving any information to the file system and instead will pass the information between the workflow code and the task form. Communications is covered in the next section.

As shown in Figure 9.19, each form (with some minor variations) consists of a title, a link, a check box used to indicate task completeness, and a submit button. The Start Evaluation form adds in text boxes to indicate who will be assigned as reviewers.

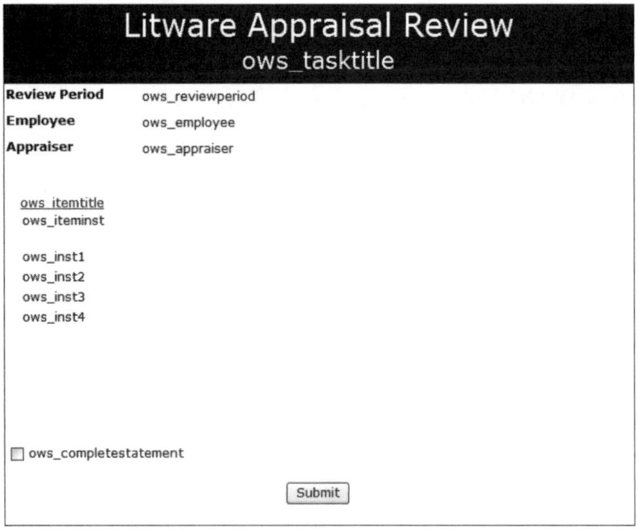

FIGURE 9.19 Complete Task form design.

Now that we have a basic understanding of where we're going, let's get started creating the first form. The other forms are basically the same with just a few variations. I'll point out those variations so you can create the other two forms on your own.

Task Form Communication

Before we jump into InfoPath form design, we need to cover communicating between InfoPath and the workflow.

To simplify our lives, we'll use the same communication structure to talk to all of the forms. This requires more work to set up task properties for each task, but it keeps the number of forms required for the solution to a minimum. This mostly applies to the Complete Task form, as we're going to change its display based upon the information we pass in.

To send information to an InfoPath form from the workflow, we need to define, and later include, a special file named ItemMetadata.xml. As the name of the file suggests, this file is an xml file. This file requires a single element with the following structure:

```
<z:row xmlns:z="#RowsetSchema"/>
```

Open Notepad (or your favorite editor) and create a text file with the code in Listing 9.26. You'll notice the single element contains attributes that are string values prefixed with "ows_".

LISTING 9.26   Form Communication File

```
<z:row xmlns:z="#RowsetSchema"

ows_reviewperiod=""

ows_employee=""

ows_manager=""

ows_appraiser=""

ows_tasktitle=""

ows_itemtitle=""

ows_itemlink=""

ows_iteminst=""

ows_inst1=""
```

```
ows_inst2=""

ows_inst3=""

ows_inst4=""

ows_completestatement=""

/>
```

Save the file to a location that you'll remember later, like c:\. Make sure the file is named exactly ItemMetadata.xml, as any other filename won't work.

The attributes are passed in as formatted strings. The first five attributes represent the review period, the employee, manager, and appraiser names, and the subtitle for the form. The `item` attributes represent the text that will be shown in a hyperlink, the actual link to where the hyperlink will be directed, and the instructions that apply to the hyperlink. The `inst` attributes represent up to four lines of instructions, and the `completestatement` attribute is the agreement statement used to indicate task completeness.

Task Form Creation

Now it's time to create the Complete Task form using the steps below:

1. Start by opening InfoPath.

2. Click Design a Form Template, as shown in Figure 9.20, and choose a blank form, as shown in Figure 9.21.

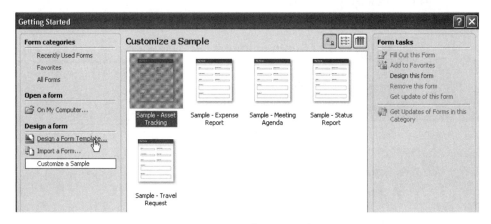

FIGURE 9.20 Design a new form.

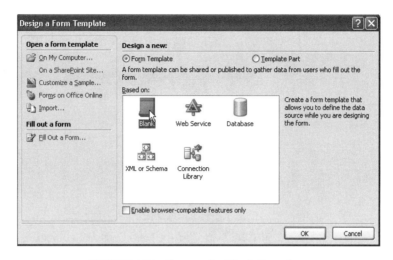

FIGURE 9.21 Choose the Blank Template.

3. Add the `TaskCompleted` field.

   For this form, the only communication that is sent back to the workflow will be an indicator that the task has been completed. We need to add a Boolean field, `TaskCompleted`, which the workflow will evaluate when the task form is closed. From the form designer's Task Pane, click Data Source, as shown in Figure 9.22.

FIGURE 9.22 Update the Form Data Source.

4. Right-click myFields and choose Add. Fill in the Add Field or Group dialog box with the following properties (see Figure 9.23). When finished, click OK.

FIGURE 9.23 Add the TaskCompleted field.

Add the Workflow Communication Data Source

The communication from the task form to the workflow is set up, so we can now set up the communication from the workflow to the task form, which will lead us to the design of the form.

1. Point at the Tools menu and choose Data Connections.

2. Click Add and select Receive data in the Data Connection Wizard, as shown in Figure 9.24.

3. Click Next.

4. Make sure that the XML document is selected as the source of data and click Next.

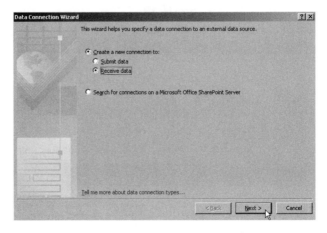

FIGURE 9.24 Data Connection Wizard, Part 1.

5. In the text box on the XML data file details page of the Data Connection Wizard, enter the path to the ItemMetadata.xml file that you saved in the previous section. Figure 9.25 assumes the file was saved in the root of the c: drive.

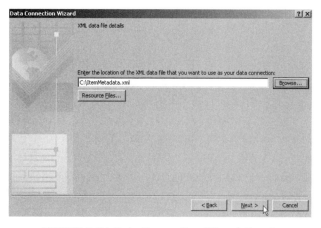

FIGURE 9.25 Data Connection Wizard, Part 2.

6. Click Next.

7. Make sure that Include the data as a resource file in the form template or template part is selected and click Next.

8. Make sure that Automatically retrieve data when form is opened is selected, as shown in Figure 9.26, and click Finish.

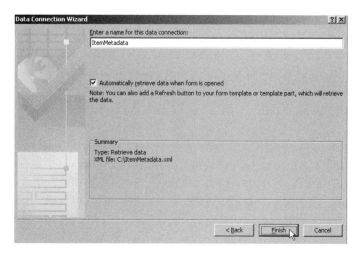

FIGURE 9.26 Data Connection Wizard, Part 3.

9. Click Close on the Data Connections dialog. To confirm the data connection completed correctly, click the Data Source drop-down list down arrow and select ItemMetadata (Secondary). The fields from the xml file are displayed, as shown in Figure 9.27.

FIGURE 9.27 ItemMetadata Data Source.

10. Click Design Tasks in the Data Source Task Pane, as shown in Figure 9.28.

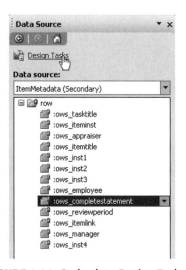

FIGURE 9.28 Go back to Design Tasks.

Creating the Form Design

Now we can move on to the form UI. The design is simple, and it is meant to provide users with the information necessary to complete their tasks and allow them to indicate when the tasks have been completed.

For this book, we chose to use a black-and-white color scheme. You're free to choose whatever scheme you want. The color scheme is chosen by pointing at the Format menu and then choosing Color Schemes. The scheme can be changed at any time.

After the color scheme has been chosen, we can create the layout of the form. To get back to the Design Tasks pane, click the down arrow next to Color Schemes and choose Design Tasks from the drop-down, as shown in Figure 9.29.

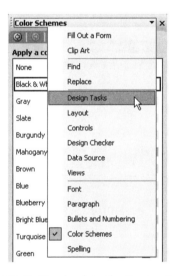

FIGURE 9.29 Getting back to the Design Tasks pane.

1. From the Design Tasks pane, choose Layout, as shown in Figure 9.30.

   Creating your layout is as simple as choosing layout tables and dragging them onto the form design page. We'll start by dragging a Table with a Title to the design form. The result is shown in Figure 9.31.

2. Click on the Click to add a title and enter **Litware Appraisal Review**. Select the entire text of the title just entered, make sure the title is centered, and change the font size to 24.

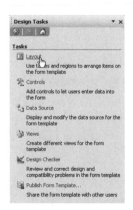

FIGURE 9.30 Layout Design Task.

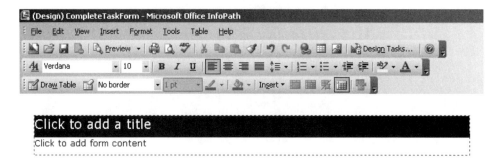

FIGURE 9.31 Initial form layout.

3. Click on Click to add form content; then click on Custom Table under Insert layout tables in the Layout task pane. Enter 2 for the number of columns and 3 for the number of rows in the Insert Table dialog box, as shown in Figure 9.32.

4. Click OK to create the table.

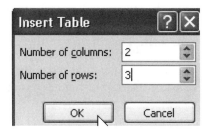

FIGURE 9.32 Custom table.

All of the layout structure is in place, and we need to add the labels and controls to the page to complete the design.

Create the labels in the three left columns by entering Review Period, Employee, and Appraiser, respectively. The labels should be bolded. The form should look like Figure 9.33.

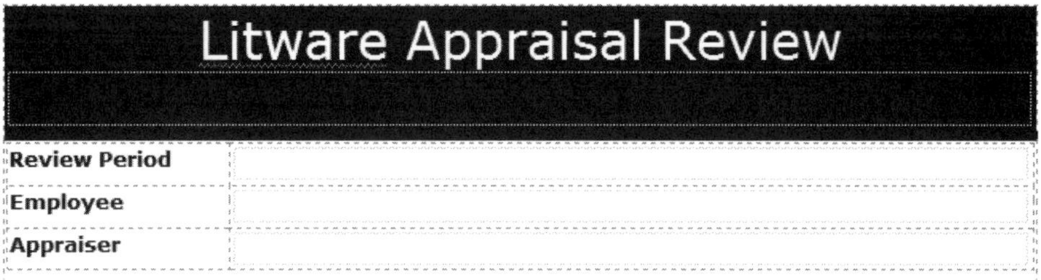

FIGURE 9.33 Form with labels.

Next, we'll be adding a few different controls including a check box, a hyperlink, a button, and expression boxes.

InfoPath controls are bound to data source items. The process of creating controls and binding them to data items can be accomplished in two ways: dragging a control from the control toolbox onto the form or dragging a data source item to the form designer. We'll be using both methods to create our design, depending on the data type and the control type.

We're going to start by adding the check box, the hyperlink, the button, and all of our expression boxes.

The check box is used to indicate when the task has been completed. As mentioned previously, there are two different methods for adding controls to the form. We're going to drag the `TaskCompleted` field to the form, as InfoPath infers which kind of control to create from the data type of the field. Some data types allow for more than one control, and in those cases, InfoPath will prompt you to choose which control to create. We don't have that issue with the `TaskCompleted` field because InfoPath will automatically create a check box for us. When the check box is created, InfoPath creates a default label next to the control with the same name as the field. We need to remove the label after creating the check box.

1. Click on Design Tasks and choose DataSource. Make sure that the Main data source is displayed and expand `myFields` if it isn't already, as shown in Figure 9.34.

FIGURE 9.34 `TaskCompleted` field.

2. Drag TaskCompleted to the bottom of the table in the form designer, as shown in Figure 9.35.

Litware Appraisal Review

Review Period	
Employee	
Appraiser	

☐ Task Completed

FIGURE 9.35 Task Completed check box.

3. Remove the check box label by clicking to the right of the label and backspacing until the label has been removed. We'll be adding a label of our own that is data-driven later. Add some space above the check box by clicking to the left of the check box and pressing Enter two or three times. We'll be adding a lot of fields below the labels and above the check box later.

Now we can add our hyperlink. Our hyperlink is used to give the user a quick way to go to either the document library, or it can be a link to the appraisal document itself. When the document is used in a hyperlink, the document is opened as read-only. This is exactly what we want when the employee is deciding whether to accept the goals, but is the exact opposite when a reviewer is expected to fill out the document. As a result, sometimes the link will point to the document, and other times it will point to the document library containing the document.

The hyperlink is added by dragging the control to the form because the hyperlink either references existing data or has hard-coded values entered. We need to get to the Controls toolbox, so click on Design Tasks in the Data Source task pane and then choose Controls.

1. Click on the Hyperlink control (located at the bottom of the control list) and drag it to the form design just below the Appraiser label and above the check box. When the control is dropped onto the form, the Insert Hyperlink dialog will be displayed, as shown in Figure 9.36.

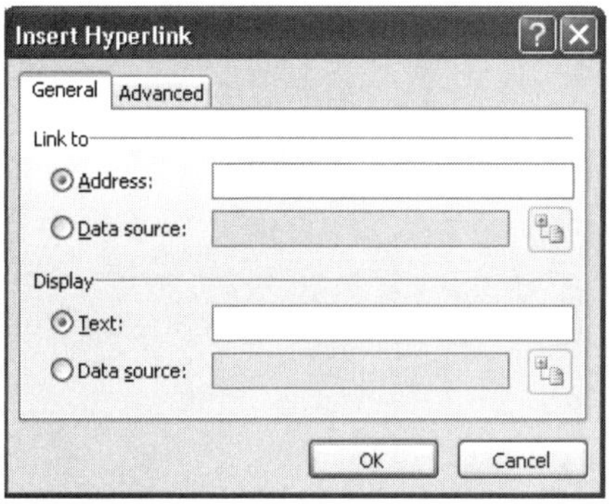

FIGURE 9.36 Add the HyperLink.

We'll be using a data source for both the Link to and Display fields. The Link to field represents the link URL, and the Display represents the text displayed for the hyperlink. Use the following step to set Link to:

2. Select Data Source and click the button to the right of the Data Source text box, as shown in Figure 9.37.

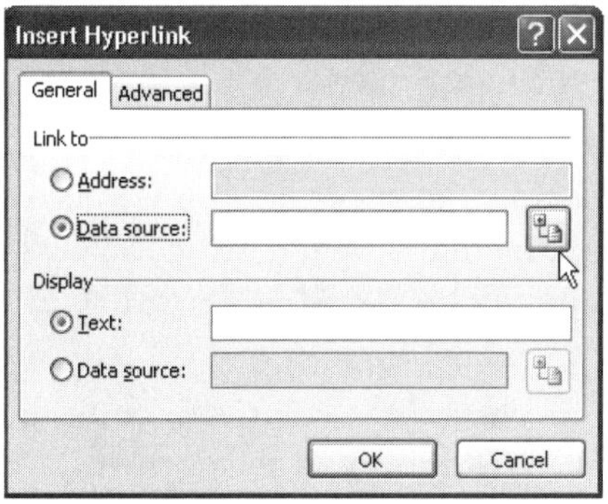

FIGURE 9.37 Form with labels.

3. When the Select a Field or Group dialog is displayed, change the Data Source to ItemMetadata (Secondary) and choose :ows_itemlink, as shown in Figure 9.38.

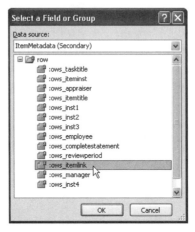

FIGURE 9.38 Choose the Link to Source Field.

4. Click OK.

For the Display value, we want to follow the same pattern.

5. Select the Data Source radio button, click on the field select button, switch the Data source to ItemMetadata (Secondary), and then choose :ows_itemtitle.

6. Click OK to close the Select a Field or Group dialog and click OK to insert the hyperlink into the form design.

The hyperlink will show up as an empty rectangle since we don't have any values in the fields the hyperlink references yet.

The button is used to submit the form to the workflow process. We're going to add the button below the check box, so we need to create some space below the check box by clicking to the right of the check box and pressing Enter two or three times. You can modify the layout of the format as you see fit.

1. Drag a Button control from the Standard controls onto the form designer below the check box. Center the button on the form using the Center command bar button on the Format toolbar. Double-click the button to display the button properties.

2. Enter Submit for the Label and click Rules, as shown in Figure 9.39.

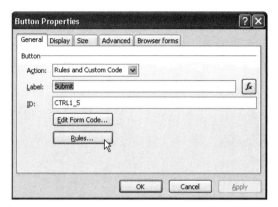

FIGURE 9.39 Submit button properties.

3. When the Rules dialog is displayed, we need to add a rule by clicking Add. The button will perform two actions. The first is to submit the form to the hosting environment, and the second action will be to close the form.

4. To add the first action, click Add Action, as shown in Figure 9.40.

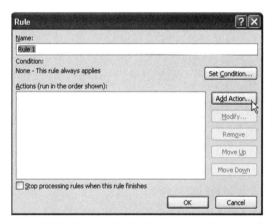

FIGURE 9.40 Submit button actions.

5. In the Action dialog box, select Submit using a data connection. We don't have a data connection to submit to, so the Data connection drop-down is disabled. We need to add a data connection by clicking the Add button. When the Data Connection Wizard dialog is displayed, leave the selections at Create a new connection to: and Submit data, as shown in Figure 9.41.

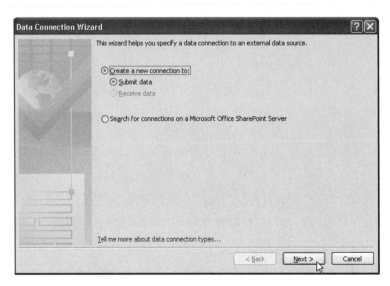

FIGURE 9.41 Data Connection Wizard, Part 1.

6. Click Next.

7. On the next wizard page, select To the hosting environment, such as an ASP.NET page or a hosting application, as shown in Figure 9.42.

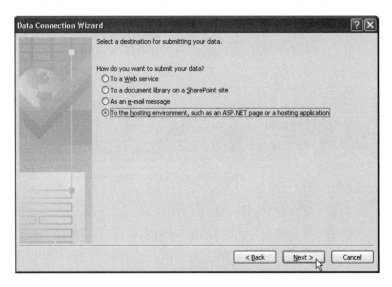

FIGURE 9.42 Data Connection Wizard, Part 2.

8. Click Next.

9. Click Finish to complete the wizard.

10. Click OK to close the Action dialog.

11. Click Add Action again to add the next action, which will close the form. Select Close the form from the Action drop-down and click OK to close the Action dialog.

12. Click OK to close the Rule dialog.

13. Click OK to close the Rules dialog.

14. Click OK to close the Button Properties dialog.

We're almost finished with the form design. We just need to add the subtitle, some appraisal information, and the instructions. This information comes from the ItemMetadata data connection, and it will be added as Expression Box controls. As mentioned previously, when you drag a data source item to the form, InfoPath creates a control based on the data source item's data type. The default control for the string data type, which is the data type for all of our metadata fields, is a text box. We don't want anyone changing these values so we have to add a control and associate it with the data for each of the fields in the form. We'll walk through the creation of one Expression Box and will give the properties for the others.

We'll add the subtitle field using the steps below.

1. Start by clicking at the end of the title and pressing Enter. A shortcut to drag a control to the form is to double-click the control in the toolbox. The control will be placed where the cursor is on the screen.

2. Double-click the Expression Box control at the bottom of the control toolbox. The Insert Expression Box dialog box will be displayed, as shown in Figure 9.43.

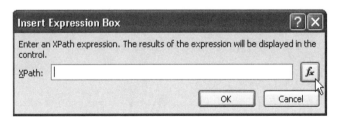

FIGURE 9.43 Insert Expression Box.

3. Click the fx button to the right of the XPath text box. When the Insert Formula dialog is displayed, click Insert Field or Group. When the Select a Field or Group dialog is displayed, change the Data Source drop-down to ItemMetadata (Secondary) and choose :ows_tasktitle, as shown in Figure 9.44.

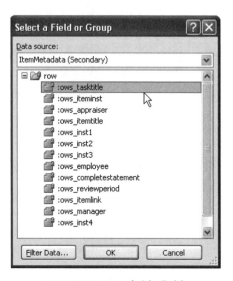

FIGURE 9.44 Subtitle field.

4. Click OK to close the Select a Field or Group dialog box.
5. Click OK to close the Insert Formula dialog box.
6. Click OK to close the Insert Expression Box dialog box.
7. Change the font size of the subtitle to 16 points.

Figure 9.45 shows the Complete Task form with the field locations. You can ignore the hyperlink. Other than that, all of the locations for the expression boxes along with the data source item (minus the leading ":") are displayed.

NOTE

My Screen Doesn't Look Like That

It's true. The screen shown in Figure 9.45 was created by adding default values for the attributes in ItemData.xml. They are only there for visual reference and are not part of the solution. While your screen will not look like Figure 9.45 completely, if you double-click (or right-click and choose Properties), the expression boxes on your form and the bindings you see should be the same as Figure 9.45.

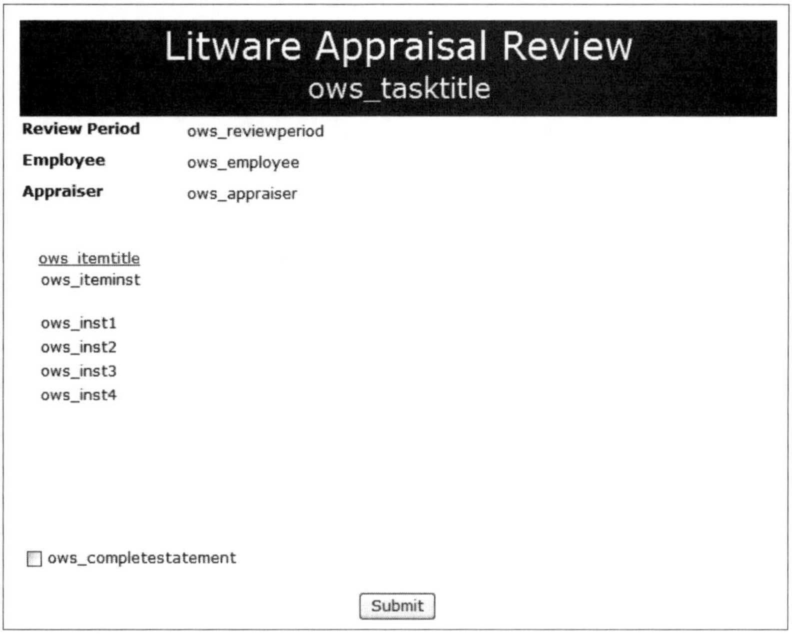

FIGURE 9.45 Form Design showing Expression Box locations and fields.

As mentioned earlier, you can format the form however you like. The important part is to make sure that you create the check box so the user can indicate when the task has been completed and make sure the Submit button is set up correctly, as described previously. Nothing else is important for the form function, although your users will appreciate instructions and links to the file or the document library where the file is located.

Publishing the Form

In order for others to use an InfoPath form, the form has to be published. In order to publish forms for workflows, the form options need to be updated to be compatible with the workflow environment before publishing:

First, we need to mark the form as being able to be opened in a browser using the steps below:

1. Point at the Tools menu and select Form Options.
2. Select Compatibility from the Category list and check Design a form template that can be opened in a browser or InfoPath, as shown in Figure 9.46.

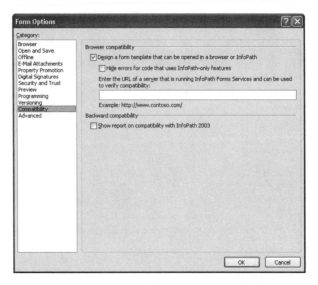

FIGURE 9.46 Create a browser-compatible form.

Next, we need to set the security level of the form to domain security.

3. Select Security and Trust from the Category list and uncheck Automatically determine security level (recommended).

4. Next, select Domain (the form can access content from the domain in which it is located), as shown in Figure 9.47.

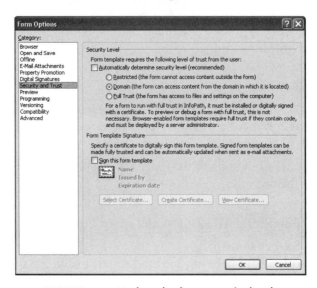

FIGURE 9.47 Update the form security level.

5. Click Close to close the Form Options dialog.

6. To publish the form, point at the File menu and choose Publish. If you haven't saved the form yet (and there have been no steps to do so), InfoPath displays a prompt to tell you to save the form before publishing. Click OK and save the file to a location that you'll remember in the future. In order to edit a form template, you'll need to open the saved version, not the published version.

   After saving the form, or if you weren't prompted to save the form, InfoPath displays the Publishing Wizard dialog.

7. Select To a network location, as shown in Figure 9.48, and click Next.

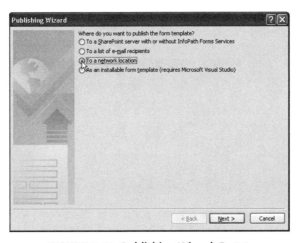

FIGURE 9.48 Publishing Wizard, Part 1.

8. Set the Form template path and file name to the SharePoint Workflow project folder with the name CompleteTaskForm.xsn, and make sure the Form template name is CompleteTaskForm, as shown in Figure 9.49.

9. Click Next.

10. Ensure that the alternate access textbox is blank, as shown in Figure 9.50. Click Next. Don't worry about any warnings you may get regarding users not being able to access the form. Just click OK if or when you get the message. Access to the form will take place within SharePoint so no alternative path is necessary.

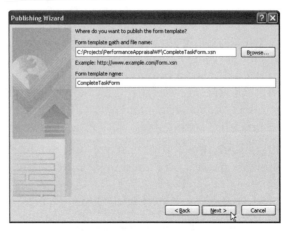

FIGURE 9.49 Publishing Wizard, Part 2.

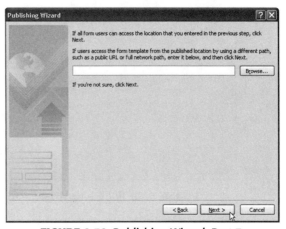

FIGURE 9.50 Publishing Wizard, Part 3.

Warning, What Warning?

If you don't receive the above warning when publishing, that probably means you didn't set the form's security to Domain. Go back and set the security level to Domain, as described in step 4.

11. Click Publish at the end of the wizard.

12. Click Close to close the Publishing Wizard.

Remember to follow the steps above for all three forms. The changes for the other two forms are covered next.

Other Task Forms

The other two forms are created in the same manner as the complete task form was in the previous section. The only differences are the metadata fields that are displayed. In the case of the start evaluation task form, a few fields are added to the main data source (where the `TaskCompleted` field was added).

Start Evaluation Task Form

The Start Evaluation Task form adds six reviewers (we only use three, but this shows how more can be added without any code changes), named Review1–6, to the main data source, as shown in Figure 9.51. The ReviewerX fields are Text(string) fields.

FIGURE 9.51 Start Evaluation Task form main Data Source.

The design does not require the hyperlink and instead puts in hard-coded instructions and adds another table (two columns, three rows) to hold reviewer information. The reviewer expression boxes are added in the same way the subtitle expression box was created in the previous section. The design is shown in Figure 9.52.

When publishing the form, make sure to name the form `StartEvaluation TaskForm.xsn`.

Employee Self-Evaluation Task Form

There are no data changes to the Employee Self-Evaluation Form compared to the Complete Task Form. The differences in the form are the lack of any instructions being brought in from the ItemMetaData data source. All of the instructions are hard-coded in the form. The form design is shown in Figure 9.53.

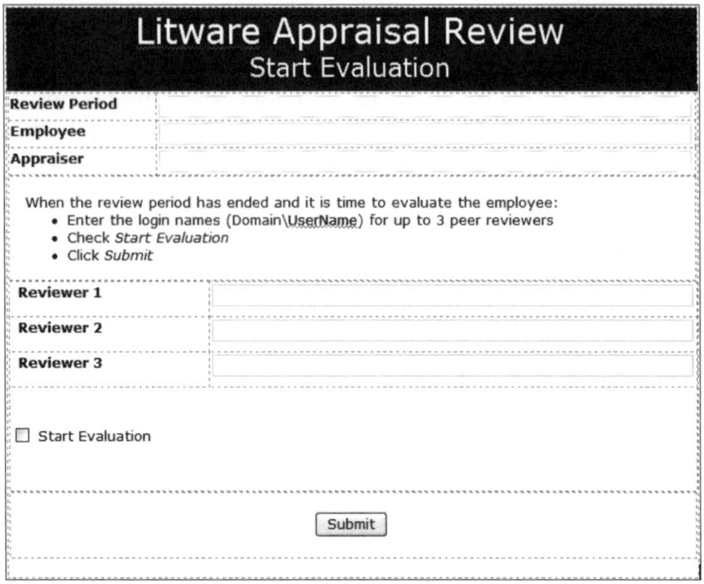

FIGURE 9.52 Start Evaluation Task form design.

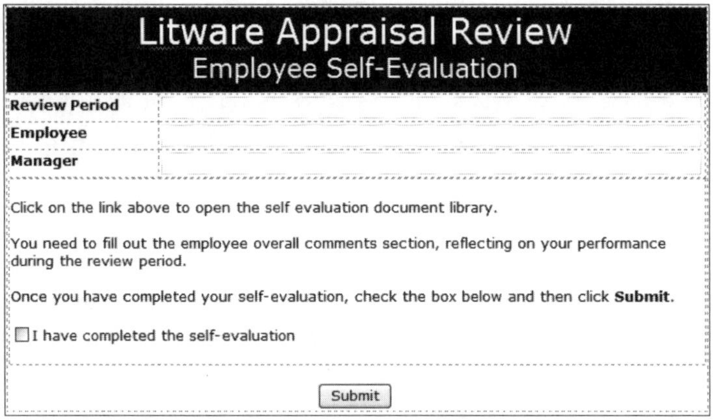

FIGURE 9.53 Employee Self-Evaluation Task form design.

When publishing the form, make sure to name the form EmployeeSelf
EvaluationTaskForm.xsn.

Add the Forms to the Workflow

Once the forms have been published, you need to associate the forms with the workflow. To do that, you need to update both `Workflow.xml` and `Feature.xml`, located in the Workflow project folder. Listing 9.27 shows the `Workflow.xml` updates, and Listing 9.28 shows the `Feature.xml` updates.

NOTE

Make Sure You Get the Correct URN Values for Your Forms

The workflow updates show the URN values for the forms we created. When you create a new form and publish it with InfoPath, you will have different values. To obtain the correct values, you need to open the form templates located in the folders they were published. Once the form is open for design, point to File and choose Properties. The URN for your form can be found in the ID section. Simply copy the value and paste it into workflow.xml.

LISTING 9.27   `Workflow.xml` Updates to Integrate the Task Forms

```
...

TaskListContentTypeId="0x01080100C9C9515DE4E24001905074F980F93160"

>

   <Categories/>

   <MetaData>

      <Task0_FormURN>

         urn:schemas-microsoft-com:office:infopath:CompleteTaskForm:
-myXSD-2008-07-30T05-17-54

      </Task0_FormURN>

      <Task1_FormURN>

         urn:schemas-microsoft-com:office:infopath:
StartEvaluationTaskForm:-myXSD-2008-07-30T18-14-16

      </Task1_FormURN>

      <Task2_FormURN>

         urn:schemas-microsoft-com:office:infopath:
EmployeeSelfEvaluationTaskForm:-myXSD-2008-08-22T17-11-02

      </Task2_FormURN>

      <StatusPageUrl>_layouts/WrkStat.aspx</StatusPageUrl>

   </MetaData>

  </Workflow>

</Elements>
```

Be Forewarned

Pay careful attention to the TaskListContentTypeId, *as it is a very long string and is required to be exact. Forms will not work if this entry is not correct. The value is specific to InfoPath forms and is an attribute of the* Workflow *element.*

Also note the <Taskx_FormURN> lines. As mentioned previously, the number in the x place is the value of the TaskType for the task properties when creating the tasks.

The task form files need to be added to the SharePoint Feature.xml files. The lines are displayed in Listing 9.28. The <ElementFile> entries show the lines that need to be added.

LISTING 9.28 Feature.xml Updates to Integrate the Task Forms

```
<ElementManifests>

    <ElementManifest Location="workflow.xml" />

    <ElementFile Location="CompleteTaskForm.xsn" />

    <ElementFile Location="StartEvaluationTaskForm.xsn" />

    <ElementFile Location="EmployeeSelfEvaluationTaskForm.xsn" />

</ElementManifests>
```

The Workflow.xml changes associate the forms with the workflow, while the Feature.xml updates get the files copied to the SharePoint Feature folder.

TESTING WHAT WE'VE GOT

At this point, our workflow should work flawlessly. Before starting a debugging session, make sure the workflow project is the startup project. Then we can test the workflow by putting a break point on the workflow activation activity (right-click on the activity and choose Breakpoints, Insert Breakpoint) and then start a debugging session using the steps below:

1. Press F5 or click Debug, Start Debugging.

An Attach Security Warning Is Displayed

If an Attach Security Warning dialog is displayed, click Attach and then click Yes to continue debugging.

When the browser displays the Appraisals_Kevin Martin document library, start a workflow on one of the appraisal documents. If there aren't any documents, you'll have to create a new one.

2. To start the workflow, click on a document and choose Workflows (see Figure 9.54).

FIGURE 9.54 Manually start a workflow on a document.

3. When the list of workflows is displayed, click on PerformanceAppraisalWF. The workflow will run and will hit the breakpoint inserted above on the onWorkflowActivated activity. You can step into or over, using commands from the Debug menu or the corresponding shortcut keys, any of the activities in the workflow.

Use Site Users for the Employee and Appraiser Names

The names that you use to test your form need to be valid users of the SharePoint site. Having valid Windows accounts is not sufficient.

If you view the document library, you'll see that the document has a new column, PerformanceAppraisalWF, and the appraisal document has a status of In Progress.

4. Click In Progress, and the workflow information is displayed.

5. Click on the Finalize Appraisal Goals Task, and the Accept Goals task form will be displayed.

6. Check Goals Accepted and click Submit.

   The workflow is still in the In Progress state, but now there is a second task. The first task is marked Completed, and the second task is marked Not Started.

7. Click on the Start Evaluation Task, and the Start Evaluation Period task form will be displayed.

8. Check Start Evaluation Period and click Submit.

The workflow is now in the Complete state and so are both tasks.

Everything is working like it's supposed to, except for security, which is our next session.

ADDING SECURITY

As mentioned earlier, security has been the sole responsibility of the manager. Whenever the appraisal moved through the different stages, the manager was responsible for enabling and disabling different people to view the document.

In this chapter, we've gotten to the point that the goals have been agreed upon and the actual period that will be reviewed has begun. We've also allowed the manager to start the evaluation period by clicking a check box on a form.

Now, we're going to use the List Item Permissions Activity that we built in the first part of this chapter to modify the permissions on the appraisal document as it moves through the workflow.

For our scenario, we allow the employee to view the document once the manager is satisfied with the draft of goals for the employee. At this point, the manager starts the workflow on the document.

Once that occurs, we want to give the employee viewing rights and the manager editing rights, but nobody else has any rights to the document.

After the employee and manager have agreed on the goals, we want to keep the security the way it is until the manager starts the evaluation period. When the evaluation period begins, the manager will still be able to edit the document, but we don't want anyone to be able to view the document presently.

When we add peer reviewers in the next section, we'll give the peer reviewers read access to the appraisal document. This allows the reviewers to comment on and score the employee on the agreed-upon goals.

To enable our custom activity, we need to add a project reference in the workflow project to the activity project. Figure 9.55 shows the project reference being added from the Projects Tab.

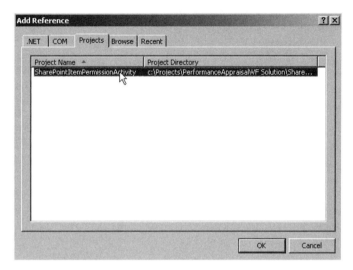

FIGURE 9.55 Add a reference to the Custom Activity.

Once we have added the reference, rebuild the solution.

Now, we are ready to add our activity to our workflow. Switch back to the Workflow Designer.

From the toolbox, find the SharePointItemPermissions section and expand it. Drag the `ItemPermissionsActivity` right under the `createAcceptedGoalsTask-Activity`, as shown in Figure 9.56.

Set the properties as follows (see Figure 9.57).

■ `Name`. Enter **setEmployeeAsReaderTaskActivity** for the name of the activity.

■ `Editors`. Click the ... button. When the Bind 'Editors' to an activity's property dialog is displayed, choose managerLoginName from the tree view.

■ `ItemId`. Click the ... button. When the Bind 'ItemId' to an activity's property dialog is displayed, choose workflowProperties.ItemId from the tree view.

■ `ListId`. Click the ... button. When the Bind 'ListId' to an activity's property dialog is displayed, choose workflowProperties.ListId from the tree view.

■ `Readers`. Click the ... button. When the Bind 'Readers' to an activity's property dialog is displayed, choose employeeLoginName from the tree view.

- **SiteId**. Click the ... button. When the Bind 'SiteId' to an activity's property dialog is displayed, choose workflowProperties.SiteId from the tree view.

- **WebId**. Click the ... button. When the Bind 'WebId' to an activity's property dialog is displayed, choose workflowProperties.WebId from the tree view.

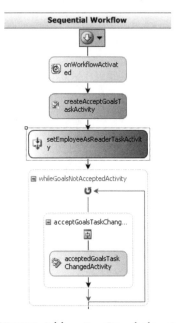

FIGURE 9.56 Add an ItemPermissionsActivity.

Properties		
setEmployeeAsReaderTaskActivity SharePointItemPermissions.ItemPermissionsActivity		
(Name)	setEmployeeAsReaderTaskActivity	
Administrators		
Description		
⊟ Editors	Activity=AppraisalWorkflow, Path=managerLoginName	
Name	AppraisalWorkflow	
Path	managerLoginName	
Enabled	True	
⊟ ItemId	Activity=AppraisalWorkflow, Path=workflowProperties.ItemId	
Name	AppraisalWorkflow	
Path	workflowProperties.ItemId	
⊟ ListId	Activity=AppraisalWorkflow, Path=workflowProperties.ListId	
Name	AppraisalWorkflow	
Path	workflowProperties.ListId	
⊟ Readers	Activity=AppraisalWorkflow, Path=employeeLoginName	
Name	AppraisalWorkflow	
Path	employeeLoginName	
⊟ SiteId	Activity=AppraisalWorkflow, Path=workflowProperties.SiteId	
Name	AppraisalWorkflow	
Path	workflowProperties.SiteId	
⊟ WebId	Activity=AppraisalWorkflow, Path=workflowProperties.WebId	
Name	AppraisalWorkflow	
Path	workflowProperties.WebId	

FIGURE 9.57 setEmployeeAsReaderTaskActivity properties.

We're halfway home with security. We just need to repeat the above process by dragging another ItemPermissionsActivity to the very last position in the workflow.

The properties are pretty much the same (see Figure 9.58), except make sure to leave Readers blank.

- ▪ `Name`. Enter **setManagerAsEditorTaskActivity** for the name of the activity.

- ▪ `Editors`. Click the ... button. When the Bind 'Editors' to an activity's property dialog is displayed, choose managerLoginName from the tree view.

- ▪ `ItemId`. Click the ... button. When the Bind 'ItemId' to an activity's property dialog is displayed, choose workflowProperties.ItemId from the tree view.

- ▪ `ListId`. Click the ... button. When the Bind 'ListId' to an activity's property dialog is displayed, choose workflowProperties.ListId from the tree view.

- ▪ `SiteId`. Click the ... button. When the Bind 'SiteId' to an activity's property dialog is displayed, choose workflowProperties.SiteId from the tree view.

- ▪ `WebId`. Click the ... button. When the Bind 'WebId' to an activity's property dialog is displayed, choose workflowProperties.WebId from the tree view.

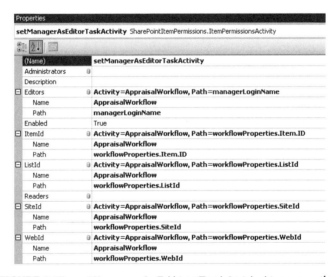

FIGURE 9.58 `setManagerAsEditorTaskActivity` properties.

Now Testing What We've Got

We have completed the workflow project for this chapter. The workflow will now work just as it had before, except that it adds security.

To test the workflow, check and record the permissions on the document that you ran the workflow on before. Run the workflow again, but this time, check the permissions when the Accept Goals task is created and again after the workflow has finished.

You should find the appraiser has Contribute (edit) rights throughout, and the employee will have read rights when the Accept Goals task is created. But when the workflow ends, you should see that while the manager still has edit rights, nobody has read rights.

Summary

We've met the goals for the chapter and have a fully functional half of an appraisal workflow process. To get here, we've completed the following tasks:

- Created a list item permissions activity to alleviate mistakes and tedium for the manager.
- Created a workflow that includes assigning tasks.
- Created InfoPath task forms and integrated them into the workflow.
- Integrated the list item permissions activity into our workflow.

In the next chapter we will be doing the following:

- Adding functionality to gather feedback from peer reviewers.
- Integrating that feedback into the original appraisal document.
- Deploying the projects.

10 Completing and Deploying the Appraisal Process

W e've created the supporting classes to get the appraisal process finished through the goal-setting phase, and the workflow has assigned the manager a task to initialize the evaluation phase.

In this chapter, we're going to finish the workflow first and then deploy the workflow with all of the activities and forms.

Let's review the AppraisalStatus field from the Performance Appraisal Content Type from Chapter 3 to see where we are and where we're going. The field contains the following values as the performance appraisal moves through five stages:

- Goals Draft
- Goals Finalized
- Collect Feedback
- Appraisal Draft
- Appraisal Finalized

To get from goals finalized to appraisal finalized, we'll need to collect feedback, incorporate the feedback into the review document, have the manager finalize the review, and collect signatures from the parties involved.

Deployment consists of packaging the activities and workflows so they can be installed.

All of our work will be modifications or additions to the solution from Chapter 9.

FINISHING THE WORKFLOW

As mentioned previously, our first goal for this chapter is to finish the workflow, which requires us to do the following:

1. Collect feedback from the reviewers.
2. Collect summary feedback from the employee.
3. Incorporate feedback into the appraisal document.
4. Collect summary feedback from the manager.
5. Collect signatures from all parties involved.

Collecting feedback will require a new activity, as well as additions to the workflow. Incorporating feedback will consist of aggregating data from various documents back into the original document. The manager feedback will be collected when the manager is finalizing the appraisal document after the employee and reviewer feedback have been integrated into the original appraisal document. The signature collection described in Chapter 8 is sufficient for our use so we won't change anything.

COLLECTING FEEDBACK FROM THE REVIEWERS

From the task form filled out by the manager, you can see that we are allowing three reviewers to be assigned to the appraisal. There is nothing magical about the number "three." As such, we'll design the activity to support as many reviewers as deemed necessary.

To support an unknown number of reviewers, we'll use the Replicator Activity. There are many references, both online and offline, to get a detailed explanation of the Replicator Activity. You can think of the Replicator as a for/each loop for activities.

NOTE

Finding Workflow Technologies Information Online

A good place to find workflow and activity information is your favorite search engine. There are many SharePoint-related sites on the Web. MSDN is a great place to get the base information. The class definition for the ReplicatorActivity *class can be found at http://msdn.microsoft.com/en-us/library/system.workflow. activities.replicatoractivity.aspx.*

Of course, links on the Internet change all the time so searching for ReplicatorActivity *within MSDN is suggested if the above link doesn't work.*

In our scenario, we need to create a custom activity that the replicator will call for each reviewer. In essence, the custom activity is required to do the following tasks:

- Create a document for the reviewer to edit.
- Assign the reviewer edit permissions for the new document.
- Create and assign the reviewer a task to indicate when he is finished.
- Wait for the reviewer to finish.
- Mark the task as completed.
- Assign the manager edit permissions for the document and remove permissions for the reviewer.

The `ReplicatorActivity` class processes the for/each loop by creating instances of the activity and sending data to each instance. The data is provided to the `ReplicatorActivity` as a property, and it is in list form. The data requirements for the data passed into the `ReplicatorActivity`, for our scenario, are listed below:

- Original review of SharePoint information
- Reviewer, employee, and manager information
- Appraisal dates
- Task type information
- New appraisal document name

We will be passing in SharePoint specific identification information (SiteId, WebId, ListId, ListItemId) so we can make a copy of the document for the reviewers to update. The new appraisal document name is included so we can calculate a related name for the copy. The appraisal dates are used exclusively for the task forms, the task type information is used to indicate which task form to display, and the reviewer, employee, and manager information are used for both task form display information and task and permission assignments.

Supporting Code

Our activity requires us to write two supporting classes. The first class is the instance data class that the replicator will pass to our activity. The other class we need is a SharePoint helper class that will give us quick and easy methods to access SharePoint list items.

The first class we'll create is a simple data class called `AppraisalInfo`. Create a new class within the workflow project and name it AppraisalInfo.cs.

Mark the class `Serializable` and be sure to make the class `public`. Add the variable declarations from Listing 10.1 to AppraisalInfo.cs.

LISTING 10.1   AppraisalInfo Class Listing

```
[Serializable]
public class AppraisalInfo
{
    public Guid SiteId = Guid.Empty;
    public Guid WebId = Guid.Empty;
    public Guid ListId = Guid.Empty;

    public int OriginalListItemId = -1;

    // People involved
    public string ReviewerLoginName = string.Empty;
    public string ReviewerFullName = string.Empty;
    public string EmployeeLoginName = string.Empty;
    public string EmployeeFullName = string.Empty;
    public string ManagerLoginName = string.Empty;
    public string ManagerFullName = string.Empty;

    // Appraisal Dates
    public string AppraisalStartDate = string.Empty;
    public string AppraisalEndDate = string.Empty;

    // Task Form Info
    public int TaskType = 0;

    // Appraisal Document Name
    public string AppraisalDocumentName = string.Empty;
}
```

Looking at the code in Listing 10.1, you can see all of the information that we require. `TaskType` is included because even though we'll be using the same activity for the employee evaluation, we'll need to use a different task form.

`SiteId`, `WebId`, `ListId`, and `ListItemId` are used together to help us find the review documents.

The user names are stored both as display name (xxxFullName) for task forms and user name (xxxLoginName) for assigning permissions and tasks.

Workflows and Serialization

If you look at the top of the class declaration, you'll see [`Serializable`], *which is required for all classes that will be referenced through workflow dehydration and rehydration. If you don't include the attribute, your class won't be able to be serialized. When the workflow dehydrates (for example, when waiting for a task to change), the workflow will encounter an exception when trying to serialize your class. The workflow will not throw an exception that you can catch and will just stop. The workflow status will be Complete, and there will be no visible history to tell you what happened.*

Whenever you encounter a workflow that just seems to stop, see if there is something obviously wrong with it. Serialization is a good starting point. However, you may have set a value while debugging and forgotten to reset it. In the event that you can't easily determine the problem, you can always look through the logs. You can find the logs in the folder located at "c:\program files\common files\microsoft shared\web server extensions\12\Logs."

Search through the log file until you get close to the time where the workflow failed. A quick check would be to search for "Dehydration" to see if there are any serialization errors.

Remember, many of the SharePoint types are not serializable. You will either need to write serialization code or find another way to represent the SharePoint types. We've chosen to use the IDs and fetch the types when we need them.

The other class we need to create is a simple static SharePoint helper class, aptly named `SharePointHelper`. Add a new class in the workflow project and name the class file **SharePointHelper.cs**.

Since this class will be accessing the SharePoint object model, we need to add a reference to SharePoint, as shown in Listing 10.2.

LISTING 10.2   Adding a Reference to SharePoint

```
using Microsoft.SharePoint;
```

The class we're creating will be static, so you'll need to update the class declaration so it matches Listing 10.3.

LISTING 10.3   Making `SharePointHelper` Static

```
public static class SharePointHelper
{
}
```

The first method we'll need to add is a supporting function to retrieve a named list item from a SharePoint list. To accomplish this, we'll loop through all of the items in the given list until we find an item with the same name. Listing 10.4 shows the code.

LISTING 10.4   Retrieving a Named List Item

```
public static SPListItem GetItemFromList(SPList list, string itemName)
{
    // Assume the item isn't found
    SPListItem retValue = null;

    // Check for valid arguments
    if (list != null && list.Items != null)
    {
        // Walk the list of items
        foreach (SPListItem item in list.Items)
        {
            // Is this the one we're looking for
            if (item.Name == itemName)
            {
                // Set the return value
```

```
            // and break from the loop
            retValue = item;
            break;
        }
    }
}


    return retValue;
}
```

The next method we need to create is the one to copy the review document. This fulfills the first requirement for our activity. Listing 10.5 shows the code for the entire function. To copy a review document, we first have to find the original document through the site, Web, list, and list item IDs. After we have the list item, we can create a copy. The copy method requires us to pass in the URL for the new file. This is calculated by appending the name of the document to Web URL and the URL of the root folder within the Web.

After the file has been copied, we have to retrieve a reference to it by calling `GetItemFromList`, which is displayed in Listing 10.4 .

LISTING 10.5   Creating a Copy of the Appraisal Document

```
public static SPListItem CopyReviewDocument(AppraisalInfo info)
{
    // Assume the review document doesn't exist
    SPListItem retValue = null;


    // Make sure we have a non-null info
    if (info != null)
    {
        // Get the site from the unique id
        using (SPSite site = new SPSite(info.SiteId))
        {
            if (site != null)
            {
```

```
                        // Get the web from the unique id
                        using (SPWeb web = site.AllWebs[info.WebId])
                        {
                            if (web != null)
                            {
                                // Get the list from the unique id
                                SPList list = web.Lists[info.ListId];

                                if (list != null)
                                {
                                    string listUrl =
                                        web.Url + "/" + list.RootFolder.Url + "/";

                                    SPFile file =
                                        list.GetItemById(info.OriginalListItemId).File;

                                    string reviewerDocumentUrl =
                                        listUrl + info.AppraisalDocumentName;
                                    file.CopyTo(reviewerDocumentUrl, true);

                                    retValue = GetItemFromList(
                                        list,
                                        info.AppraisalDocumentName
                                        );
                                }
                            }
                        }
                    }
                    return retValue;
                }
```

The final method we'll be adding will be used to retrieve the collected feedback so it can be integrated into the original appraisal document. The code, as shown in Listing10.6, looks very similar to `CopyReviewDocument`. The only difference is that the file is not copied, just retrieved using `GetItemFromList`.

LISTING 10.6   Retrieving a Review Document

```
public static SPListItem GetReviewDocument(AppraisalInfo info)
{
    // Assume the review document doesn't exist
    SPListItem retValue = null;

    // Make sure we have a non-null info
    if (info != null)
    {
        // Get the site from the unique id
        using (SPSite site = new SPSite(info.SiteId))
        {
            if (site != null)
            {
                // Get the web from the unique id
                using (SPWeb web = site.AllWebs[info.WebId])
                {
                    if (web != null)
                    {
                        // Get the list from the unique id
                        SPList list = web.Lists[info.ListId];
                        if (list != null)
                        {
                            retValue = GetItemFromList(
                                list,
                                info.AppraisalDocumentName
                                );
                        }
```

```
            }
         }
      }
   }
}
   return retValue;
}
```

Create the Activity

Our new activity will be created as a new item within the workflow project. This activity can be considered a mini-workflow because it inherits from `SequenceActivity` instead of `Activity`.

The activity is being designed to run multiple instances in parallel inside of a Replicator Activity. The major complication is that we have to get the current instance of the caller from the sender parameter of the methods.

Since you are familiar with adding activities to workflows, we'll change the way we approach implementing this activity. The process will consist of creating a new activity, creating all of the class member variables, creating the activity workflow within the designer, and finally assigning activity properties and creating the support code.

The first step is to create the activity itself. Right-click PerformanceAppraisalWF, choose Add, and then choose Activity, as shown in Figure 10.1.

FIGURE 10.1 Add a new activity to the workflow project.

When prompted for the name, enter **ReviewerApprovalActivity.cs**, as shown in Figure 10.2.

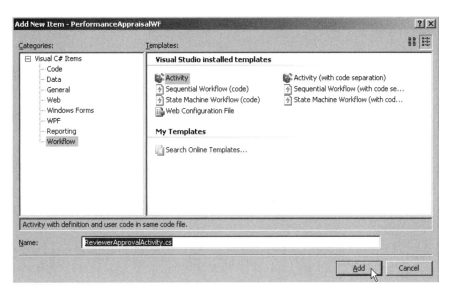

FIGURE 10.2 Name the new activity.

Go to the code view and add the required using directives, as shown in Listing 10.7.

LISTING 10.7   References Required for `ReviewerApprovalActivity`

```
using Microsoft.SharePoint.Workflow;

using Microsoft.SharePoint.WorkflowActions;

using Microsoft.Office.Workflow.Utility;

using Microsoft.SharePoint;

using SharePointItemPermissions;

using System.Collections.Generic;

using System.Text;
```

To make our property settings easier when adding activities in the workflow designer, we'll add all of the properties that we'll need for the activity now, as shown in Listing 10.8.

LISTING 10.8	Workflow Variables and Properties for the Reviewer Approval Activity

```
#region Member Variables and Properties
public bool reviewerIsFinished = false;
public string reviewerDocumentUrl = string.Empty;
public string reviewerDocumentName = string.Empty;
public int reviewerDocumentItemId = 0;


public AppraisalInfo AppraisalInfo = default(AppraisalInfo);


public Guid reviewerTaskId;


public SPWorkflowTaskProperties taskProperties =
    new Microsoft.SharePoint.Workflow.SPWorkflowTaskProperties();
public SPWorkflowTaskProperties taskChanged_AfterProps =
    new Microsoft.SharePoint.Workflow.SPWorkflowTaskProperties();
public SPWorkflowTaskProperties taskChanged_BeforeProps =
    new Microsoft.SharePoint.Workflow.SPWorkflowTaskProperties();
#endregion
```

The task ID and task property properties should be familiar by now. We'll use these when we create the task for the reviewer. The `bool`, `reviewerIsFinished`, is also familiar because it will be used to determine when the while loop can exit. The next three variables are related to the document that we are creating by copying the original appraisal document. Later, we'll set those values and also use them to retrieve the document to assign permissions.

The final variable is the `AppraisalInfo`, which is the instance data being assigned to this activity by the `Replicator` activity.

Add Activities to the Reviewer Approval Activity

With our properties in place, we can design the Reviewer Approval Activity. Switch back to the design mode for the activity and drag activities to the Reviewer Approval Activity so it looks like Figure 10.3. Don't worry about names and properties at the moment. We'll set each of them in the next sections.

The activities to add in order are the following:

1. Code Activity
2. ItemPermissions Activity
3. CreateTask Activity
4. While Activity
5. Sequence Activity
6. OnTaskChanged Activity
7. CompleteTask Activity
8. ItemPermissions Activity

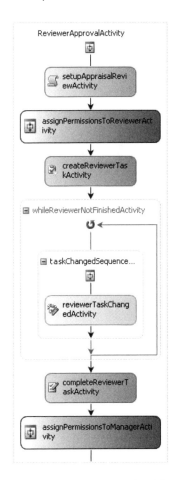

FIGURE 10.3 ReviewerApprovalActivity design.

Set Up the Appraisal Review

Click the code activity and set the following properties (see Figure 10.4):

- `Name`. Type **setupAppraisalReviewActivity** for the name of the activity
- `ExecuteCode`. Type **OnSetupAppraisalReview** for the name of the method. After entering the value and pressing Enter, Visual Studio will drop you into the code editor. The code that needs to be added is shown in Listing 10.9.

FIGURE 10.4 Create the workflow solution and activity project.

Within the code, we'll give the reviewer a copy of the original review to work on. We do that by calling into the `SharePointHelper` class that we created earlier. `AppraisalInfo` contains the name of the new document. We'll store the reviewer's document information to be used later. The reviewer name for the appraisal document is stored in the appraisal document, but it is also a property of the content type. As a property, we can easily update the appraiser name to be the current reviewer.

LISTING 10.9   Initialization Code for the Reviewer Approval Activity

```
private void OnSetupAppraisalReview(object sender, EventArgs e)
{
    // Copy the original review to a new document for
    // the current reviewer
    SPListItem reviewerItem =
        SharePointHelper.CopyReviewDocument(AppraisalInfo);
```

```
    // Save the information about the new item

    reviewerDocumentItemId = reviewerItem.ID;

    reviewerDocumentUrl = reviewerItem.ParentList.ParentWeb.Url + "/" +
        reviewerItem.ParentList.RootFolder.Url;


    // Update the appraiser name in the new document

    SPUser user =
        reviewerItem.Web.Users[AppraisalInfo.ReviewerLoginName];

    reviewerItem["AppraiserName"] = user;

    reviewerItem.Update();

}
```

Assign Permissions

When the review is copied, the permissions are not set correctly, at least not for what we need. We're going to give the reviewer editor rights and nobody else gets any rights.

Switch back to the designer view and click ItemPermissionsActivity1 located just below the code activity. Setting properties is easy since we have set up all of the member variables and properties. For all but the name, click the ... button and choose the existing member, according to the Path properties that follow (see Figure 10.5):

- `Name`. Enter **assignPermissionsToReviewerActivity** for the name of the activity.
- `Editors`. Click the ... button. When the Bind 'Editors' to an activity's property dialog is displayed, choose AppraisalInfo.ReviewerLoginName from the tree view.
- `ItemId`. Click the ... button. When the Bind 'ItemId' to an activity's property dialog is displayed, choose reviewerDocumentItemId from the tree view.
- `ListId`. Click the ... button. When the Bind 'ListId' to an activity's property dialog is displayed, choose AppraisalInfo.ListId from the tree view.
- `SiteId`. Click the ... button. When the Bind 'SiteId' to an activity's property dialog is displayed, choose AppraisalInfo.SiteId from the tree view.
- `WebId`. Click the ... button. When the Bind 'WebId' to an activity's property dialog is displayed, choose AppraisalInfo.WebId from the tree view.

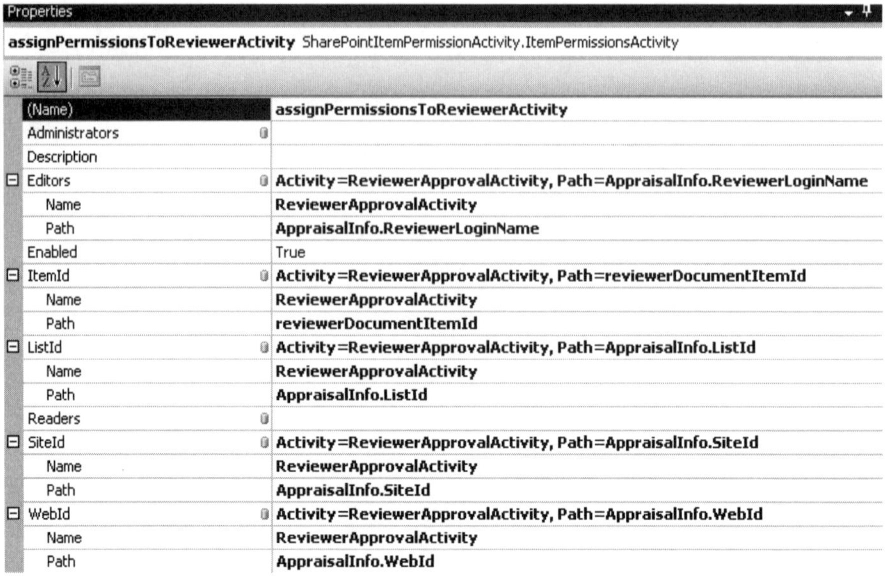

FIGURE 10.5 `assignPermissionsToReviewerActivity` properties.

Create Task for the Reviewer

After the file has been copied and the reviewer has edit rights, we need to assign the reviewer a task to let him know the document is ready for him to update, as well as to find out when he is finished.

The properties for this task are similar to the tasks created in Chapter 9. Click createTask1 and set properties, as defined below (see Figure 10.6).

- `Name`. Type **createReviewerTaskActivity** for the name of the activity.

- `CorrelationToken`. Type **reviewerTaskCorrelationToken** for the value of the Correlation Token. Next, you'll need to expand the Correlation Token, click in the OwnerActivityName property value, and choose ReviewerApprovalActivity from the drop-down.

- `TaskId`. Click the ... button. When the Bind 'TaskId' to an activity's property dialog is displayed, choose reviewerTaskId from the tree view.

- `TaskProperties`. Click the ... button. When the Bind 'TaskProperties' to an activity's property dialog is displayed, choose taskProperties from the tree view (similar to the TaskId).

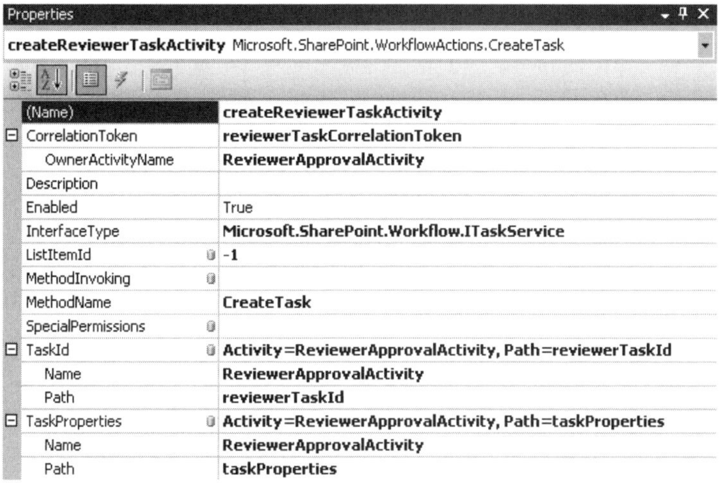

FIGURE 10.6 `createReviewerTaskActivity` properties.

Enter OnCreateReviewerTask as the value for the `MethodInvoking` property. After entering the MethodInvoking value and pressing Enter, Visual Studio drops you into the code editor ready to add the source code.

Listing 10.10 shows the code required to create the task. The structure is similar to what we've previously created. A new task ID is created, the task is assigned, the task title is set, the task type is set, and all of the instructions are set.

The difference is that we have to cast the sender object to a `CreateTask` so we can be sure we are accessing our instance of the activity within the workflow.

LISTING 10.10   OnCreateReviewTask Method

```
private void OnCreateReviewerTask(object sender, EventArgs e)
{
    CreateTask createTaskActivity = sender as CreateTask;

    // Create a new Id for the task
    createTaskActivity.TaskId = Guid.NewGuid();

    // Assign the task to the manager
    createTaskActivity.TaskProperties.AssignedTo =
        AppraisalInfo.ReviewerLoginName;
```

```
// Set the title and description with hard-coded strings. In a true
// production environment these strings would either be configurable
// or would at least be in resources
createTaskActivity.TaskProperties.Title =
    "Appraisal information needed for " +
    AppraisalInfo.EmployeeFullName;
createTaskActivity.TaskProperties.Description =
    AppraisalInfo.ManagerFullName +
    " has requested you to fill out an appraisal for " +
    AppraisalInfo.EmployeeFullName;


createTaskActivity.TaskProperties.TaskType =
    AppraisalInfo.TaskType;


// Set the information for the task form through
// the extended properties
createTaskActivity.TaskProperties.ExtendedProperties["tasktitle"] =
    "Peer Review";
createTaskActivity.TaskProperties.ExtendedProperties["employee"] =
    AppraisalInfo.EmployeeFullName;
createTaskActivity.TaskProperties.ExtendedProperties["appraiser"] =
            AppraisalInfo.ReviewerFullName;
createTaskActivity.TaskProperties.ExtendedProperties["reviewperiod"] =
    AppraisalInfo.AppraisalStartDate + " - " +
    AppraisalInfo.AppraisalEndDate;
if(AppraisalInfo.TaskType == 0)
{
    createTaskActivity.TaskProperties.ExtendedProperties["itemtitle"] =
        "Peer Review Document";
}
else
{
        "Self Evaluation Document ";
}
```

```
createTaskActivity.TaskProperties.ExtendedProperties["itemlink"] =
    reviewerDocumentUrl;
createTaskActivity.TaskProperties.ExtendedProperties["iteminst"] =
    "Click on the link above to review the employee.";
createTaskActivity.TaskProperties.ExtendedProperties["inst1"] =
    "Please comment on the employee for each goal in the review.";
createTaskActivity.TaskProperties.ExtendedProperties["inst2"] = "";
createTaskActivity.TaskProperties.ExtendedProperties["inst3"] =
    "Once finished, check the box below and click \"Submit\".";
createTaskActivity.TaskProperties.ExtendedProperties["inst4"] = "";
createTaskActivity.TaskProperties.ExtendedProperties["completestatement"]
    =
    "I have reviewed the employee to the best of my abilities.";
}
```

Wait for the Task to Be Completed

Waiting for the reviewer to complete his evaluation of the employee follows a familiar pattern. We have a while loop that waits for the reviewer to indicate the task is complete, and we have some code that checks to see if the reviewer has finished whenever the task changes.

The While activity waits for the reviewer to finish his evaluation. Switch back to the designer and click whileActivity1 and set the properties as follows (see Figure 10.7):

- Name. Type **whileReviewerNotFinishedActivity** for the value.
- Condition. Choose Code Condition.

FIGURE 10.7 whileReviewerNotFinishedActivity properties.

Expand the `Condition` property and enter **ReviewerNotFinished** for the Condition sub property value. When you press Enter, you'll be dropped into the code editor. The code for `ReviewerNotFinished` is in Listing 10.11.

LISTING 10.11   `ReviewerNotFinished` Method

```
private void ReviewerNotFinished(object sender, ConditionalEventArgs e)
{
    e.Result = !reviewerIsFinished;
}
```

Switch back to the designer and click `sequenceActivity1` and enter **taskChangedSequenceActivity** as the activity name.

Click `onTaskChanged1` to update the activity's properties:

- `Name`. Type **reviewerTaskChangedActivity** for the name of the activity.
- `AfterProperties`. Click the ... button. When the Bind 'AfterProperties' to an activity's property dialog is displayed, choose taskChanged_AfterProps from the tree view.
- `BeforeProperties`. Click the ... button. When the Bind 'BeforeProperties' to an activity's property dialog is displayed, choose taskChanged_BeforeProps from the tree view.
- `CorrelationToken`. Choose reviewerTaskCorrelationToken from the drop-down.
- `TaskId`. Click the ... button. When the Bind 'TaskId' to an activity's property dialog is displayed, choose reviewerTaskId from the tree view.

The property values for the activity should look like Figure 10.8.

The last property that needs to be set is the `Invoked` property. `Invoked` represents the method in the workflow code that will be called when the activity is executed. Enter **OnReviewerTaskChanged** as the value for the `Invoked` property. After entering the Invoked value and pressing Enter, Visual Studio drops you into the code editor ready to add the source code, as shown in Listing 10.12.

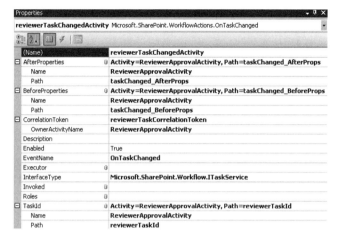

FIGURE 10.8 reviewerTaskChangedActivity properties.

OnReviewerTaskChanged Method

```csharp
private void OnReviewerTaskChanged(object sender,
    ExternalDataEventArgs e)
{
    SPTaskServiceEventArgs taskEventArgs = e as SPTaskServiceEventArgs;
    SPWorkflowTaskProperties afterProps = taskEventArgs.afterProperties;

    // Check the task properties to see if the review
    // has been completed.
    string s = afterProps.ExtendedProperties["TaskCompleted"] as string;

    bool result = false;

    if (bool.TryParse(s, out result))
    {
        reviewerIsFinished = result;
    }
    else
    {
        reviewerIsFinished = true;
    }
}
```

Complete the Task

As we did earlier, we're going to complete the reviewer task.

Switch back to the designer view and click completeTask1 to set the following properties (see Figure 10.9 for help):

- `Name`. Enter **completeReviewerTaskActivity** for the name of the activity.
- `CorrelationToken`. Choose reviewerTaskToken from the drop-down
- `TaskId`. Click the ... button. When the Bind 'TaskId' to an activity's property dialog is displayed, choose reviewerTaskId from the tree view

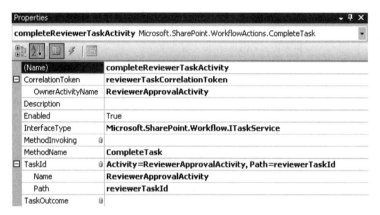

FIGURE 10.9 `completeReviewerTaskActivity` properties.

Assign Permissions to the Manager

After the reviewer has finished, we give permissions back to the manager. The setup is the exact same as earlier in this section with the exception of setting the editor to the manager instead of the reviewer. Set the properties of the permissions activity using the following steps:

1. Click ItemPermissionsActivity2 (the last in the design).
2. For all but the name, click the ... button and choose the existing member, according to the Path properties that follow (see Figure 10.10):
   - `Name`. Enter **assignPermissionsToManagerActivity** for the name of the activity.
   - `Editors`. Click the ... button. When the Bind 'Editors' to an activity's property dialog is displayed, choose AppraisalInfo. ManagerLoginName from the tree view.

■   `ItemId`. Click the ... button. When the Bind 'ItemId' to an activity's property dialog is displayed, choose reviewerDocumentItemId from the tree view.

■   `ListId`. Click the ... button. When the Bind 'ListId' to an activity's property dialog is displayed, choose AppraisalInfo.ListId from the tree view.

■   `SiteId`. Click the ... button. When the Bind 'SiteId' to an activity's property dialog is displayed, choose AppraisalInfo.SiteId from the tree view.

■   `WebId`. Click the ... button. When the Bind 'WebId' to an activity's property dialog is displayed, choose AppraisalInfo.WebId from the tree view.

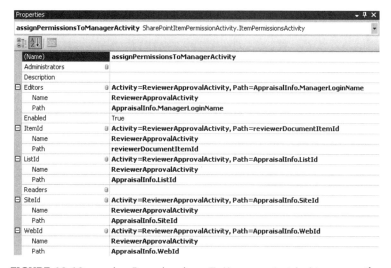

FIGURE 10.10 `assignPermissionsToManagerActivity` properties.

The Reviewer Approval Activity is finished and is ready to use in the appraisal workflow. The next sections will finish the workflow.

Adding the Replicator Activity to the Workflow

We will be adding a Replicator Activity that has an `ExecutionType` of `Parallel` to allow all of our reviewers to review the employee at the same time. To give each of our ReviewerApproval activities an `AppraisalInfo` instance, we need to add an `AppraisalInfo` list member variable. Later on, we're going to need an `AppraisalInfo` member variable for the employee to perform a self-evaluation, so we'll create it at this time as well.

Open AppraisalWorkflow.cs in code view.

Since this class will be creating lists of `AppraisalInfo` objects, we need to add a reference to `System.Collections.Generic`. We'll also be using `StringBuilder` so we need to add a reference to `System.Text`. The code is shown in Listing 10.13.

LISTING 10.13   Adding References to `System.Collections.Generic` and `System.Text`

```
using System.Collections.Generic;
using System.Text;
```

Add the code from Listing 10.14 to the Member Variables region.

LISTING 10.14   AppraisalInfo Declarations for AppraisalReview Activity

```
// Appraisal information for other reviewers
public List<AppraisalInfo> reviewerInformation;
public AppraisalInfo employeeAppraisalInfo;
```

Next, we need to update `OnStartEvaluationTaskChanged` method to create both the reviewers and the employee `AppraisalInfo` class instances. The code for `OnStartEvaluationTaskChanged` is shown in Listing 10.15.

LISTING 10.15   `OnStartEvaluationTaskChanged` Method

```
private void OnStartEvaluationTaskChanged(
object sender,
ExternalDataEventArgs e)
{
    // Check the task properties to see if the goals have been accepted
    string s = startEvaluationTaskChanged_AfterProps.ExtendedProperties
    ["TaskCompleted"].ToString();

    SPFile file = workflowProperties.Item.File;
    string fileName =
        System.IO.Path.GetFileNameWithoutExtension(file.Name);
    string extension = System.IO.Path.GetExtension(file.Name);
```

```
bool result = false;

if (bool.TryParse(s, out result))
{
   startEvaluation = result;

   if (result == true)
   {
      string reviewerName;
      string propertyName;

      reviewerInformation = new List<AppraisalInfo>();

      int i = 1;
      bool processReviewers = true;

      while(processReviewers)
      {
         propertyName = "Reviewer" + i.ToString();

         reviewerName =
            startEvaluationTaskChanged_AfterProps.ExtendedProperties
               [propertyName] as string;

         AppraisalInfo info;
         if (reviewerName != null && reviewerName.Length > 0)
         {
            SPUser reviewer =
               workflowProperties.Web.AllUsers[reviewerName];

            info = new AppraisalInfo();
            info.SiteId = workflowProperties.SiteId;
            info.WebId = workflowProperties.WebId;
            info.ListId = workflowProperties.ListId;
```

```
        info.OriginalListItemId = workflowProperties.ItemId;

        info.ReviewerLoginName = reviewer.LoginName;

        info.ReviewerFullName = reviewer.Name;

        info.EmployeeLoginName = employeeLoginName;

        info.EmployeeFullName = employeeFullName;

        info.ManagerFullName = managerFullName;

        info.ManagerLoginName = managerLoginName;

        info.AppraisalStartDate =
            appraisalPeriodStart.ToShortDateString();

        info.AppraisalEndDate =
            appraisalPeriodEnd.ToShortDateString();

        info.AppraisalDocumentName = fileName + " Peer Review_" +
            reviewer.Name + extension;

        info.TaskType = 0;

        reviewerInformation.Add(info);

    }

    else

    {

        processReviewers = false;

    }

    i++;

}

employeeAppraisalInfo = new AppraisalInfo();

employeeAppraisalInfo.SiteId = workflowProperties.SiteId;

employeeAppraisalInfo.WebId = workflowProperties.WebId;

employeeAppraisalInfo.ListId = workflowProperties.ListId;

employeeAppraisalInfo.OriginalListItemId =
    workflowProperties.ItemId;

employeeAppraisalInfo.ReviewerLoginName = employeeLoginName;

employeeAppraisalInfo.ReviewerFullName = employeeFullName;

employeeAppraisalInfo.EmployeeLoginName = employeeLoginName;

employeeAppraisalInfo.EmployeeFullName = employeeFullName;

employeeAppraisalInfo.ManagerFullName = managerFullName;

employeeAppraisalInfo.ManagerLoginName = managerLoginName;
```

```
            employeeAppraisalInfo.AppraisalStartDate =
                appraisalPeriodStart.ToShortDateString();
            employeeAppraisalInfo.AppraisalEndDate =
                appraisalPeriodEnd.ToShortDateString();
            employeeAppraisalInfo.TaskType = 2;
            employeeAppraisalInfo.AppraisalDocumentName =
                fileName + "_Self Evaluation" + extension;
            reviewerInformation.Add(employeeAppraisalInfo);
        }
    }
    else
    {
        startEvaluation = false;
    }
}
```

Build the solution to make sure you have entered the code correctly.

Now that all of the Replicator Activity prerequisites are taken care of, we need to add the Replicator Activity to our workflow. Open AppraisalWorkflow in workflow designer and add the Replicator Activity using the following steps:

1. Drag a `Replicator` Activity from the Windows Workflow v3.0 section of the Toolbox to the bottom of the workflow in the designer.

2. Select replicatorActivity1 and update the properties (see Figure 10.11), as indicated below:

   ■ `Name`. Enter **reviewerReplicatorActivity** for the name of the activity.

   ■ `ExecutionType`. Click the ... button. Choose Parallel from the drop-down.

   ■ `InitialChildData`. Click the ... button. When the Bind 'InitialChildData' to an activity's property dialog is displayed, choose reviewerInformation from the tree view

3. Enter **OnReplicatorChildInitialized** for the `ChildInitialized` property.

4. When you press Enter, you will be dropped into the code editor, and you'll need to add the lines from Listing 10.16 to the `OnReplicator ChildInitialized` method. Whenever a review approval activity is instantiated by the Replicator, this code will be called to initialize the properties for the instance.

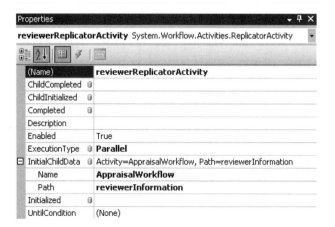

FIGURE 10.11 `reviewerReplicatorActivity` properties.

LISTING 10.16 `OnReplicatorChildInitialized` Method

```
private void OnReplicatorChildInitialized(object sender,
    ReplicatorChildEventArgs e)
{
    AppraisalInfo info = e.InstanceData as AppraisalInfo;
    ReviewerApprovalActivity reviewerActivity =
        e.Activity as ReviewerApprovalActivity;
    reviewerActivity.AppraisalInfo = info;
}
```

Add the Reviewer Approval Activity to the Replicator

With the Replicator in place, all we need to do is drag a ReviewerApprovalActivity as the only activity within `reviewerReplicatorActivity`.

1. Switch back to the workflow designer.
2. Drag a ReviewerApprovalActivity from the PerformanceAppraisalWF Controls section of the Toolbox inside `reviewerReplicatorActivity`.
3. Set the name of the activity to **reviewerApprovalActivity** (see Figure 10.12).
4. The Replicator takes care of the rest of it by passing the initialization data to each instance of the ReviewerApprovalActivity.

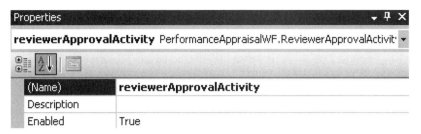

FIGURE 10.12 `reviewerApprovalActivity` properties.

Incorporate Feedback into the Appraisal Document

At this point, we have all of the review information from the reviewers as well as the employee. We're going to integrate all of that information into the original document so the manager can finish the appraisal process working from a single document. We'll be dragging a code activity onto the workflow designer and then writing code that is basically an aggregating copy/paste routine. We're going to copy all of the reviewers' goal and overall comments and the employee's overall comments from the respective documents and paste them into the original document.

1. Drag a Code activity from the Windows Workflow v3.0 section of the Toolbox onto the designer as the last activity in the workflow.

2. In the Properties window for the code activity, enter **integrateFeedbackCodeActivity** for the `Name` property and then enter **OnIntegrateFeedback** for the `ExcecuteCode` property.

3. When you press Enter, you'll be dropped into the code editor.

The code for this activity, as shown in Listings 10.17–10.20, is broken up into three distinct tasks:

1. Copy the employee's overall comments into the original document.

2. Copy the reviewers' goal comments into the original document.

3. Copy the reviewers' overall comments into the original document.

While the code listing is long, the code itself is pretty straightforward. First, we get the employee's self evaluation review document and copy the comments from that document into the original document.

LISTING 10.17 Copying the Employee's Comments

```
private void OnIntegrateFeedback(object sender, EventArgs e)
{
   // Get the employee comments and add them to the
   // original appraisal document
   SPListItem employeeReview =
      SharePointHelper.GetReviewDocument(employeeAppraisalInfo);

   workflowProperties.Item["EmployeeOverallComments"] =
   employeeReview["EmployeeOverallComments"];

   workflowProperties.Item.Update();
```

The next two tasks require us to keep references to all of the reviewers' documents. Since we appended the employee review to reviewerInformation, we need to get all but the last one.

LISTING 10.18 Getting References to the Reviewers' Documents

```
SPListItem[] reviewItems =
   new SPListItem[reviewerInformation.Count - 1];

// Get all of the reviewer documents
for (int i = 0; i < reviewerInformation.Count - 1; i++)
{
   reviewItems[i] = SharePointHelper.GetReviewDocument(
      reviewerInformation[i]);
}
```

We'll copy the comments from the reviewer documents for only those goals that are defined in the original document. We find all the goals by appending the goal index to the end of "GoalComments" to form the property name for the goals, as defined in the content type. We continue processing goals until the original document does not contain the named goal property.

The goal comments from each reviewer are appended together with each comment being prefixed with the reviewer's name.

LISTING 10.19	Processing the Goals

```
// Walk through the original document updating the goal results
int goalIndex = 1;
bool validGoal = true;
StringBuilder sb;
string goalPropertyName;

while (validGoal)
{
   // Get the goal property from the original
   // document
   goalPropertyName = "GoalComments" + goalIndex.ToString();

   if (workflowProperties.Item[goalPropertyName] != null)
   {
      sb = new StringBuilder();

      for (int j = 0; j < reviewerInformation.Count - 1; j++)
      {
         sb.Append(GetConsolidatedPropertyValue(
            reviewerInformation[j].ReviewerFullName,
            reviewItems[j],
            goalPropertyName));
      }

      workflowProperties.Item[goalPropertyName] = sb.ToString();
   }
   else
   {
      validGoal = false;
   }

   goalIndex++;
}
```

Our final task is to get the reviewers' overall comments into the original appraisal document. The overall comments are stored in a single field so we only need to loop through the reviews, not any properties as we did with the goals.

Once again, the comments from each reviewer are appended together with each comment being prefixed with the reviewer's name.

LISTING 10.20   Processing the Reviewers' Overall Comments

```
// Walk through the review documents and update the overall comments
sb = new StringBuilder();


for (int j = 0; j < reviewerInformation.Count - 1; j++)
{
   sb.Append(GetConsolidatedPropertyValue(
      reviewerInformation[j].ReviewerFullName,
      reviewItems[j],
      "AppraiserOverallComments"));
}


workflowProperties.Item["AppraiserOverallComments"] = sb.ToString();
workflowProperties.Item.Update();
}
```

Listing 10.21 contains the help function called by both the goal and overall processing methods above.

LISTING 10.21   GetConsolidatedPropertyValue Method

```
private string GetConsolidatedPropertyValue(string name,
   SPListItem item,
   string propertyName)
{
   string retValue = name + " - ";
```

```
    try
    {

       retValue += item[propertyName].ToString();

    }
    catch (Exception)
    {
    }


    return retValue;
}
```

Build the solution again to verify the code has been entered correctly.

FINALIZING THE REVIEW

At this point in the review process, all that's left is for the manager to finalize the appraisal document. To do this, the manager needs to examine the comments the reviewers and employee made and create the scores and add his own comments.

Fortunately for us, there isn't a lot to do except to create a task for the manager to let him know when everyone else has finished commenting on the review. The task creation follows the same pattern as the others: create the task, wait for the task to be marked complete, and then complete the task. Once again, we'll make property setting easy by creating the design and all of our properties ahead of time.

1. To get started, make sure that `AppraisalWorkflow.cs` is open in the designer mode.

2. Drag a `CreateTask` Activity, a `While` Activity, a `Sequence` Activity, an `OnTaskChanged` Activity, and a `CompleteTask` Activity to the designer so it looks like Figure 10.13. Don't worry about the names because we'll set the properties in the next few sections.

3. Switch to the code editor and add the code in Listing 10.22 to the Member Variables and Properties regions.

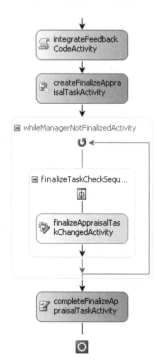

FIGURE 10.13 Finalize review workflow design.

LISTING 10.22 Member Variables and Properties Required for Manager Finalize Task

```
public bool appraisalFinalized = false;
public Guid finalizeAppraisalTaskId;

public SPWorkflowTaskProperties finalizeAppraisalTaskProps =
    new Microsoft.SharePoint.Workflow.SPWorkflowTaskProperties();
public SPWorkflowTaskProperties finalizeAppraisalTaskChanged_AfterProps =
    new Microsoft.SharePoint.Workflow.SPWorkflowTaskProperties();
public SPWorkflowTaskProperties
    finalizeAppraisalTaskChanged_BeforeProps =
        new Microsoft.SharePoint.Workflow.SPWorkflowTaskProperties();
```

Set the Properties for the Finalize Appraisal Task

Since the activities have already been added to the workflow, we only need to set the properties for each activity. Set the createTask1Activity properties using the following steps:

1. Switch back to the designer view.

2. The properties for the Finalize Appraisal task follow the same pattern as before. Click createTask1 and set properties as defined below (see Figure 10.14).

   ■ Name. Type **createFinalizeAppraisalTaskActivity** for the name of the activity.

   ■ CorrelationToken. Type **finalizeAppraisalTaskCorrelationToken** for the value of the Correlation Token. Next, you'll need to expand the Correlation Token, click in the OwnerActivityName property value, and choose AppraisalWorkflow from the drop-down.

   ■ TaskId. Click the ... button. When the Bind 'TaskId' to an activity's property dialog is displayed, choose finalizeAppraisalTaskId from the tree view.

   ■ TaskProperties. Click the ... button. When the Bind 'TaskProperties' to an activity's property dialog is displayed, choose finalizeAppraisalTaskProps from the tree view (similar to the TaskId).

3. Enter **OnCreateFinalizeAppraisalTask** as the value for the MethodInvoking property. After entering the MethodInvoking value and pressing Enter, Visual Studio drops you into the code editor ready to add the source code.

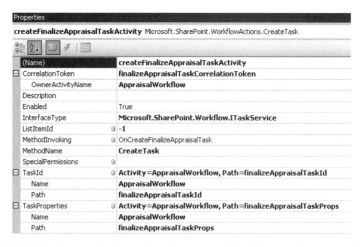

FIGURE 10.14 createFinalizeAppraisalTaskActivity properties.

Listing 10.23 shows the code required to create the task. The structure is similar to what we've previously created. A new task ID is created, the task is assigned, the task title is set, the task type is set, and all of the instructions are set.

LISTING 10.23 Creating the Finalize Task for the Manager

```
private void OnCreateFinalizeAppraisalTask(object sender, EventArgs e)
{
    // Create a new Id for the task
    finalizeAppraisalTaskId = Guid.NewGuid();

    // Assign the task to the manager
    finalizeAppraisalTaskProps.AssignedTo = managerLoginName;

    // Set the title and description with hard-coded strings. In a true
    // production environment these strings would either be configurable
    // or would at least be in resources
    finalizeAppraisalTaskProps.Description =
        "Complete this task once the appraisal has been finalized.";
    finalizeAppraisalTaskProps.Title = "Finalize Appraisal";
    finalizeAppraisalTaskProps.TaskType = 0;

    // Set the information for the task form through
    // the extended properties
    finalizeAppraisalTaskProps.ExtendedProperties["tasktitle"] =
        "Finalize Appraisal";
    finalizeAppraisalTaskProps.ExtendedProperties["employee"] =
        employeeFullName;
    finalizeAppraisalTaskProps.ExtendedProperties["appraiser"] =
        managerFullName;
    finalizeAppraisalTaskProps.ExtendedProperties["reviewperiod"] =
        appraisalPeriodStart.ToShortDateString() + " - " +
        appraisalPeriodEnd.ToShortDateString();
    finalizeAppraisalTaskProps.ExtendedProperties["itemtitle"] =
        "Appraisal Document for " + employeeFullName;
```

```
finalizeAppraisalTaskProps.ExtendedProperties["itemlink"] =
    workflowPropertiesItem.ParentList.ParentWeb.Url  + "/" +
    workflowProperties.Item.ParentList.RootFolder.Url;
finalizeAppraisalTaskProps.ExtendedProperties["iteminst"] =
    "Click on the link above to edit the appraisal document.";


finalizeAppraisalTaskProps.ExtendedProperties["inst1"] =
    "Please ensure that all feedback is represented.";
finalizeAppraisalTaskProps.ExtendedProperties["inst2"] =
    "Make sure you fill out the manager comments section.";
finalizeAppraisalTaskProps.ExtendedProperties["inst3"] = "";
finalizeAppraisalTaskProps.ExtendedProperties["inst4"] =
    "When the review has been finalized, check the box " +
    "below and click \"Submit\" below.";
finalizeAppraisalTaskProps.ExtendedProperties["completestatement"] =
    "The appraisal has reached final draft.";



}
```

Wait for the Task to Be Completed

Set the whileActivity1 properties using the following steps:

1. Click whileActivity1 and set the properties as follows (see Figure 10.15):
   - Name. Type **whileManagerNotFinalizedActivity** for the value.
   - Condition. Choose Code Condition.

FIGURE 10.15 whileManagerNotFinalizedActivity properties.

2. Expand the `Condition` property and enter **ManagerNotFinalized** for the Condition subproperty value.

3. When you press Enter, you'll be dropped into the code editor. The code for `ManagerNotFinalized` is in Listing 10.24.

LISTING 10.24 `ManagerNotFinalized` Method

```
private void ManagerNotFinalized(object sender, ConditionalEventArgs e)
{
    e.Result = !appraisalFinalized;
}
```

4. Switch back to designer view and click sequenceActivity1 and enter **finalizeTaskCheckSequenceActivity** as the activity name.

5. Click onTaskChanged1 to update the activity's properties:

   ■ Name. Type **finalizeAppraisalTaskChangedActivity** for the name of the activity.

   ■ `AfterProperties`. Click the ... button. When the Bind 'AfterProperties' to an activity's property dialog is displayed, choose finalizeAppraisal-TaskChanged _AfterProps from the tree view.

   ■ `BeforeProperties`. Click the ... button. When the Bind 'BeforeProperties' to an activity's property dialog is displayed, choose finalizeAppraisal-TaskChanged _BeforeProps from the tree view.

   ■ `CorrelationToken`. Choose finalizeAppraisalTaskToken from the drop-down.

   ■ `TaskId`. Click the ... button. When the Bind 'TaskId' to an activity's property dialog is displayed, choose finalizeAppraisalTaskId from the tree view.

6. The property values for the activity should look like Figure 10.16.

The last property that needs to be set is the `Invoked` property. Invoked represents the method in the workflow code that will be called when the activity is executed.

1. Enter **OnFinalizeAppraisalTaskChanged** as the value for the `Invoked` property. After entering the `Invoked` value and pressing Enter, Visual Studio drops you into the code editor ready to add the source code, as shown in Listing 10.25.

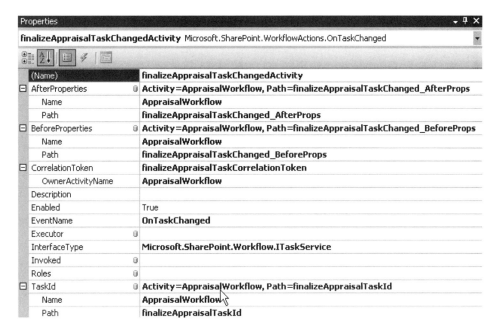

FIGURE 10.16 finalizeAppraisalTaskChangedActivity properties.

LISTING 10.25   OnFinalizeAppraisalTaskChanged Method

```
private void OnFinalizeAppraisalTaskChanged(object sender,
   ExternalDataEventArgs e)
{
   // Check the task properties to see if the goals have been accepted
   string s =
   finalizeAppraisalTaskChanged_AfterProps.ExtendedProperties
      ["TaskCompleted"].ToString();

   bool result = false;

   if (bool.TryParse(s, out result))
   {
      appraisalFinalized = result;
   }
```

```
    else
    {

      appraisalFinalized = false;

    }

}
```

Complete the Task

No code is required for us to complete the task, so all we need to do is set the properties.

1. Switch back to the designer view and click completeTask1 to set the following properties (see Figure 10.17):

   - ■ Name. Enter **completeFinalizeAppraisalTaskActivity** for the name of the activity.

   - ■ CorrelationToken. Choose finalizeAppraisalTaskToken from the drop-down.

   - ■ TaskId. Click the ... button. When the Bind 'TaskId' to an activity's property dialog is displayed, choose finalizeAppraisalTaskId from the tree view.

FIGURE 10.17 completeFinalizeAppraisalTaskActivity properties.

Collect Signatures from All Parties Involved

Signatures will be collected using the Collect Signatures workflow, as described in Chapter 6. Since there aren't any more requirements beyond what was required in Chapter 6, there is nothing to extend or replace.

TEST THE WORKFLOW

Testing the workflow to incorporate all of the additions in Chapter 10 requires us to follow the tests from Chapter 9 and then continue. This time we want to start by putting the debug breakpoint on the "completeStartEvaluationTaskActivity" activity.

1. Press F5 to start the process.

An Attach Security Warning Is Displayed

If an Attach Security Warning dialog is displayed, click Attach and then click Yes to continue debugging.

2. When the browser displays the Appraisals_Kevin Martin document library, start a workflow on one of the appraisal documents.

3. When the list of workflows is displayed, click PerformanceAppraisalWF.

4. Complete the Finalize Appraisal Goals task.

5. Click the Start Evaluation task, and the Start Evaluation task form will be displayed.

6. Enter a name of a reviewer. (Remember to use the login name in the form "litwareinc\username.")

7. Check Start Evaluation and click Submit.

There will now be two new tasks, one for the reviewer and one for the employee. Open the employee task, click the document library link, and edit the review with "SelfEvaluation" in the title by using the following steps:

1. Add a comment in the employee overall comments field.

2. Save and close the document.

3. Mark the task as completed in the task form.

Process the reviewer task similarly. The only difference is that the reviewer has to comment on each goal, as well as giving feedback for the overall review period.

After the reviewer task is marked complete, the integrate feedback code will run, and the original document will contain all of the comments.

The manager will have a new task assigned to finalize the appraisal named Finalize Appraisal.

1. Open the task.

2. Open the original document and check to be sure the information has been integrated.

3. Normally, the manager would finalize the document, but we're more interested in the workflow than the manager's edits to the document.

4. Mark the manager's task as complete and submit the task form.

The workflow is now in the Complete state and so are all of the tasks.

As in Chapter 9, you should put break points both on the activities in the designer, as well as into the code, to see how the different parts interact.

DEPLOYING THE WORKFLOW AND ACTIVITIES

We now have a fully functioning development workflow, and we need to deploy it to a staging environment. It would be nice to think we could go directly to production, but there's a bit more testing that would need to occur before that happens.

To get our hard work deployed to another system, we need to perform a few tasks:

- Clean up the name of our workflow and associated feature.
- Create a WSS Solution Package (WSP).
- Create a short set of instructions to install the WSP.

MAKING THE WORKFLOW AND FEATURE NAMES ATTRACTIVE

Open `workflow.xml` and `feature.xml` and update the `Name`, `Title`, and `Description` attributes to something that better describes the workflow functionality. In the book project, I chose to use something very long and descriptive, but not necessarily too catchy.

In `feature.xml`, I set `Title` to "Content Types Book Performance Appraisal Workflow" and `Description` to "Content Types book performance appraisal workflow created in Visual Studio 2008."

In `workflow.xml`, I set `Name` to "Content Types Book Performance Appraisal" and `Description` to "Content Types book performance appraisal workflow created in Visual Studio 2008."

You'll want to set the attributes to whatever makes the most sense for your organization.

CREATING A WSS SOLUTION PACKAGE

To create the WSP package, I used WSPBuilder. WSPBuilder is an open source code project located on CodePlex. The URL to the project is http://www.codeplex.com/wspbuilder. I'm sure there are other solutions out there, but this one works and is very straightforward to use.

After downloading and expanding the project, perform the following steps: (I installed the x86 version and extracted the files to "c:\wspbuilder.")

1. Create the following folder structure in the solution folder: 12\Templates\Features\PerformanceAppraisalWF.

2. Copy the following files into the folder created in step 1:

   `Feature.xml`, `Workflow.xml`, `CompleteTaskForm.xsn`, `EmployeeSelfEvaluation.xsn`, and `StartEvaluationTaskForm.xsn`.

3. Create a folder in the solution folder named "GAC."

4. Copy `PerformanceAppraisalWF.dll` and `SharePointItemPermissions.dll` from the bin\debug folder into the GAC folder created in step 3.

5. From a command prompt, located in the solution folder, type **c:\wspbuilder\buildx86\wspbuilder.exe** and press Enter. (Replace \wspbuilder\buildx86 with the path to wspbuilder.exe that you installed.)

You now have a WSP file located in the solution folder and are ready to install it, following the guidelines in the next section.

INSTRUCTIONS TO INSTALL THE WSP

To install the workflow WSP, we'll need to add the solution to SharePoint, deploy the solution, and activate the workflow feature. The tool we'll use to perform those actions is stsadm.exe. Stsadm is a versatile tool with many command options. You can find many resources on the Internet to describe all of the commands.

We're only going to concern ourselves with the ones that we need. You can get an abbreviated description for all of the options by typing "stsadm /?" at the command prompt.

Before doing anything else, you'll need to find where stsadm.exe is located on the installation machine. Most of the time, it is located at "c:\program files\ common files\Microsoft Shared\web server extensions\12\bin." You can either add the folder to the system environment path variable or copy the executable to another folder that is easier to type and easier to remember.

Deploy the solution to SharePoint using the following steps. (For all of the URL parameters I've used the one I installed to. Change appropriately for your environment):

1. Open a command window.

2. Change directories to the directory where the .WSP file is located.

3. Type **stsadm –o addsolution –filename "PerformanceAppraisalWF Solution.wsp"** and press Enter.

4. Type **stsadm –o deploysolution –name PerformanceAppraisalWF Solution –url http://moss.litwareinc.com –immediate -allowGACDeployment**, and press Enter.

5. Type **stsadm –o activatefeature –name "Content Types Book Performance Appraisal Workflow" –url http://moss.litwareinc.com -force**, and press Enter.

After steps 1–5 have been implemented the workflow can be attached to the document library using the following steps:

6. Open the browser and navigate to the document library; in our example, the document library is located at http://moss.litwareinc.com/hr/Appraisals_ Kevin Martin/forms/allitems.aspx.

7. Click Settings, Document Library Settings, and then Workflow Settings, as shown in Figure 10.18.

8. Choose "Content Types Book Performance Appraisal Workflow" from the Select a workflow template list box, type **Performance Appraisal Workflow** for the name of the workflow, and click OK to add the workflow to the document library (see Figure 10.19).

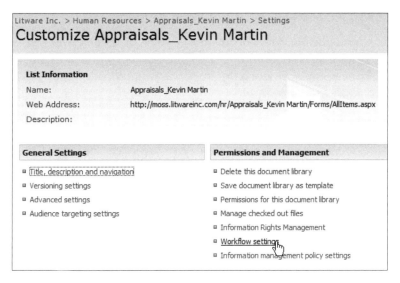

FIGURE 10.18 Document Library Workflow settings.

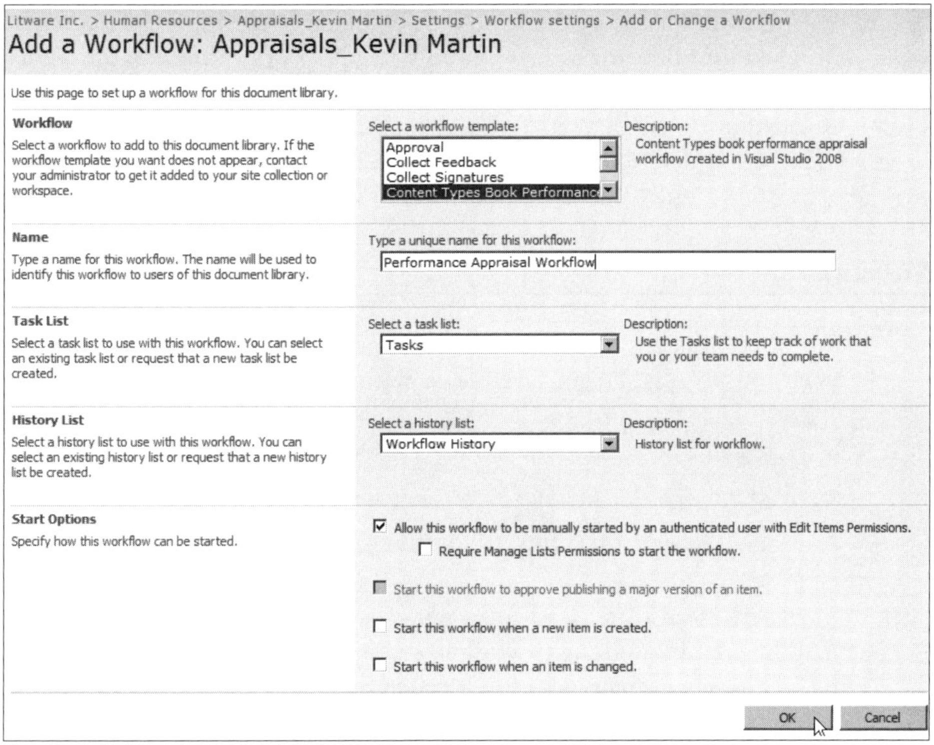

FIGURE 10.19 Add the Performance Appraisal Workflow to the document library.

NOTE

Removing What You Just Installed

Installing the workflow solution is only half of what you need to know. You may decide at some point to remove the workflow from the system. When that time comes, you'll remove it just like it was installed, only in reverse. Remove the workflow using these steps:

1. Open a command window.

2. Change directories to the directory where the .WSP file is located.

3. Type **stsadm –o deactivatefeature –name "Content Types Book Performance Appraisal Workflow" –url http://moss.litwareinc.com - force** and press Enter.

4. Type **stsadm –o retractsolution –name "PerformanceAppraisalWF Solution.wsp" –immediate** and press Enter. Type **stsadm –o deletesolution –name PerformanceAppraisalWF Solution** and press Enter.

Just like the install process, make sure that stsadm.exe *is either in the directory where you're running it, or is in a folder listed in the path environment variable.*

After adding the workflow to the document library, you can manually start the installed workflow the same way you started the workflow with the debugger. You can always change the workflow behavior by having it start whenever a document is added or updated, or both. This specific workflow is meant to run when documents are added to the document library.

Summary

We've met the goals for the chapter and should have a fully functional appraisal workflow process. To get here, we've performed the following tasks:

■ Created a new activity to collect feedback from the reviewers and employee.

■ Written a code activity to incorporate the feedback into the appraisal document.

■ Collected signatures from all parties involved.

There are also areas that were not covered, such as proper error and exception handling, fault handling in workflows, detailed InfoPath form design, workflow history logs, and many others. One area that might be beneficial would be a state machine workflow. If the process we covered in these last two chapters had very many more steps or was extremely complicated, a state machine probably would have been required.

Index

X